Reading the New Global Order

Reading the New Global Order

Textual Transformations of 1989

Edited by Kirrily Freeman and John Munro

BLOOMSBURY ACADEMIC
LONDON • NEW YORK • OXFORD • NEW DELHI • SYDNEY

BLOOMSBURY ACADEMIC
Bloomsbury Publishing Plc
50 Bedford Square, London, WC1B 3DP, UK
1385 Broadway, New York, NY 10018, USA
29 Earlsfort Terrace, Dublin 2, Ireland

BLOOMSBURY, BLOOMSBURY ACADEMIC and the Diana logo are
trademarks of Bloomsbury Publishing Plc

First published in Great Britain 2023
This paperback edition published 2024

Copyright © Kirrily Freeman and John Munro, 2023

Kirrily Freeman and John Munro have asserted their right under the
Copyright, Designs and Patents Act, 1988, to be identified as Editors of this work.

For legal purposes the Acknowledgments on p. x constitute
an extension of this copyright page.

Cover design: Terry Woodley
Cover image © Berlin wall in winter with mist and nightlights. Spreephoto.de/Getty.

All rights reserved. No part of this publication may be reproduced or transmitted
in any form or by any means, electronic or mechanical, including photocopying,
recording, or any information storage or retrieval system, without prior permission
in writing from the publishers.

Bloomsbury Publishing Plc does not have any control over, or responsibility for,
any third-party websites referred to or in this book. All internet addresses given in
this book were correct at the time of going to press. The author and publisher regret
any inconvenience caused if addresses have changed or sites have ceased to exist,
but can accept no responsibility for any such changes.

A catalogue record for this book is available from the British Library.

A catalog record for this book is available from the Library of Congress.

ISBN:	HB:	978-1-3502-6493-9
	PB:	978-1-3502-6496-0
	ePDF:	978-1-3502-6494-6
	eBook:	978-1-3502-6495-3

Typeset by Integra Software Services Pvt. Ltd.

To find out more about our authors and books visit www.bloomsbury.com
and sign up for our newsletters.

*To the memory of Gladys and Maurice Purtill,
James and Claire Freeman, and Jann Knijnenburg,*

*and to the memory of Eddie Hanley, Bobby McNickle, Molly McNickle,
Anne Munro, Billy Munro, Billy Wright, and Connie Wright*

Contents

List of Illustrations	ix
Acknowledgments	x
Introduction *Kirrily Freeman and John Munro*	1
Part 1 Intellectual Production	15
1 The End of History? *Molly Geidel*	17
2 The Rushdie Affair, the Threat of a Globalized Islam, and the Retreat from Multiculturalism *Rita Chin*	39
3 Total Critique: *The Condition of Postmodernity* at the End of History *Don Mitchell*	59
4 Beyond Binaries: Stuart Hall and the History of Science *Michell Chresfield*	79
5 Intersectionality as Heuristic: A Conversation *Phanuel Antwi and Amira Ismail*	101
Part 2 Culture and Politics	117
6 The New Concerned Intellectuals and Civil Society: Democracy Movements in Taiwan *Song-Chuan Chen*	119
7 The Guildford Four and *First Tuesday: Free to Speak* *Frances Pheasant-Kelly*	143
8 George H. W. Bush's Panama War Speech: Realist Policy as "Just Cause" *Wassim Daghrir*	161
9 Poptivism on the Cold War's Edge: *Breakthrough/Rainbow Warriors* and the "1989" Sound *Roxanne Panchasi*	183
10 A Tale of Two Periodicities: Indigenous and Settler Continuities amid Neoliberal Transformation at the St. Alice Hotel *John Munro*	203
11 Germany, the Environment, and the End of Communism: A Conversation *Julia Ault and Thomas Fleischman*	227

Conclusion *Ned Richardson-Little* 241

Contributors 253
Select Bibliography 256
Index 261

Illustrations

6.1 Yeh and comrades with Cheng's charred body beneath the flag   130

6.2 Front cover of *The Freedom Era Weekly* (May 21, 1989) showing Chan's self-immolation   132

10.1 St. Alice Hotel, 1980s   206

10.2 The Observatory, 2013   206

10.3 Municipality of North Vancouver. This 1899 map indicates land subdivision in North Vancouver and provides a sense of the spatial relationship between North Vancouver and Vancouver, which are separated by Burrard Inlet. The St. Alice was located within the densely plotted area of North Vancouver close to the straight line that spans Burrard Inlet on this map   210

10.4 St. Alice Hotel, ca. 1913   211

10.5 View from the St. Alice Hotel of North Vancouver Shipyards, Burrard Inlet, and Vancouver (across the inlet) during the Second World War   213

10.6 St. Alice Hotel, 1960s   214

10.7 St. Alice Hotel interior, 1980s   216

10.8 St. Alice Hotel demolition, 1989   217

Acknowledgments

This volume is the second in a planned trilogy that began with *Reading the Postwar Future: Textual Turning Points from 1944* (2020). That collection looked at 1944 as a key moment in intellectual history, one which saw a profusion and variety of texts that were remarkably visionary and future-oriented. In choosing a date for our "sequel" volume, 1989 jumped out at us as a—or perhaps even the—landmark year of the twentieth century because of the sheer magnitude of its world-historical eventfulness. Yet we wanted to retain our focus on texts, including unconventional ones, and so pursued the question of whether 1989 was as significant intellectually as it was politically, economically, socially, and culturally. The extent to which 1989 represented a turning point, textually or otherwise, ultimately became a central concern of the book.

While our intention for this volume was to follow the same trajectory we did for the 1944 project, the eventfulness of 2020–21 made the process of completing this book markedly different from the previous one. Gone was the in-person workshop initially scheduled for Brussels in summer 2020 and then Berlin in summer 2021. Gone, too, was the institutional and external grant funding that would have supported such a meeting. Instead, our international group of contributors met remotely, while negotiating all the challenges and difficulties—personal and professional—of the Covid-19 pandemic. We lost some contributors along the way, and gained others as we went, and we are grateful for our authors' patience and persistence, their faith in us and in this project, and their willingness to tackle 1989 in 2020/21. We are likewise very grateful to our editors at Bloomsbury Academic: Maddie Holder, who proposed the idea of a trilogy in the first place and has been patient, encouraging, and flexible, is a joy to work with. Abigail Lane has shepherded us through the production process with kindness and efficiency. We would like to thank our colleagues and students at our respective institutions, the University of Birmingham and Saint Mary's University, in particular Elise Blacker for her artful and speedy transcription of the interviews that feature in the volume. But our greatest debt, as always, is to our families. We dedicated the 1944 volume to our children and the future. This book is dedicated to the elders in our families, and to the past that will always be present.

Introduction

Kirrily Freeman and John Munro

Text and Transformation

Among the texts of 1989, some of the most iconic are images. From the Exxon Valdez oil spill to Tank Man in Tiananmen Square to the fall of the Berlin Wall, 1989 may well have been the year of the photograph. These images contributed to the sense of eventfulness and immediacy that characterize 1989: we are on tenterhooks as we watch Tank Man face down the People's Liberation Army; like the Alaska wildlife choked with crude oil, we are overwhelmed by yet another corporate environmental disaster; we share in the hopeful jubilation of crowds in Eastern Europe and Germany as they press for change; we cheer the Guildford Four as they emerge from an English jail after fifteen years of wrongful imprisonment. These photographic texts are powerful to look at now, and many had power in 1989, as press coverage shaped public reactions to and understandings of global events and spurred further action. But contradictions abound. Here, momentous transformation and "immediate effect," there, more of the same. Our cover image—of the Berlin wall before it came down—reflects just such ambiguity. Less famous than other photographs of its moment, it nevertheless has a haunting quality that also characterizes 1989. The throngs of people and their acts of defiance are missing. With hindsight, we know they will come and that the wall will disappear. But formidable security structures, politicized and militarized spaces, and the footprint of the Cold War, however, are clearly in view. And they remained so after Communism was declared defeated and the Cold War proclaimed over. The wall opened, but the future was foreclosed.

No one was naïve in greeting with glee the end of the unfreedoms that defined life under Communism as it existed. State surveillance, interminable lines for food and other necessities, access to travel and education limited by lack of loyalty, political elites protecting their own out-of-touch privileges: history's dustbin was the appropriate repository for such things. And yet in them had been another way, an outside. After the fall of the Berlin Wall, such alternatives were unavailable in the face of an unopposed capitalism that was intensifying inequality, devouring the planet's resources, and possessed of an inbuilt tendency to expand and consolidate power by imperial means. Berlin was 1989's brightest flashpoint, but Washington and Wall Street were certainly significant to the proceedings of that year. As the view from Panama brought into focus within mere weeks of the fall of the Wall, in the absence of the Communist villain, the sheriff of US empire could now patrol the global village seemingly at whim. The terms of such a unipolar Pax Americana were those of a liberal individualism unfettered by either Communism's overweening control or its stated concern with collective interests. From 1989, whatever the future was to be, it would unfold under one overarching system in which the scope of freedom widened in some senses and particularly for some people, while with no meaningful outside to that system, horizons of possibility narrowed. Well-placed individuals might be at liberty to maximize their potential after 1989, in other words, but under a now globally governing logic, the sense of what people might owe each other and the natural world was diminished. The texts taken up in the following chapters indicate some of the structural continuities and continua of resistance that weathered a moment of epochal change, and these texts reveal in their moment the contradictions attending the concurrent defeat of a kind of hope-stifling autocratic rule and the victory of another kind of rule that also dwindled optimism and has shown itself to be quite compatible with authoritarianism. These contradictions, we suggest, are not resolvable, but they comprise the ideological constellation of our times.

This volume is the second in a series that looks at the textual production of landmark years.[1] *Reading the Postwar Future* treated 1944 as a significant date in intellectual history.[2] An astoundingly generative year, 1944 (even more than the year that followed), was a moment of radical openness in which a stunning variety of texts proposed plans for and visions of the postwar future. In selecting a subject year for the present volume, 1989 struck us as perhaps having the same potential: as a moment alive with possibility and hope, a seismic year of world-historical events and major texts that inspired or were inspired by those events. In this, we were both right and wrong, as the texts and chapters assembled here, and the contradictions they exemplify and analyze will make clear.

In our volume on 1944, we embraced a broad and capacious definition of what constitutes a "text." From monographs and novels to speeches and poetry, films, policy platforms, and pamphlets, we explored and interpreted myriad programs that envisioned the postwar future on a global scale. In this volume, we have likewise maintained our global outlook (highlighting events in Taiwan, Panama, Canada, Iran, the UK, and the United States in addition to those in the Soviet Union, Eastern Europe, and China) and our broad conception of "text": scholarly articles and academic monographs meet infamous novels and popular pamphlets, presidential speeches, television documentaries, fundraising pop albums, and the press. To these we have also added—following Paul Ricoeur—"meaningful action considered as text": the self-immolations of two pro-democracy dissidents in Taiwan, the displacement of poor and Indigenous residents in gentrifying Vancouver, and in Germany, *die Wende* (the turn) itself.[3] These texts and the chapters that treat them—chapters authored by an array of international scholars at a range of points in their careers—are organized in two sections. The first treats the intellectual production of 1989 and assembles chapters on Francis Fukuyama's "End of History?" (by Molly Geidel), "The Rushdie Affair" (by Rita Chin), David Harvey's *Condition of Postmodernity* (by Don Mitchell), Stuart Hall's "New Ethnicities" (by Michell Chresfield), and Kimberlé Crenshaw's "Demarginalizing the Intersection of Race and Sex" (in a conversation between Phanuel Antwi and Amira Ismail), each text a key intellectual intervention of 1989. The second section examines 1989's reverberations in culture and politics: the pro-democracy movement in Taiwan (by Song-Chuan Chen); the release of the Guildford Four examined through the *First Tuesday* television documentary "Free to Speak" (by Frances Pheasant-Kelly); the US invasion of Panama analyzed through President George H. W. Bush's speech announcing "Operation Just Cause" (by Wassim Daghrir); Greenpeace's *Breakthrough* and *Rainbow Warriors* fundraising albums (by Roxanne Panchasi); the demolition of the St. Alice Hotel in North Vancouver (by John Munro); and the collapse and erasure of the German Democratic Republic in East Germany (explored in a conversation between Julia Ault and Thomas Fleischman).

Ours is, of course, not the first book to take up the significance of 1989, the nature or character of that year, its major events, or its cultural and intellectual products and implications.[4] As George Lawson notes, 1989 has become something of a "cottage industry."[5] Nor are we the first to broach the year in terms of change and continuity, or from a global perspective.[6] Perhaps the dominant interpretive tradition—beginning in the year itself—has been to see 1989 as a watershed. President George H. W. Bush's inaugural address on January 20, 1989, proclaimed,

> A new breeze is blowing, and a world refreshed by freedom seems reborn; for in man's heart, if not in fact, the day of the dictator is over. The totalitarian era is passing, its old ideas blown away like leaves from an ancient, lifeless tree. A new breeze is blowing, and a nation refreshed by freedom stands ready to push on. There is new ground to be broken, and new action to be taken. There are times when the future seems thick as a fog; you sit and wait, hoping the mists will lift and reveal the right path. But this is a time when the future seems a door you can walk right through into a room called tomorrow.[7]

Popular and scholarly understandings of 1989 have seized on this threshold quality, buttressing public perceptions. Some commentators see the "long 1989" as the end of the "short twentieth century."[8] Others see in 1989 the birth of the present.[9] Some observers have cautioned that interpretations of 1989 as transformational or disruptive often hew toward the triumphalist and romantic, and run the risk of ignoring local realities and global experiences, or obscuring structures and timelines (such as those of colonialism) that, while imbricated with the Cold War, were neither tethered to nor reliant upon it. Others retain the notion of rupture but are more pessimistic about the changes wrought: there was no inexorable progress toward prosperity, freedom, and democracy, no real relaxation of tensions, nor the dawn of a new era of peace and cooperation. Instead, the liberal democracies of the West became less democratic and more illiberal; capitalism, rather than democracy, filled the spaces opened up by the "End of History"; and post-communist states forged their own distinctive paths, many shaped by nationalism, plutarchy, and repression. Indeed, for those who had lived under Communism, one of the consequences of its collapse was an immediate, sharp decline in life expectancy.[10] As we write this introduction, Russian forces are invading Ukraine, revealing the Soviet Union's successor to be a carbon autocracy possessed of neither economic nor political democracy but ready to resume dreams of conquest. This time, tragedy followed farce: first, shallow proclamations about Communism's demise signaling history's terminus; later, horrific wars of imperial aggression. That a GDR-based KBG agent would, in formulating Russian policy, go on to prompt the full remilitarization of a united Germany is but one illustration of the fact that history remains ongoing and unpredictable.

Our emphasis on contradiction, on how 1989 represents the promise of expanded liberatory potential accompanied by its clear contraction, marks a perspective made possible from a temporal distance of over three decades. The chapters collected here explore many interpretive avenues raised by the contradictions of 1989. We see moments of change, rupture, and transformation. Taiwan became more democratic. The USSR collaborated with Greenpeace on a compilation of Western pop music. For the first time, DNA evidence overturned a conviction—technology that would also buttress new ethnicities and sense of belonging. "Intersectionality" brought new a language and framework for understanding and expressing power and identity. Eastern Europeans were no longer behind an Iron Curtain. The Guildford Four were no longer behind bars. In a military engagement that sat comfortably in a long list of imperialist interventions that spanned and preceded the Cold War, the United States made good on Bush's promise to "take new action" by invading Panama. And, of course, the German Democratic Republic and its ruling party would soon cease to exist.

But the volume also makes clear that optimism quickly faded, radical opportunities were soon foreclosed, and much of the promise of 1989 remained unfulfilled. In many post-Communist states, corruption and inequality intensified.[11] Many alternative projects and innovative ideas for reform were sidelined, as Julia Ault and Thomas Fleischman highlight in the case of Germany. Some innovations were largely superficial. Roxanne Panchasi's chapter notes that Greenpeace's fundraising albums contained no new songs, only repackaged hits from the previous decade. Greenpeace International did innovate, however, in its embrace of a gamut of marketing strategies to promote the albums, a commitment to consumerism that some saw as a departure from the organization's mission and values. Neoconservative and neoliberal policymakers continued to simultaneously abuse and disregard the global South, as Ambalavaner Sivanandan chronicled in 1989, resulting in pressures that drove human migrations on ever larger scales and under increasingly perilous conditions.[12] The dynamics of these forces are made clear in Molly Geidel's chapter on Fukuyama, Wassim Daghrir's chapter on the US invasion of Panama, and Rita Chin's chapter on British responses to the Ayatollah Khomeini's fatwa against Salman Rushdie. As Phanuel Antwi and Amira Ismail discuss in relation to intersectionality, and John Munro outlines in connection to settler colonialism and gentrification in Canada, the oppression of Black and Indigenous people remained a persistent and pervasive structure that the liberations of 1989 did little to displace. Even the experience of the Guildford Four, detailed by Fran Pheasant-Kelly, encapsulates the simultaneous promise and disappointment of 1989: after their long-fought battle for freedom, the Four found themselves facing the future under the weight of an inescapable, sometimes unbearable, past.

Symbolism and Cynicism

Other contradictions also emerge in the texts and chapters that follow. One is the year's heavy investment with symbolism and cynicism in almost equal measure. The year's relationship with commemoration functions in two directions: anniversary commemorations were generative of many of the momentous events of 1989 and feature in many of the texts explored here; and what 1989 means, the way it is understood, has shifted with time in such a way that each major anniversary brings its own interpretive valences. Cynical responses to 1989 began in the year itself and continue unabated.

Commemorations and anniversaries were without doubt key to the eventfulness and character of 1989. Pro-democracy protests in China and Taiwan were linked to "May Fourth movement" commemorations, the observance of Human Rights Day, and, in Taiwan, the memory of the violent suppression of Taiwanese protesters by the Republican Chinese government in 1947, known as the "228 Incident." Demonstrations in Czechoslovakia were ignited by the observance of the fiftieth anniversary of International Students' Day, commemorating the Nazi suppression of student demonstrations at Prague University in 1939. The fatefulness of November 9—Germany's *Schicksalstag* (Day of Fate)—was reinforced by Günter Schabowski's accidental opening of East Germany's borders. The year 1989 was also, of course, the bicentenary of the French Revolution, the lessons and legacy of which loomed large.[13] More subtly, but nevertheless persuasively, Don Mitchell explores the 1989 centenary commemorations of the Johnstown (Pennsylvania) flood as an expression of postmodernity in a postindustrial American city. Michell Chresfield highlights Ghana's Year of Return in 2019, which marked 400 years since the first enslaved Africans arrived in Virginia.

The anniversaries of 1989 itself have also had a role to play in how the year's importance is understood. Every June 4, rallies and candlelight vigils are held in Hong Kong to mark the Tiananmen Square massacre. For the tenth anniversary, there was a crackdown on dissidents in China itself, though the vigil in Hong Kong (which had just recently experienced its own momentous transition from British to Chinese possession in 1997) continued, with heightened solemnity.[14] For China, these commemorations clearly represent a threat (despite Zhu Rongji's quip that he had "almost forgotten" what they were about). For the crowds in Hong Kong, however, "remembrance is resistance."[15]

The tenth anniversary celebrations in Berlin featured a concert and fireworks at the Brandenburg gate—the Scorpions played *Wind of Change*—and the newly elected Gerhard Schröder joined Helmut Kohl, George Bush senior, and Mikhail Gorbachev in a celebration of reunification and Europeanization. The twentieth anniversary in Berlin, however, had a more playful tenor, though a similar message. The "Festival of Freedom" once again featured a concert at the Brandenburg gate, a Berlin Twitter Wall, and 1,000 eight-foot foam dominoes that toppled along the footprint of the Berlin Wall in a whimsical inversion of the "domino effect."[16] Some of these bricks were decorated by artists in countries where "walls still divide people."[17] In the United States, the Spy Museum in Washington, DC, held its inaugural Trabant car rally.[18] As some of these initiatives suggest, the postmodern "kitschification" of the Wall, and of the GDR more generally, was by this point well underway.

National Geographic's 2019 documentary, *1989: The Year That Made Us*, marked the thirtieth anniversary by taking a broad view of 1989's geopolitical and cultural legacies but—perhaps fittingly—within a narrower, American, frame: the Soviet withdrawal from Afghanistan sowed the seeds of Islamic fundamentalism, 9/11, and the War on Terror; the ascent of TV tabloids with the launch of *A Current Affair* permanently changed the journalistic landscape in the US and popular understandings of what news is and should be; *Batman*, *The Little Mermaid* and *The Simpsons*—as "global, branded franchises"—transformed the entertainment industry, particularly through merchandizing; Spike Lee, Public Enemy, and Arsenio Hall challenged white racism in the United States and brought Black urban culture into suburban living rooms; the World Wide Web, the first computer virus, the launch of a network of GPS satellites, and the release of Nintendo's Gameboy established the "miniaturization, personalization, mobility, and connectedness," alongside the threats to cyber security, that now define our digital lives.[19]

The Personal and the Provocative

Taylor Swift named her 2014 album *1989* because that was the year she was born. Indeed, for many people, the personal 1989 is inextricable from the historical 1989. There is a strikingly autobiographical dimension to much of the scholarship on 1989, including in this volume.[20] Song-Chuan Chen witnessed the massacre in Beijing over a phone line from Taiwan. John Munro experienced the collision of neoliberal gentrification and Indigenous dispossession in North Vancouver. Roxanne Panchasi reflects on encountering 1989 through the poptivism, soundscapes, and materiality of a record; Phanuel Antwi and Amira

Ismail discuss what intersectionality has meant for them as Black intellectuals. The personal was central for Fay Weldon as she excoriated Khomeini's fatwa against her friend Salman Rushdie; for Kimberlé Crenshaw and, as Ismail asserts, for many Black women scholars whose "political and social thought is fed through their personal experiences" and is marginalized as a result; for the Black Americans looking to DNA testing for clues to their ancestral pasts and connections to community in the present; even for George H. W. Bush in combatting his own "wimp factor." Gorbachev's personal appeal was a driver of events in 1989, from his meetings with Margaret Thatcher and Pope John Paul II to the ubiquitous posters and chants of "Gorbi" that sprang up in demonstrations around the world.

But, as Antwi and Ismail inquire, if a keyword, or a theory, or a text, or a year is simply an aggregation of the personal and individual, does it have heuristic value? On the other hand, as Ned Richardson-Little asks in the conclusion to this volume, can the eventfulness and specificity of 1989 be extricated from meta-discursive attempts to ascribe it a singular meaning? Linked to these questions is another: to what extent are intellectual, cultural, and even political products of 1989 truly of their moment? As Don Mitchell notes, David Harvey's manuscript for *Condition of Postmodernity* went to press on the eve of Tiananmen and was published on the eve of the fall of the Berlin Wall, and therefore engages with neither. Rather than broach the watershed of 1989, Harvey's concern is the sea-change that began "around 1972." Molly Geidel engages accusations of "lateness" made against Fukuyama's "End of History." Salman Rushdie's *Satanic Verses* was published in 1988 and generated only localized responses until the fatwa in February 1989. The Guildford Four had been fighting, and *First Tuesday* had been reporting on, judicial malpractice for over a decade. These efforts culminated in 1989, but were they "of" it?

The same could be said of 1989's other events: despite their quality of surprise, many had been brewing for years. The road to June 1989 was a long one for Solidarity in Poland and the pro-democracy movements in China and Taiwan alike. The St. Alice Hotel in North Vancouver was demolished in 1989, but the demolition was part of a broader process of urban redevelopment that had intensified in the city in preparation for Expo '86 and continued through the 2010 Vancouver Olympics and beyond. So, is there a *Zeitgeist* to 1989? Is there something that unites the events and texts of the year beyond their ambiguity and their moment of arrival?

If there is a discernible "spirit" of 1989 in the year's political, cultural, social, and economic products, it is one conjured by a liberal individualism globally ascendant and yet inescapably vulnerable to the antagonistic pull of its multiple meanings of "freedom." There is no direct line of historical causation running from 1989 to the likes of Boris Johnson and Donald Trump, but the extreme self-centeredness of leaders who put personal gain before even the dominant set of interests they are meant to represent must be counted as a morbid symptom of a hegemonic ideology cracking under the weight of its own contradictions. The texts gathered here are provocations which speak to the reconfigurations of power that made the world less oppressive for some and yet limited liberation for others, all while deepening hierarchies that often represented more of the same. Francis Fukuyama's "The End of History?", analyzed by Molly Geidel in Chapter 1, might perhaps be best remembered as 1989's most high-profile attempt to iron out the contradictions in which the Iron Curtain's end was ensnared. The smug and gimmicky quality of Fukuyama's essay provoked the derision of a legion of commentators, from Margaret Thatcher to Jacques Derrida. Geidel argues that "The End of History" was both symptom and agent of tendencies far more serious than its pop sensibility suggests, however: its updating of Cold War modernization theory both provoked and disavowed myriad forms of violence inflicted on the global South and relegated much of the globe to "not mattering."

In Chapter 2, by Rita Chin, Salman Rushdie's *The Satanic Verses*, Ayatollah Khomeini's fatwa against Rushdie, and Fay Weldon's pamphlet on the affair, *Sacred Cows*, are hardly the stuff of celebratory triumphalism. Rushdie's book featured a dream sequence in which a character invoking the Prophet Muhammad is lampooned and sexualized. Khomeini issued a fatwa condemning Rushdie to death for blasphemy. The ensuing controversy, into which feminist Fay Weldon interjected her "counterblast," drew attention to the large number of Muslim immigrants settled across Western Europe and the United Kingdom, provoking liberal doubts and debates about multiculturalism, integration, and the compatibility of Islam with "Western" values, and fueling anti-Muslim and ant-immigration sentiments. In the controversy that Chin expertly charts, we see not the freedom wrought by a falling wall but the ideological hardening of the walls surrounding Fortress Europe.

For Don Mitchell, in Chapter 3, David Harvey's *Condition of Postmodernity* is both provocative and prescient. Harvey's rethinking of Marxist theories in light of the shifting experiences of late capitalist cities and his assertion of a new form of "time-space compression" delineated the coming culture wars and made *Condition* a "lightning rod for criticism." Despite its totalizing theory and vision, Mitchell argues, Harvey's work is nevertheless strikingly prescient of the forms that postmodern, postindustrial, post-Cold War capitalism were about to take.

Stuart Hall's "New Ethnicities"—which Michell Chresfield puts in conversation with one of 1989's major developments in the history of science (the application of DNA testing to confirm/refute the identity of a perpetrator in a court of law)—is very much of its moment in Hall's assertion that binary frameworks no longer suffice. Chresfield uncovers the provocative possibilities of "new ethnicities" by exploring the potential of ancestry DNA testing for Black American root-seekers in uncovering their identities and articulating demands for justice and redress. Kimberlé Crenshaw's "Demarginalizing the Intersection," discussed by Phanuel Antwi and Amira Ismail in Chapter 5, also provoked reassessments of identity and demands for representation and justice. Central to Antwi and Ismail's analysis is the fact that intersectionality, despite its current ubiquity—even co-option—as a "buzzword," nevertheless retains its provocative, heuristic power, especially for the Black women it was coined to serve. As a term of analysis devised in service of liberation but also serviceable for liberal individualism, intersectionality marks the continuities of counterhegemonic thought as well as the contradictions of its era.

The depth of provocation that pro-democracy protests represent for China is perhaps best underscored by the regime's response to the protests in Tiananmen Square—a massacre in which thousands were killed and injured—and related arrests and imprisonments that continue to this day. But as Song-Chuan Chen describes in Chapter 6, the "new concerned intellectuals" who were the lifeblood of dissent in Taiwan saw it as their duty and their right to speak truth to power: it is hard to imagine a more provocative act than setting oneself on fire in the name of political ideals. The *First Tuesday* television documentaries discussed by Fran Pheasant-Kelly in Chapter 7 were provocative in their filmmaking techniques as well as their assertions of corruption and malpractice in the British legal system. They provoked not only the release of the Guildford Four from prison, but a judicial review, and the reform of interrogation and evidentiary procedures. And yet, police and prisons in the UK and beyond remain comprehensible only within the terms of the order of global racial capitalism in which they operate.

The contradictions inherent in George H. W. Bush's "world refreshed by freedom" and the ongoing exigencies of empire were nowhere better in evidence than in Panama. Manuel Noriega, long a protected CIA asset, thumbed his nose at American demands. The US government invaded Panama and deposed him. Bush's "Operation Just Cause" speech, as a piece of political propaganda justifying military intervention abroad, is also inherently provocative, as Wassim Daghrir illustrates. Bush himself may have been provoked to take military action by media discussion of his "wimp factor" and by a lack of clear foreign policy direction following Communism's demise, but behind these more immediate factors was a structural one. The manly maintenance of markets and of white racial domination were themselves a kind of pursuit of freedom for the beneficiaries of racial capitalism, as had long been the case in "America's backyard."

Greenpeace's 1989 "poptivism," meanwhile, was more subtly provocative but equally locatable within heightened contradictions. Greenpeace itself had long been a confrontational organization, but its fundraising albums were less so: *Breakthrough/Rainbow Warriors* contained not only no new songs, but also none of the rap, hip hop, metal, or alternative rock artists who were the provocateurs of the 1980s. The assembled pop music was conscientious, but benign. In their mobilization on both sides of the geopolitical divide, these albums rejected the Cold War status quo, even if they did so on terms increasingly defined by capitalist consumerism and commodification. For its part, the St. Alice Hotel in North Vancouver was caught in contradictions of long standing, as John Munro illustrates in Chapter 10. That settler freedom on stolen land could never liberate everyone within the territory of "Canada" was a political fact in 1989, as it had been since the arrival of the Europeans and as it is today. This hotel's construction and demolition alike necessitated multiple evictions of Indigenous people on whose land the hotel stood: the St. Alice's construction claimed Squamish land for white settlers, its demolition involved the eviction of Indigenous residents and patrons for whom the hotel had become home. While it stood, the St. Alice and its neighborhood provoked fear, anxiety, and vitriol. When it fell, it was a domino in the total transformation of North Vancouver.

Germany is perhaps where 1989 mattered most, but as the essays of this book and the contributions from Julia Ault, Thomas Fleischman, and Ned Richardson-Little all testify, the way Germany has come to stand in for the year as a whole has obscured significant dynamics. As Ault and Fleischman's conversation suggests, with the fall of the Wall and ultimate German reunification went numerous missed opportunities to deepen democracy without completely capitulating to capitalism. The environmental implications of this situation remain to be fully reckoned with. At the same time, as this volume demonstrates, 1989 mattered much well beyond Germany. After November, the citizens of the GDR would indeed breathe more freely, but they did so within a global system in which the slogan "I can't breathe" would later emerge from a literal plea in the face of ongoing police brutality to recognize that Black lives matter. Also within this global system, by the time Germany became reunified in the autumn of 1990, the United States was gearing up for an invasion in the Middle East which, even more than in Panama, emblematized the terms of a new global order in which the Soviet-led check on US empire was no more. The path of imperialism connected Berlin to Baghdad after all.

Lecturing a few years before the year this book considers, Stuart Hall noted that counterhegemonic cultural formations "are required for the construction of new kinds of societies. But every such formation, every struggle for change, has contradictory effects as well as limits."[21] The events and the textual record of 1989 show how systems of power were challenged within the First, Second, and Third Worlds of the day. They also show the contradictions that structured those challenges. The provocations of that year took shape amid a winnowing of the very possibility to provoke. Such contradictions were perhaps 1989's most durable legacy. And we live with them to this day.

Notes

1. Publications such as Margaret MacMillan's *Paris 1919: Six Months That Changed the World* (New York: Penguin, 2003); Ian Buruma's *Year Zero: A History of 1945* (New York: Penguin, 2014); Simon Hall's *1956: The World in Revolt* (London: Faber, 2016), alongside the ever-growing list of titles on 1968, have led the way in focusing on the historical significance of a single year. Their approach is to chronicle the events that made a given year momentous. Our approach takes the events of the year as a starting point to engage with their cultural and intellectual resonance and legacies.
2. Kirrily Freeman and John Munro, *Reading the Postwar Future: Textual Turning Points from 1944* (London: Bloomsbury Academic, 2020).
3. Paul Ricoeur, "The Model of the Text: Meaningful Action Considered as a Text," *Social Research* 28, no. 3 (1971): 529–62.
4. See Ronald Beiner, "1989: Nationalism, Internationalism and the Nairn-Hobsbawn Debate," *European Journal of Sociology* 40, no. 1 (1999): 171–84; Mary Elise Sarotte, *1989: The Struggle to Create Post-Cold War Europe* (Princeton: Princeton University Press, 2014); Stephen Kotkin, *Uncivil Society: 1989 and the Implosion of the Communist Establishment* (New York: Penguin, 2010); Jeffrey A. Engel, *The Fall of the Berlin Wall: The Revolutionary Legacy of 1989* (Oxford: Oxford University Press, 2012); Piotr H. Kosicki and Kyrill Kunakhovich, *The Long 1989: Decades of Global Revolution* (Budapest: Central European University, 2019); Chris Armbruster Lawson and Michael Cox, eds., *The Global 1989: Continuity and Change in World Politics* (Cambridge: Cambridge University Press, 2012).
5. Lawson, *Global 1989*, 4.

6   See especially Kosicki and Kunakhovich, *The Long 1989: Decades of Global Revolution* and Lawson, Armbruster and Cox, eds., *The Global 1989: Continuity and Change in World Politics*.
7   Inaugural Address of George H. W. Bush, January 20, 1989. Available online: https://avalon.law.yale.edu/20th_century/bush.asp (accessed December 5, 2021).
8   See Timothy Garten Ash, "1989!" *The New York Review of Books*, November 5, 2009.
9   See, for example, Time, *1989: The Year That Defined Today's World* (New York: Time, 2009); National Geographic, *1989: The Year That Made Us* (2019).
10 Vladimir Popov, "Mortality and Life Expectancy in Post-Communist Countries," *Dialogue of Civilizations Research Institute*, March 5, 2018. Available online: https://doc-research.org/2018/06/mortality-life-expectancy-post-communist/ (accessed March 3, 2022).
11 See, for example, Stephen McGrath, "Executing a Dictator: Open Wounds of Romania's Christmas Revolution," *BBC News*, December 25, 2019.
12 Ambalavaner Sivanandan, "New Circuits of Imperialism," *Race & Class* 30, no. 3 (1989): 1–19.
13 Georgia Hesse, "La Vive France 1789–1989: The New Year Marks the Beginning of Twelve Months of Festivals, Exhibitions, Art Shows and Musical Performances throughout France and in the United States to Commemorate the Bicentennial of the French Revolution," *Los Angeles Times*, January 1, 1989; Hugh Gough, "France and the Memory of the Revolution: 1789–1989," *History of European Ideas* 15, no. 4–6 (1992): 811–16; Karen Offen, "Women's Memory, Women's History, Women's Political Action: The French Revolution in Retrospect, 1789–1889–1989," *Journal of Women's History* 1, no. 3 (Winter 1990): 211–30; Jurgen Wilke, "The Example of the French Revolution," *European Journal of Communication* 4, no. 4 (December 1, 1989): 375–91.
14 Mark Landler, "A Quiet Tiananmen Anniversary in China," *The New York Times*, June 5, 1999.
15 "Jimmy Lai and Two Other Hong Kong Democracy Activists Found Guilty over June 4 Assembly," *Reuters*, December 9, 2021.
16 Eric Westervelt, "Berlin Marks 20th Anniversary of Wall's Fall," *NPR Special Series: After the Fall: 20 Years after the Berlin Wall*, November 9, 2009; "Fall of the Berlin Wall: 20th Anniversary Celebrations" *The Guardian*, November 9, 2009; "The Wall Project," *Wende Museum*, https://artsandculture.google.com/exhibit/the-wall-project-wende-museum/QQspCdVW?hl=en
17 Kim Se-jeong, "Three Koreans Will be Part of German Unification Ceremony," *The Korea Times*, September 6, 2009.
18 Laura Kiniry, "Thirty Years On, the 'Worst Car Ever Built' Has a Fervent Fan Club," *Atlas Obscura*, August 5, 2019. Available online: https://www.atlasobscura.com/articles/trabant-cars-east-germany (accessed December 5, 2021).

19 National Geographic, *1989: The Year That Made Us* (2019).
20 See, for example, Michael Meyer, *The Year That Changed the World: The Untold Story behind the Fall of the Berlin Wall* (New York: Schribner, 2012); Timothy Garton Ash, *The Magic Lantern: The Revolution of '89 Witnessed in Warsaw, Budapest, Berlin and Prague* (London: Vintage, 1993); Victor Sebestyen, *Revolution 1989: The Fall of the Soviet Empire* (London: Vintage, 2010); Craig Calhoun, "Tiananmen, Television, and the Public Sphere: Internationalization of Culture and the Beijing Spring of 1989," *Public Culture* 2, no. 1 (Fall 1989): 54–71.
21 Stuart Hall, *Cultural Studies 1983* (London: Duke University Press, 2016), 189.

Part One

Intellectual Production

1

The End of History?

Molly Geidel

In summer 1989, "The End of History?" by RAND Corporation Sovietologist-turned US State Department planner Francis Fukuyama was published in the conservative magazine *The National Interest*.[1] The article declared "the unabashed victory of political and economic liberalism" and "the triumph of the West— the Western *idea*," evident in both the "total exhaustion of viable systematic alternatives" to capitalist democracy and the global ubiquity of consumer goods, rock music, and television.[2] Drawing on a somewhat simplified version of GWF Hegel's contention that Napoleon's victory at Jena in 1806 had marked history's end, Fukuyama declared that, where it mattered—famously excluding pockets of socialism in "Managua, Pyongyang, or Cambridge Massachusetts"— history in 1989 had settled into an era in which it remained only to work out the technical details rather than big questions about how societies should be organized.[3] Despite the relatively minor status of both writer and journal (*The National Interest* had been founded only four years earlier by neoconservative Irving Kristol), the article quickly became a sensation; Louis Menand writes that the essay "turned the foreign-policy world on its ear."[4] The *New York Times*' James Atlas similarly recounts that "within weeks, 'The End of History?' had become the hottest topic around," and its fame quickly extended beyond US policy circles:

> 'The End of History?' had become ... this year's answer to Paul Kennedy's phenomenal best seller, 'The Rise and Fall of the Great Powers.' George F. Will was among the first to weigh in, with a *Newsweek* column in August; two weeks later, Fukuyama's photograph appeared in *Time*. The French quarterly *Commentaire* announced that it was devoting a special issue to 'The End of History?' The BBC sent a television crew. Translations of the piece were scheduled to appear in Dutch, Japanese, Italian and Icelandic. Ten Downing Street requested a copy. In Washington, a newsdealer on Connecticut Avenue

reported, the summer issue of *The National Interest* was 'outselling everything, even the pornography.' ... By mid-September, Peter Tarnoff, president of the Council on Foreign Relations, could speculate on the Op-Ed page of *The New York Times* that 'The End of History?' was 'laying the foundation for a Bush doctrine.'[5]

Fukuyama's star rose even higher when the Berlin Wall fell just months later, seemingly confirming his pronouncements. The reception of the article, however, and subsequently of the bestselling 1992 book *The End of History and the Last Man*, in which Fukuyama clarified and extended his propositions, was more mixed, and its translation into concrete policy directives less clear than the above breathless account suggests. Perry Anderson writes that "for different reasons, liberals, conservatives, social democrats, communists all expressed incredulity or abhorrence of Fukuyama's arguments."[6] The conservatives in power, as Atlas reports, refrained from translating Fukuyama's grand pronouncements into policy prescriptions; he quotes Kristol saying "flatly" that "no one in the administration has read it."[7] Fukuyama attested to this remove in his own response to his critics, protesting that he was "a relatively junior official with little impact on policy," and that the "article has not been read by many of my superiors."[8] This was perhaps no surprise, as Fukuyama credited not at all the United States' Cold War aggression (in which he had played a part as a RAND analyst and Reagan-Bush State Department official) with the West's victory; his pronouncements thus imagined little for interventionist right-wing administrations to do. Internationally, the piece met with similar derision, even from conservatives: Margaret Thatcher reportedly marked up the article angrily when she read it, insisting that "the battle is not won," while, in Andrey Kortunov's words, Fukuyama became "a popular punching bag for Russian social scientists," in part "for his free interpretations of Hegel."[9]

This dual quality characterizes the reception of Fukuyama's end-of-history thesis, both in its moment and since. It is at once incoherent and deeply resonant with its moment, demobilizing and influential, widely mocked and referenced everywhere. Its sound-byte-readiness fit with the first Bush administration's penchant for one-liners, but also inspired in-depth exegeses from the likes of both Anderson and Jacques Derrida; Derrida declared Fukuyama's 1992 book-length expansion of the essay a "media gadget" which was "all the rage in the ideological supermarkets of the worried West," but also devoted a significant portion of his book *Specters of Marx* to refuting Fukuyama's propositions.[10] This chapter attempts to explain the stubborn persistence of Fukuyama's thesis despite its gimmicky quality that infuriated many, considering it in relation to his intellectual trajectory and influences, and paying particular attention to the piece's attempts to return to and update Cold War modernization theory.[11] I go on to situate the essay, and to a lesser extent the book that followed, as deeply embedded in, but also helping to destroy, an era of postwar Northern prosperity and welfarist planning that felt much more permanent than it turned out to be.

The End of Modernization

The ambivalent response to "The End of History?" partly stemmed from the hybrid nature of Fukuyama's text: it was neither reactionary jeremiad, nor philosophical tract, nor policy planning paper, but combined elements of all three. The title of Atlas' piece "What Is Fukuyama Saying? And to Whom Is He Saying It?" captures this confusion well. The article synthesizes the formal properties of Fukuyama's major influences: as an undergraduate at Cornell in the early 1970s, he studied with charismatic conservative philosopher Allan Bloom, author of the bestselling 1987 screed against cultural pluralism *The Closing of the American Mind*; Bloom became Fukuyama's mentor in his first year and was later responsible for the 1989 University of Chicago invitation for the talk on which "The End of History?" was based.

Fukuyama and Bloom's bond was forged in opposition to student radicalism: Fukuyama arrived the semester after the spring 1969 takeover of an administrative building by armed Black activists, an event which had bitterly divided the faculty and student body. Despite having missed the takeover by a few months, Fukuyama recalled the incident more than thirty years later as "a horrible spectacle because basically the whole university administration capitulated to them. They admitted it was a racist institution, and that academic freedom didn't exist. Bloom was part of a group of professors who were outraged by the whole thing and left Cornell, but he owed one more semester, which I took."[12] After Cornell, Fukuyama briefly went on to do graduate work in comparative literature at Yale, spending a few months in Paris where he sat in on lectures by Derrida and Roland Barthes. "I was turned off by their nihilistic idea of what literature was all about," he later recalled. "It had nothing to do with the world. I developed such an aversion to that whole over-intellectual approach that I turned to nuclear weapons instead."[13] If Fukuyama's claim that the nihilism of deconstructionism led him to a career re-igniting a Cold War and dealing with world-ending weapons seems contradictory, his story follows a well-known neoconservative trajectory: his brush with leftist intellectual life happened in a later era, and more briefly, than for an earlier generation of neoconservatives like Kristol, almost as if he had contrived an encounter (or at Cornell, conjured second-hand outrage at one) with left-academic circles in order to burnish his resume.[14]

Disillusioned with literature and philosophy, Fukuyama began a PhD at Harvard, where he studied with conservative political scientist Samuel P. Huntington and wrote a dissertation on Soviet influence in the Middle East. This training led him into a job at the RAND corporation, the archetypal think tank that shaped US military and development policy during the Cold War and beyond. There he worked as a policy analyst, producing reports on the Soviet presence in the Third World and US chances for swaying or pressuring Soviet "clients" there. The 1980s was not an easy time for Sovietologists. Chronicling the ideological divides in Sovietology after the Reagan administration's post-détente ratcheting up of tensions, David Engerman argues that these splits contributed to a crisis in the discipline as it utterly failed "to predict or explain Gorbachev."[15] If history was not ending for everyone in 1989, it certainly seemed to be ending for Sovietologists. "The End of History?", then, was a second self-reinvention for Fukuyama, this time as a public intellectual at the intersection of philosophy and geopolitics.

While part of the novelty of "The End of History?" came from its mix of policyspeak and philosophical conceptual framing, Fukuyama also brought a unique tone to this synthesis, inflecting the piece with a breezy optimism that Bloom and Huntington, along with most other conservatives, eschewed. Fukuyama's argument, which he accurately accuses many of his critics of mischaracterizing, is that the ideals of capitalism and democracy are not just the high point of modernity but the last word in ideal societies. While there are undoubtedly more ideals and goals to realize, he contends, there is no more to be thought or known about what a good society looks like than we, meaning Westerners, know now. Whatever events and conflicts might arise, "the victory of liberalism has occurred primarily in the realm of ideas or consciousness and is as yet incomplete in the real or material world. But there are powerful reasons for believing that it is the idea that will govern the material world *in the long run*."[16] If some, like Nelson Lichtenstein, identified this optimism as a "maddening piece of ideological larceny" in which "the principal asset of the left—the stamp of historical inevitability"—is appropriated by the right, this appropriation fit very much in the tradition of Cold War modernization theory, which, despite its liberal orientation, had both drawn on and attempted to counter Marx's ideas about social development.[17]

Fukuyama's assertion of the total ideological supremacy of Western ideas also shares much with the proposition advanced in *The Closing of the American Mind*, in which Bloom, counterintuitively given the book's title, denounces a new openness in academia in the form of "relativisms."[18] Rather than taking a similar denunciatory stance, however, Fukuyama generally pretends that relativist and anti-Western views of cultural and social difference—from the Boasian anthropology that challenged civilizational hierarchies in the early twentieth century to the Black Power tracts that accused "the Euro-American cultural sensibility" of being "anti-human in nature"—either do not exist or are unimportant enough not to be mentioned.[19] The 1992 book contains some denunciation of "relativisms," but they are not specifically named or dwelt upon there either. Instead, in both the article and the book, Fukuyama advances the proposition that while "relativisms" are now in vogue, especially in universities, they are also fundamentally illogical, and that educated people only pretend to believe in them. This incredulity is on display in his 1989 rejoinder to critics of the essay:

> Anyone who accepts the historicist premise—that is, that truth is historically relative—faces the question of the end of history even if he is not aware of it. For unless one posits something like an end of history, it is philosophically impossible to prevent historicism from degenerating into simple relativism, or from undermining any notion of progress. Anyone who believes that earlier thinkers were simply 'products of their time' must, if he is honest and consistent, ask whether he and his own historicism are not also products of their times. The present-day feminist who looks with condescension and disdain at the antiquated views of her grandparents regarding the role of women must ask whether her views are 'absolute,' or whether there are yet more progressive views that will render them just as quaint in the eyes of her granddaughter. And if that is so, why devote one ounce of effort, why argue passionately in favor of today's cause?
>
> For historicists, there are two ways out of this conundrum. The first is the path chosen by Hegel, to declare that history had come to an end .... The other path was the one chosen by Nietzsche and his twentieth-century followers like Heidegger, who accepted fully the consequences of radical historicism and realized that it makes impossible any sort of conventional ethics or morality ... Let me simply suggest that the attempt to work out the political implications of historicism without a concept of an end of history leads to consequences (fascism and the glorification of war) which few of us would be willing to stomach.[20]

Fukuyama's claims here leap from the modest but illogical (historicism implies an "end") to the murky and hyperbolic (historicism with no "end" leads to fascism and war). To do this he must posit that fascism and war have not constantly been driven by moral, civilizational, and millenarian certainties (or, alternatively, that war and fascism are generally driven by an excess of respect for cultural difference). Why the end should be now, whether the "now" is Hegel's 1806 or Fukuyama's 1989 (and why it should be one and not the other) also remains unclear. The example he offers of "the role of women," given the epistemological and ethical debates over gender and feminism roiling 1980s academic and activist scenes in the United States but also globally—all sides of which would have contested the visions of women's empowerment being concurrently advanced by corporations and even conservatives—is almost laughably inapt.[21] However, Fukuyama's strategy here is not so much logical or historically grounded argumentation, but rather an appeal to the common sense of modernization theory in the face of what he saw as wrongheaded political correctness. As Nils Gilman writes, "Fukuyama claimed that only bashfulness prevented American intellectuals from admitting that modernization theory formed their basic philosophy of history."[22]

Despite Fukuyama's self-identification as a modernization theorist, Gilman is one of the few scholars to place him in this context, partly because his arrival on the scene so far postdates modernization theory's heyday in the late 1950s, when social scientists in well-funded university centers and think tanks schematized and updated the logic Johannes Fabian calls "the spatialization of time."[23] Like the discourse of racial civilization that preceded it as an organizing logic of pre–Second World War empire, modernization theory imagined that the peoples of the world did not exist at the same time across geographical space, nor in any sort of antagonistic or exploitative relationship to one another, but rather along a universal path of human perfectibility. However, modernization largely rejected the biological racism of civilizational thinking, imagining the world in terms of nations, rather than races, advancing together, though from different starting points, along a fixed trajectory whose endpoint looked something like the rich societies of the West. Modernization theory thus posited a degree of racial and cultural mutability while still insisting that some nations and cultures were "behind" others and needed to be forcibly transformed. Particularly in the 1960s, modernization theorists dictated Cold War policy, most prominently Walt Rostow, who used his schematic theories to push John F. Kennedy and then Lyndon Johnson to escalate the Vietnam War.[24] The United States' failure to proffer capitalist modernity at gunpoint in Vietnam, along with Johnson's inability to pacify the poor at home with paternalistic uplift programs, shook the confidence of many modernizers, while on an intellectual level, dependency and world-systems theory challenged the neat trajectories of modernization theory. As a formal theory, modernization had been discredited in most quarters by the late 1970s.

Fukuyama, however, remained undeterred in his commitment to the tenets of modernization theory: in "The End of History?" he denounced "materialist theories of economic development," arguing for the primacy of "culture and consciousness" in explaining economic success or failure; in the subsequent book, he more straightforwardly bemoaned the "charge of ethnocentrism" that "spelled the death knell" for modernization theory.[25] As Gilman describes, Fukuyama set himself the task of trying single-handedly "to resurrect modernization theory by placing it on a firmer philosophical grounding."[26] This seemingly naïve project was cannier than it might at first seem, and more significant than Gilman's formulation gives credence, given the wild popularity of "The End of History?" Fukuyama's determined revival of modernization theory's schematic teleological narrative, after the many failures of the United States to bring capitalist modernity to the Third World, was a powerful and resonant move in 1989, one that helped usher in a remarkably uncritical triumphalism.[27] The powerful resonance of Fukuyama's recuperation of modernization theory resulted from its instatement of a remarkable level of amnesia about the many right-wing dictatorships, wars, and military coups that had decimated the international left; a neat teleology of capitalist democracy allowed even fairly recent memories of capitalist regimes attempting to contravene popular will in Chile and Vietnam to be replaced with a simple narrative of people wanting, and finally getting, capitalist freedom.

Well before he wrote his famous treatise, in his capacity as a Sovietologist and Third World expert at RAND in the early 1980s, Fukuyama had already adopted modernization theory's commitment to ostensible antiracism and schematic social science.[28] Fukuyama's commitment to modernization theory's tenets and practices can be found across his RAND reports, as when he wrongly characterizes Afghanistan as "untouched by modern culture" in a show of modernization theory's conviction that "untouched" traditional societies abound, disregarding Third World peoples' many encounters with colonial wars and other "modern" encroachments.[29] Also in line with modernization theory's dictates, he generally does not characterize Third World nations as independent or capable (or deserving) of forging their own policies, instead considering them simply to be Soviet clients: "In Grenada, the Soviets had no choice but to sit back and watch the United States overthrow one of their most recent acquisitions," he writes.[30] At the same time, when Fukuyama did make policy recommendations, he encouraged aggressive US military intervention in what he called Soviet "clients" in the Third World, as in this 1983 paper:

> Whether one's objective is to wean away the client or to try to replace it altogether, the US approach must be one which combines diplomacy and force simultaneously. These are not alternative methods but two sides of the same dialectical coin: Sandinista interest in the Contadora process or direct talks with the United States, far from being incompatible with US support for the *contras*, is in fact motivated by the latter.[31]

We might notice here Fukuyama's casual use of Hegelian dialectics to describe how the United States might achieve a synthesis between diplomacy and force. Equally significant, though, is his easy praise for this kind of brutality, as well as for regime change, here glossed as "replacing [the client] altogether." It is perhaps true, as he writes in "The End of History?", that "VCRs" more than the colossal military might of the United States won the Cold War. But this straightforward recommendation that "Soviet clients" be undermined militarily suggests a shadow history of his lofty proclamation in the 1989 essay that "events" have undeniably and inexorably proven the correctness of "the Western idea." At work in this claim is the dialectic, or maybe more accurately the one-two-punch, of modernization theory: here we apply deadly force to stymie or overthrow a regime attempting to make socialism work; there we proclaim capitalist modernity inevitable. There is "the Western idea," but there are also armaments to force its adoption.

These armaments, this force, entirely disappear from "The End of History?" and the subsequent book. Instead, Fukuyama's absolute faith in the tenets of modernization theory manifests not only in his uncomplicated recourse to a narrative of natural historical progress, but also in his conviction that poverty stemmed from cultural stagnation and a lack of ingenuity. These aspects of Fukuyama's modernizing ethos are most evident in "The End of History?" when he describes the "egalitarian" United States:

> The egalitarianism of modern America represents the essential achievement of a classless society envisioned by Marx ... the root causes of economic inequality do not have to do with the underlying legal and social structure of our society, which remains fundamentally egalitarian and moderately redistributionist, so much as with the cultural and social characteristics of the groups that make it up, which are in turn the historical legacy of premodern conditions. Thus black poverty in the United States is not the inherent product of liberalism, but is rather the "legacy of slavery and racism" that persisted long after the formal abolition of slavery.[32]

Fukuyama refers here to fellow neoconservative Daniel Patrick Moynihan's contention in his infamous 1965 report "The Negro Family: The Case for National Action" that Black poverty in America stemmed from a "tangle of pathology," at the heart of which was a "matriarchal" or female-headed family.[33] If this insistence on Black poverty as only residual and cultural, even as the Reagan and Bush administrations attacked welfare provision and ramped up the so-called drug war, was common among conservatives and even liberals in the 1980s (and persists today, invoked by Joe Biden in his famously garbled "play the record player" pivot in answer to a 2019 question about reparations for slavery), it is also indicative of the continuing influence of modernization theory's self-serving historical narrative, its insistence that poverty has nothing to do with systemic exploitation or dispossession.[34]

If "The End of History?" can be situated well within the lineage of modernization theory, there are also ways in which it departs from, or shuts the door on, that body of work. The most remarkable of the essay's foreclosures of modernization ideology is, perhaps, its open disregard for the Third World, its rhetorical re-expulsion of the majority of the world's people from history. If modernization theory had ushered the Third World into history, forcefully if necessary, Fukuyama signaled that its peoples had ceased largely to matter. "For our purposes," he sweepingly opines in the original essay, "it matters very little what strange thoughts occur to people in Albania or Burkina Faso, for we are interested in what one could in some sense call the common ideological heritage of mankind."[35] Albania and Burkina Faso, of course, were not randomly chosen far-flung places. Rather, they were existing (in the former case) and recent (in the latter, under the leadership of Thomas Sankara) leftist nations. Albania had been, as Elidor Mëhilli writes, "a kind of laboratory for transnational collaboration and confrontation during the Cold War," before breaking with the Soviets and then China to pursue its own insular socialist path, while Sankara had inspired a continent with his commitments to abolishing imperialism and corruption, his refusal to repay IMF debts, and his institution of a more direct and participatory democracy.[36] His 1987 assassination, Brian J. Peterson writes, "sent shockwaves throughout Africa."[37] Given the force of the post-assassination erasure of Sankara from the scene, perhaps it was fitting that his ambitious program would be quickly reduced to the status of a "strange thought" from an exotic land. Still, in an essay committed in theory to liberal principles of human equality, it was a bold move to declare outright that entire regions and nations were of no significance. Fukuyama returns to the line in his

"Reply to Critics," where he backtracks slightly but also digs in his heels about the primacy of Western ideas:

> My remarks about Albania and Burkina Faso were not meant to denigrate the importance of these countries or of the Third World more generally, but simply to register the self-evident fact that the major ideologies around which the world frames its political choices seem to flow primarily from the First World to the Third, and not the reverse. I do not know why this should be so, but it is nonetheless remarkable how persistently Third World revolutionaries continue to study the works of long-dead white male philosophers and polemicists.[38]

This rhetorical shrug resonates more generally with modernization theory's sleight-of-hand, its attempt to both frame processes as inexorable and force them into being. However, Fukuyama's particular situation—as someone who spent his career studying ways to exert military pressure on the Third World—makes his "I do not know why this should be so" seem particularly disingenuous. (Fukuyama's framing also prematurely erases the Second World, redrawing global boundaries to consign Albania to the Third.)

The article's explicit discounting and re-consignment of Third World peoples into not mattering again, despite its stated concern with universal human desire for recognition (which in the book Fukuyama calls *thymos* and spends considerable time discussing), might have been recognized as a racist denial of recognition, and by his own logic also humanity, to the majority of the world's people. But Fukuyama was not accused of racism, even by critics, due at least in part to his own Asianness and familial ethnic traumas: his grandparents and uncle had been displaced during the Second World War and imprisoned in an internment camp, a fate his father had narrowly avoided. In a process Emily Raymundo has theorized in her work on Asian American conservatism, Fukuyama did not attempt to access whiteness to argue on behalf of the West but rather mobilized his Japanese-Americanness in several ways against other "others."[39] He was uniquely positioned among neoconservatives to glorify a Western heritage not explicitly organized around whiteness, but also to make blanket statements about ethnic groups, as when he contends that "the cultural heritage of those Far Eastern societies, the ethic of work and saving and family, a religious heritage that does not, like Islam, place restrictions on certain forms of economic behavior, and other deeply ingrained moral qualities" explains the "economic performance" of East Asian nations. He adds to this statement a superfluous footnote that "one need look no further than the recent performance of Vietnamese immigrants in the US school system when compared to their Black or Hispanic classmates to realize that culture and consciousness are absolutely crucial to explain not only economic behavior but virtually every other important aspect of life as well."[40] Fukuyama here mobilizes his Asianness to make dubious comparisons that wield the model minority myth to cast aspersions on Black and Latinx "culture and consciousness," but also to pronounce on the comparative national achievement of Asian countries (over and against Muslim ones) on which he had no particular expertise.[41]

Fukuyama's dismissiveness of the Third World both indexed and bolstered a process already taking place in neoliberalism, after the failure of large-scale development schemes. Gilman writes that "the tragedy of modernization theory is that while its misleading understanding of the historical process still underpins much Western (and postcolonial) thinking about postcoloniality, its secular reformist ideas have died without being replaced with a positive alternative."[42] While I am less admiring of the modernizers' grand project than Gilman, he is perceptive in noting that many of modernization theory's assumptions—its idea of modern democracy as a top-down process controlled by experts (as opposed to "populisms" which constitute too much popular participation to be properly democratic), its insistence that wealth is somehow deserved and poverty a result of cultural dysfunction and disorganization—remain operational long after the Cold War's end and IMF and World Bank dictates have made state-run development planning an impossibility. This is a dynamic James Ferguson notes in his devastating study of miners on the Zambian copperbelt: with the economic decline, poverty, and indebtedness they experienced after the postwar flurry of modernization's investments and promises came a loss not just of any secure means of day-to-day subsistence but also of "a certain ethos of hopefulness, self-respect, and optimism." For the mineworkers, "the breakdown of the myth of modernization" amounted to "a world-shattering life experience."[43] It is this experience of mattering and then suddenly not mattering, of being violently yanked into and then violently cast out of the global modernization process, that Fukuyama senses and facilitates, however glibly, when he redraws the boundaries of history.

The Liberal Moment That Was History

If Fukuyama's "End of History?" tells us something about modernization theory—its premises, its persistence and shifts, its cultural work—it also tells us something about the global transition to neoliberalism as it was at once facilitated and underestimated by intellectuals. Both Derrida and Anderson sense, and are fascinated by, a certain untimeliness in Fukuyama's work. "How can one be late to the end of history?" Derrida asks, recounting how "the eschatological themes of the 'end of history,' of the 'end of Marxism,' of the 'end of philosophy,' of the 'ends of man,' of the 'last man' and so forth were, in the 1950s, that is, forty years ago, our daily bread."[44] Throughout *Specters* Derrida marvels at Fukuyama's lateness, comparing his work to "the disconcerting and tardy byproduct of a footnote" and "the grammar school exercise of a young, industrious, but come-lately reader of Kojève."[45] For Anderson, Fukuyama is even further out of time, expressing a "serene Enlightenment confidence" that "had fallen into discredit by the close of the last century."[46]

What did it mean that Fukuyama's pronouncements were too late? This lateness, Derrida and Anderson both ultimately argue, is a result of Fukuyama's certainty, even at the late date of 1989, that capitalist states, and specifically the New Deal order for the global North, would continue on more or less as they were. His account of the United States as a "fundamentally egalitarian and moderately redistributionist" society, used to bolster his "culture of poverty" claims, betrays his conviction that aspects of mid-century welfare states constituted genuine historical progress—that they were thus stable and could not be fully undone, even as Reagan and Thatcher's supply-side policies were decimating them. If Fukuyama is particularly late here as he celebrates the global triumph of capitalist democracy, he seems to have also activated a certain sense of alarm in his critics—a sense that they, too, were caught off guard or had been worried about the wrong threats.

As Anderson perceptively notes, Fukuyama's linkage of "the progress of political democracy" globally with "the spread of capitalist prosperity" constitutes "a fallacy of composition," in that there was no "material possibility" that the Third World would ever achieve material equality with the First World.[47] Rather, he explains that Fukuyama's vision is dual, of a rich "post-historical" zone cordoning off and policing an immiserated and historically enmeshed one:

> The ever tighter integration of the world capitalist economy, as it now for the first time comes within sight of encompassing the whole earth, and the increasingly visible polarizations of wealth within it, are generating tremendous pressures for entry into the privileged zones. Already there are some 25 million refugees from political and economic despair in the poor countries. Flows of immigration on a tidal scale are the logical outcome of a bifurcation of the globe that makes residence in the rich countries—of any kind, even as an underclass—of incomparable value, for the positional benefits of their

infrastructures and social services alone. Since the First World cannot be reproduced in the Third, without common ecological ruin, increasing numbers from the Third, and the Second, will try to come to the First ... The relations between the post-historical zone of a fortunate liberal capitalism and the zone of misfortune still enmeshed in history will, he suggests, not be close. But they will involve collisions along three axes. Oil supplies must be safeguarded; immigration must be filtered; and advanced technologies—especially, but not exclusively, armaments—must be blocked, where necessary ... After effectively criticizing the basis of Kissinger-style 'realism,' Fukuyama admits that such policy recommendations scarcely differ from it. What this amounts to, of course, is a set of border patrols.[48]

The world Anderson accuses Fukuyama of ushering into being in 1992 is of course the world in which we all live now. The egalitarian economic prosperity and democracy Fukuyama predicted, which he avowed that "modernizing societies" could share in if they would only stop lagging behind culturally, was exactly the opposite of the direction in which the world was moving. The very attempt by decolonizing Third World nations to follow modernization theory's dictates and "arrive" into history was in part what made the system untenable. As dependency theorists explained, modernization theory's premises and promises were not only wrong, but exactly wrong. Part of this impossibility was the faulty assumption by modernizers as well as economists, beginning in the 1930s and 1940s, of infinite natural resources, the idea that national economies could grow infinitely and "human capital" was the main factor that would have to be enhanced through the erasure of traditional cultures.[49] But part of it was also by design: as Quinn Slobodian demonstrates, "neoliberal critics stalked the vision of a New Deal for the world from the start."[50] Neoliberal planners anticipated and responded deliberately to decolonization with their plans to protect markets from the democratic impulses of newly independent peoples.

It was not just modernization theory and economics that were constructed on these faulty premises of replicability, the idea that everyone could have what the rich West had while the rich West gave up nothing, and that furthermore the world was moving in a direction that would make this possible. Political philosophy, a field with which Fukuyama is sometimes identified, was also constructed according to these seemingly immutable principles, an apparent culmination of history that instead turned out to be a twenty-five-year interlude. Katrina Forrester writes, with regard to the thought of John Rawls, of a "broader problem in which abstract philosophical principles are constructed against the backdrop of a society whose basic underpinnings are assumed to be stable or moving in a particular (progressive) direction."[51] Forrester argues that the discipline of political philosophy was shaped by worries about totalitarianism rather than fears of states' protection of corporate profit at all costs. However, as Forrester argues, "the idealizations on which liberal egalitarianism relied were formulated in a society that had little in common with that of later decades."[52] Even as neoliberal states destroyed the grounding for the kind of state-guided redistribution carried out in the global North at mid-century, a liberal philosophy became dominant, the premises of which presumed the ongoing expansion of that distributional logic. Rawls, along with other liberal-left thinkers and planners, spun out their philosophies as the world changed drastically. They chafed against restrictions on "liberty" in the name of redistribution that were already giving way to a different kind of socioeconomic order entirely; these philosophers' championing of individual freedom dovetailed with neoliberal planners' emphasis on freeing markets and entrepreneurial subjects alike, thus facilitating a more drastic undoing of public services than they ever thought possible. Thus, Fukuyama's extensive worries in his book that the egalitarian comfort of Northern capitalist democracies would mean the end of the recognition of exceptional men can be understood as a sillier version of Rawls' cautions about too many redistributive policies encroaching on individual liberty: these thinkers both misjudged the times in which they lived and helped usher in a very new era.

Part of the reason these thinkers underestimated the upheavals of the neoliberal order was that they retained an implicit certainty about the flow of ideas from North to South. Fukuyama states this most explicitly, but even Anderson imagines the global crisis to come as a problem primarily of rich nations immiserating and policing citizens of and refugees from poor ones. Contrary to this assumption, neoliberal austerity and crumbling infrastructure have traveled in the other direction: the rollback of social welfare famously began in the Global South, but it has returned with a vengeance to the Global North. Similarly, the strengthening of democratic rights and freedoms that Fukuyama observed in the Global North and imagined would sweep through as-yet-undemocratic capitalist states in the global South has not materialized; instead, such rights and freedoms have been attenuated in the global capitalist North. This difficulty of any continuity of democracy and capitalism even in wealthy states, while lost on Fukuyama, has long been understood by neoliberal thinkers. As Slobodian writes and Naomi Klein and David Harvey also demonstrate, neoliberal planners "did not see democracy and capitalism as synonymous," but rather engaged in deeply and deliberately undemocratic projects. Democracy, for the planners, "meant successive waves of clamoring demanding masses, always threatening to push the functioning market economy off its tracks."[53] The undemocratic nature of neoliberal governance has also not been lost on ordinary people around the world, from Jamaica to Greece to even the reactionary movements pushing back against "free" trade. It is perhaps only the experts, particularly of the political center, who maintain the fiction that capitalism and a genuinely participatory democracy might coexist for very long without one hampering and eventually destroying the other.

Trouble Imagining: Culture and the Left

In a time of pandemic, as the effects of the climate crisis have become universally felt, the specter of Francis Fukuyama seems ubiquitous. In a 2021 *Baffler* essay, Brendan O'Connor credits Bernie Sanders' 2020 US presidential campaign with "helping to kickstart the rebirth of history," praising the campaign for reinvigorating the socialist imagination (however New Deal-ish that imagination looked).[54] Matthew Karp, in one of the more elliptical Fukuyama references, writes in a 2021 *Harper's* article about US conservative and liberal mobilizations of the American past: "leaving behind the End of History, we have arrived at something like History as End."[55] In *The Nation*, Maggie Doherty also signals the end of the end, by looking back at the left's moment of political despair:

> Not so long ago, there seemed to be something radical in rejecting the future. Looking back, it's easy to see why. In the 1990s, history was over; the United States and capitalism had won. Strutting conservative televangelists and smug liberal technocrats took turns running the world. In response, a reasonable nihilism emerged in the era's counterculture.[56]

This memory of "reasonable nihilism" is not very different from what Joshua Clover and Mark Fisher diagnosed in their discussions, both in 2009, of Fukuyama-era pop music and "capitalist realism," respectively: a certain lack of imagination on the left, and everywhere, that made life into passive spectatorship. Clover and Fisher's pronouncements came at the end of what was a bleak decade for much of the global left; Clover was right in identifying an incapacitation of Euro-American popular culture to articulate dissent and imagine anticapitalist worlds, an incapacitation that occurred, oddly and infelicitously, at the very moment when leftist academia was taking its "cultural turn," attempting to detect resistance in unlikely texts and subcultures. Both Clover and Fisher found in Fukuyama a grain of truth, an inchoate understanding of the impoverishment of the Western cultural imaginary.

But despite the brilliance of Clover and Fisher's formulations, the important thing to note is that history never really ended, even if political imaginations are always being deadened somewhere. Even when the left does not win, and it has always lost more than it has won, struggles often seem to proceed dialectically, if not, as George Ciccariello-Maher also notes, in the unified, teleological, and easily closed way imagined by Fukuyama. Even in the moments of Clover and Fisher's writing, indigenous and leftist movements swept South America, notably mobilizing indigenous culture and epistemology to fight global capitalism. In other regions, the left would be reinvigorated by both the Arab Spring and the Occupy movement, which broke through the smooth technocratic, finance driven, and highly secretive veneer of Obama-era US hegemony. In response to highly undemocratic attempts by "globalization" advocates to encase markets, the unruly leaderless alternative globalization movement emerged. Likewise, more recently, children have gone on strike, leaving schools and filling streets worldwide; this is a perfect dialectical response to the disingenuous framing of climate change as the technocratic province of scientists, policy wonks, and Davos innovators.

"Defund the police" is perhaps an even clearer example. During the mass mobilizations in 2020 that followed Minneapolis cop Derek Chauvin's murder of George Floyd, this seemingly innocuous slogan was perceived by its critics as radical and destructive only because of its dialectical relationship to neoliberal imperatives to defund (and thus, it is now understood, craftily destroy) everything *but* the police; the slogan's power, its threat, come from this understanding. We might see the Black Lives Matter movement protests this way too, as they claim the world-historical importance of those informally employed and improperly consuming Black people (cigarette buyers and sellers, counterfeit bill passers) who have been cast out of the global economy, asserting through action that these lives are more important than the existence of a Wendy's or a police station. That even this movement, which began in the global North but has forged international ties from Palestine to Nigeria, is not counted as properly historical in the above accounts indicates that these popular leftist understandings of history might draw more from Fukuyama and, in Ciccariello-Maher's words, his "bad dialectics," than they'd like to admit.[57]

This, then, is the trap intellectuals set themselves when they glibly invoke "the end of history"; the lure of the joke allows the political order and the recent past to remain framed in Fukuyama's terms even as writers mock his formulations. These recent and ongoing struggles of the left elude history which seems forever in need of restarting, even though, as the many leaderless movements of the post-1989 world have shown, restarting history, in the sense of a coherent power bloc and vision countering today's staggeringly violent and oligarchic overlords, would seem to require the spatialization of time and the attendant relegation of so many to the status of not-mattering. Rather than reach for the gimmick, we might do better to remember not only that we are in history still, and have been all along, but that the current struggles occurring beyond the narrow field of Euro-American vision are of world-historical importance.

Notes

1. Francis Fukuyama, "The End of History?" *The National Interest* 16 (Summer 1989): 3–18.
2. Fukuyama, "The End of History?" 3.
3. Ibid., 18.
4. Louis Menand, "Francis Fukuyama Postpones the End of History," *The New Yorker*, August 27, 2018. Available online: https://www.newyorker.com/magazine/2018/09/03/francis-fukuyama-postpones-the-end-of-history (accessed October 14, 2021).
5. James Atlas, "What Is Fukuyama Saying? And to Whom Is He Saying It?" *New York Times Magazine*, October 22, 1989. Available online: https://www.nytimes.com/1989/10/22/magazine/what-is-fukuyama-saying-and-to-whom-is-he-saying-it.html (accessed October 14, 2021).
6. Perry Anderson, *A Zone of Engagement* (New York: Verso, 1992), 284.
7. Atlas, "What Is Fukuyama Saying?"
8. Francis Fukuyama, "A Reply to My Critics," *The National Interest* 18 (Winter 1989/90): 21–8. He was, in fact, so little convinced of his impact on the State Department that when he got an advance to write the book-length version of the essay, he resigned from the George H. W. Bush administration, more comfortable at the edges of academia and the think-tank world than in politics.
9. Robert Saunders, "Britain at the End of History," *The New Statesman*, October 7, 2020. Available online: https://www.newstatesman.com/politics/uk/2020/10/britain-end-history (accessed October 14, 2021); Andrey Kortunov, "A Few Words

in Defence of Francis Fukuyama," *Russian Council*, June 19, 2019. Available online: https://russiancouncil.ru/en/analytics-and-comments/analytics/a-few-words-in-defence-of-francis-fukuyama/ (accessed October 14, 2021).
10 Jacques Derrida, *Specters of Marx: The State of the Debt, the Work of Mourning, and the New International*, trans. Peggy Kamuf (New York: Routledge, 1994), 85.
11 Sianne Ngai's theorization—that "protected by its own slickness, as a thing whose sheer stupidity neutralizes the critical feeling it incites, the gimmick defends itself from intellectual curiosity in a way that puts any person seeking to analyze it at a comical disadvantage"—sums up the Fukuyama effect well. Sianne Ngai, *Theory of the Gimmick: Aesthetic Judgment and Capitalist Form* (Cambridge: Harvard University Press, 2020), 9.
12 Nicholas Wroe, "History's Pallbearer," *The Guardian*, May 11, 2002. Available online: https://www.theguardian.com/books/2002/may/11/academicexperts.artsandhumanities (accessed October 14, 2021). For an account of the Cornell building takeover, see George Lowery, "A Campus Takeover That Symbolized an Era of Change," *Cornell Chronicle*, April 16, 2009. Available online: https://news.cornell.edu/stories/2009/04/campus-takeover-symbolized-era-change (accessed October 14, 2021).
13 Atlas, "What Is Fukuyama Saying?"
14 See Andrew Hartman, *A War for the Soul of America: A History of the Culture Wars* (Chicago: University of Chicago Press, 2015), 38–69.
15 David Engerman, *Know Your Enemy: The Rise and Fall of America's Soviet Experts* (Oxford: Oxford University Press, 2009), 332.
16 Fukuyama, "The End of History?" 4.
17 Nelson Lichtenstein, "Market Fundamentalism and the Wishful Liberals," in *Cold War Triumphalism: The Misuse of History after the Fall of Communism*, ed. Ellen Schrecker (New York: New Press, 2004), 104.
18 See Allan Bloom, *Closing of the American Mind: How Higher Education Has Failed Democracy and Impoverished the Souls of Today's Students* (New York: Simon & Schuster, 1987).
19 Larry Neal, "The Black Arts Movement," *Drama Review* 12, no. 4 (Summer 1968): 30. For an account of race in Boasian anthropology, see David Luis-Brown, *Waves of Decolonization: Discourses of Race and Hemispheric Citizenship in Mexico, Cuba and the United States* (Durham: Duke University Press, 2008).
20 Fukuyama, "A Reply to My Critics," 23.
21 See Alice Echols, *Daring to Be Bad: Radical Feminism in America 1967–1975* (Minneapolis: University of Minnesota Press, 1989); Domitila Barrios de Chungara, *Let Me Speak!* (New York: Monthly Review Press, 1978); Clare Hemmings, *Why Stories Matter: The Political Grammar of Feminist Theory* (Durham: Duke University Press, 2010); Chandra Mohanty, *Feminism without*

Borders: Decolonizing Theory, Practicing Solidarity (Durham: Duke University Press, 2003), 17–42; Patricia Stuelke, *The Ruse of Repair: US Neoliberal Empire and the Turn from Critique* (Durham: Duke University Press, 2021).

22 Nils Gilman, *Mandarins of the Future: Modernization Theory in Cold War America* (Baltimore: Johns Hopkins University Press, 2007), 268.
23 Johannes Fabian, *Time and the Other: How Anthropology Makes Its Object* (New York: Columbia University Press, 1983).
24 See David Milne, *America's Rasputin: Walt Rostow and the Vietnam War* (New York: Hill and Wang, 2008).
25 Fukuyama, "The End of History?" 7; Francis Fukuyama, *The End of History and the Last Man* (1992; New York: Free Press, 2006), 69.
26 Gilman, *Mandarins*, 267.
27 This is partly due to Fukuyama's rhetorical sleight-of-hand: when discussing the collapse of the Soviet Union, he argues for the importance of actual world-historical events, while he discounts all failures of liberal-capitalist democracy by claiming that he is only referring to its triumph in the realm of ideas.
28 Engerman argues that Cold War Sovietology was generally committed to social science modeling and modernization theory's schematic methods, moving away from the characterological assessments and "elegant prose" like that of founding figure George Kennan. Engerman, *Know Your Enemy*, 3.
29 Francis Fukuyama, *The New Marxist-Leninist States in the Third World* (Santa Monica: RAND Corporation, September 1984), 33. Available online: https://apps.dtic.mil/sti/pdfs/ADA152546.pdf (accessed October 14, 2021).
30 Ibid., 42.
31 Francis Fukuyama, *US-Soviet Interactions in the Third World* (Santa Monica: RAND/UCLA Center for the Study of Soviet International Behavior, 1985), 21. Available online: https://www.rand.org/content/dam/rand/pubs/occasional_papers-soviet/2006/OPS004.pdf (accessed October 14, 2021).
32 Fukuyama, "The End of History?" 9.
33 Moynihan's rebirth as a neoconservative was spurred in a large part by Black and leftist dismay and rejection of his thesis: like Lyndon Johnson, he simply could not understand how his diagnosis of dysfunctional "cultures of poverty" could be received as paternalistic, racist, and sexist. See Hartman, *Soul of America*.
34 See Marcia Chatelain, "Joe Biden Isn't the Only Democrat Who Has Blamed Black America for Its Problems," *Washington Post*, September 17, 2019. Available online: https://www.washingtonpost.com/outlook/2019/09/17/joe-biden-isnt-only-democrat-who-has-blamed-black-america-its-problems/ (accessed October 14, 2021).
35 Fukuyama, "The End of History?" 9.
36 Elidor Mëhilli, *From Stalin to Mao: Albania and the Socialist World* (Ithaca: Cornell University Press, 2017), 4. For a lovely piece on the aftermath of socialism

36 in Albania and how the "strange thoughts" of Albanians might be more global than Fukuyama suggests, see Joshua Clover, "Meant to Be," *Popula*, March 6, 2019. Available online: https://popula.com/2019/03/06/meant-to-be/ (accessed October 14, 2021).

37 Brian J. Peterson, *Thomas Sankara: A Revolutionary in Cold War Africa* (Bloomington: Indiana University Press, 2021), 1.

38 Fukuyama, "A Reply to My Critics," 24.

39 Emily Raymundo, "The Monster Minority: Multiculturalism in John Yoo's Torture Memos," *Review of International American Studies* (forthcoming).

40 Fukuyama, "The End of History?" 7.

41 For a good account of the fallacies inherent in comparing the "culture" of Asian immigrant populations to that of Black and Latinx non-immigrant populations, see Vijay Prashad, *The Karma of Brown Folk* (Minneapolis: University of Minnesota Press, 2001).

42 Gilman, *Mandarins*, 20. Despite these perceptive comments, Gilman reserves special vitriol in his work for scholars like Arturo Escobar who critique modernization epistemology, accusing them of "moral cowardice" for not advancing their own overarching programs. Gilman, *Mandarins*, 266.

43 James Ferguson, *Expectations of Modernity: Myths and Meanings of Urban Life on the Zambian Copperbelt* (Berkeley: University of California Press, 1999), 14.

44 Derrida, *Specters*, 16.

45 Ibid., 70. Alexandre Kojève, Hegel's twentieth-century translator and his best known interpreter after Marx, is discussed at length in *The End of History and the Last Man*. Fukuyama argues that Kojève shared his certainty that liberal capitalist democracy constituted the final stage of human progress, though Anderson points out that Kojève only abandoned his socialism near the end of his life.

46 Anderson, *A Zone of Engagement*, 280.

47 Ibid., 354.

48 Ibid.

49 See Timothy Mitchell, *Carbon Democracy: Political Economy in an Age of Oil* (New York: Verso, 2011).

50 Quinn Slobodian, *Globalists: The End of Empire and the Birth of Neoliberalism* (Cambridge: Harvard University Press, 2018).

51 Katrina Forrester, *In the Shadow of Justice: Postwar Liberalism and the Remaking of Political Philosophy* (Princeton: Princeton University Press, 2019), 4.

52 Forrester, *In the Shadow of Justice*, 271–2.

53 Slobodian, *Globalists*, 17. Kanishka Goonewardena makes a similar point in an article on Fukuyama and the architects of UK Third Way politics, citing a 1997 economist piece worried about democracy's incompatibility with "liberty," meaning capitalism. Kanishka Goonewardena, "The Future of Planning after the 'End of History,'" *Planning Theory* 2, no. 3 (2003): 214.

54 Brendan O'Connor, "When the Party's Over: Organizing after Bernie," *The Baffler* 57 (May 2021). Available online https://thebaffler.com/salvos/when-the-partys-over-oconnor (accessed October 14, 2021).

55 Matthew Karp, "History as End: 1619, 1776 and the Politics of the Past," *Harper's* (July 2021). Available online: https://harpers.org/archive/2021/07/history-as-end-politics-of-the-past-matthew-karp/ (accessed October 14, 2021).

56 Maggie Doherty, "Adjunct Hell: The Rise of a New Kind of Campus Novel," *The Nation*, May 3, 2021. Available online: https://www.thenation.com/article/culture/smallwood-steger-strong-adjunct/ (accessed October 14, 2021).

57 Ibid., 9.

2

The Rushdie Affair, the Threat of a Globalized Islam, and the Retreat from Multiculturalism

Rita Chin

The year 1989 has long been understood as transformational. Even as it unfolded, it was clear that world-historical changes were afoot. For most witnesses with an eye to Europe, though, the events that galvanized attention took place along the Iron Curtain: in April, the Polish Communist government concluded the Roundtable Agreement with the Solidarity Trade Union; in June, the borders between Hungary and Austria reopened; and, most dramatically, in November, the Berlin Wall fell. What has been less recognized is that the collapse of communism in Eastern Europe occurred simultaneously with another set of crucial events that came to be known as the Rushdie affair. This controversy heralded a new, more explicitly global conflict, as the Cold War, whose geographical poles were clearly associated with the United States and Soviet Union, was quickly superseded by a protracted clash with Islam, whose adherents were scattered across the world.

In February 1989, Ayatollah Khomeini of Iran issued a fatwa, which condemned the British-Indian writer Salman Rushdie for blasphemy contained in his novel, *The Satanic Verses*. This legal ruling sentenced Rushdie and his publishers to death, accelerating the storm around the author and his book that had already been brewing in India and Britain for several months. Khomeini's edict effectively transformed a localized set of disputes into a major global controversy. Debate dominated the international press during the first part of 1989, focusing primarily on free speech and the putative intolerance of Islam. As the dispute escalated, it drew attention to the large numbers of Muslim immigrants settled in the United Kingdom (and throughout Western Europe), forcing Britons to grapple with the fact that issues which had seemed distant and even irrelevant actually had major ramifications for their society and culture. The affair laid the groundwork for new questions in Europe (and the so-called Western world more generally) about whether Muslims and Islam were compatible with the core principles of liberalism and democracy.

Rushdie's *The Satanic Verses* lay at the center of this global controversy. Yet the novel itself was largely an afterthought in the ensuing affair. A postmodern work of fiction, the book employed magical realism to explore themes of divine revelation, faith, and doubt in the context of multicultural Britain. For many, the novel felt impenetrable, full of inside jokes, strange juxtapositions, and non-sequiturs. It was no easy read. Few commentators at the time—beyond professional literary critics—offered sustained discussion of the book, its style, or even the offending passages. Rushdie's skewering and sexualization of the Prophet Muhammad served to catalyze a furious debate not so much about the novel itself, but rather about the nature of Islam, Islamic religious authority, and its reach across secular state boundaries, particularly in relation to Muslim immigrants who resided throughout Europe. These issues were articulated more explicitly by two other texts: Khomeini's fatwa and a pamphlet penned by the British feminist author Fay Weldon, *Sacred Cows*. Together, the legal ruling and the booklet raised the specter of fanatical Muslim zealots squared off against Europeans—even those left of center—seeking to defend their core values, especially freedom of speech. They catalyzed doubts about the viability of multiculturalism as a social model and ultimately set the terms of debate about Muslim immigrants in Europe for decades to come.

Rumblings of a Global Controversy

When Penguin Books released *The Satanic Verses* in the United Kingdom at the end of September 1988, the press had already been made aware of the novel's potential for controversy. An editorial consultant in India had warned the publishers that parts of the story would deeply upset many Muslims. The sections of the novel that caused offense were written as dream sequences, which combined historical names and fantastical situations. Here, Rushdie introduced Mahound, a character whose name invoked the medieval Christian epithet that vilified Muhammad and was easily read by religious insiders as a stand-in for the prophet. He depicted the recently widowed Mahound engaging in a promiscuous sex binge at a brothel where the prostitutes bore the names of the prophet's wives. The swirling language of these dreams signaled a playfulness that masked a highly pointed critique of fanatical religious belief. Yet the cerebral logics of the novel were beside the point. Many of those most disturbed by the book openly admitted that they had not read it in its entirety; instead, they had examined the passages purported to be problematic in order to confirm the offense. They did not engage with the literary project of the novel. They took the depiction of Mahound and the prostitutes literally.

Reaction came swiftly in countries around the world with large Muslim populations.[1] On the subcontinent, where Rushdie was born and spent his early years, Muslim communities in both India and Pakistan pressed their governments to ban the novel. Two Muslim members of the Indian parliament successfully lobbied their colleagues to embargo Rushdie's book in October 1988. Meanwhile, the Pakistani National Assembly voted unanimously to condemn the novel and formally prohibited it in November. Over the next month, other Muslim-majority states followed suit, including Bangladesh, Sudan, Sri Lanka, Egypt, and Saudi Arabia.

In Britain, word of *The Satanic Verses'* provocative sections began to circulate among various groups of Muslim immigrants in early October, when an administrator for the Islamic Federation in Leicester sent photocopies of the objectionable passages to Muslim organizations around the country. Within days, Syed Pasha, secretary of the Union of Muslims in London, called a meeting to organize a response to the book in the United Kingdom. Initially, Muslim leaders approached Penguin Press behind the scenes to explain the offense caused by the novel, request its retraction, and demand a public apology from Rushdie. The hope was that once the publishers understood the deeply insulting nature of the offending passages, Penguin would withdraw the book willingly and without a major fuss. When the publishing house failed to respond or treat the situation with urgency, some approached the British government for redress. Pasha, for instance, wrote to Prime Minister Margaret Thatcher and entreated her to ban the novel under England's blasphemy law. He argued that the law should be extended to protect all faiths, not just Christianity. Others lobbied their local members of parliament. According to the British political scientist Bhikhu Parekh, these Muslim protests were characterized not so much by "their intolerance as their timidity, not their feeling of rage but a sense of hurt, not their anger but their distress."[2] What seemed especially upsetting about the novel, then, was that it had been written by one of their own, an immigrant from the subcontinent, who knew very well that his words would cause offense.[3]

When these quiet efforts failed to produce the desired changes or even a response, a small group of offended Muslims burned a copy of *The Satanic*

Verses in the northern town of Bolton, an attempt to focus public attention on the community's upset over the novel. Frustrated that such a provocation still did not grab national headlines, Muslim leaders in Bradford orchestrated another mass demonstration with a planned ritual burning of the book for January 1989. This time, the organizers notified media outlets of their intentions beforehand.[4] The symbolic book burning at Bradford garnered a handful of small stories, some letters to the editor, and a couple of editorials in the *Times* that month. The protest was covered in more detail by *The Guardian*, prompted by the short-lived decision by the bookseller W. H. Smith to remove the novel from its shelves in Bradford in advance of the demonstration. But through the month of January, the dispute—while now finally generating British press attention—remained limited to the UK and subcontinent.

The event that transformed the localized debates over Rushdie into a full-blown global controversy was the public pronouncement of a fatwa by Iran's spiritual leader Ayatollah Khomeini. Transmitted across the airwaves on February 14 by Radio Tehran, the legal ruling itself was terse and provided no justification for its verdict. "In the name of God," read the announcer, "we are from God and to God we shall return." The decree followed:

> I am informing all brave Muslims of the world that the author of *The Satanic Verses*, a text written, edited, and published against Islam, the Prophet of Islam, and the Qur'an, along with all the editors and publishers aware of its contents, are condemned to death. I call on all valiant Muslims wherever they may be in the world to kill them without delay, so that no one will dare insult the sacred beliefs of Muslims henceforth. Whoever is killed in this cause will be a martyr, God Willing. Meanwhile if someone has access to the author of the book but is incapable of carrying out the execution, he should inform the people so that [Rushdie] is punished for his actions.[5]

Sentencing Rushdie and all those who had been involved in the publication of his novel to death seemed shocking, especially to Western ears. But as the Islamic scholar Yaqub Zaki noted in a commentary for the *Times*, "on the penalty for apostasy there is complete unanimity between all five schools of law in Islam." He further explained, "Khomeini has only stated what every Muslim knows to be the case, and his fatwa on the subject is no different from what would be issued by some village mullah in Pakistan were the matter referred to him."[6] The punishment for sacrilege dictated by Khomeini, in short, was not particularly extreme or unusual within the Islamic world.

A number of conditions, however, made this fatwa different. For one thing, Rushdie was a celebrated literary figure, acclaimed for his previous books and lauded for *The Satanic Verses*. For another, he did not reside in a Muslim-majority country, nor was his readership primarily Muslim. Rushdie's status as a well-known, London-based intellectual meant that the fatwa immediately attracted far more public attention in Europe and the United States than it might have otherwise. Western ears, in other words, were primed to take note of this particular decree. And take note they did. The fatwa provoked a veritable cavalcade of media coverage and commentary from the Western world. Articles and opinion pieces appeared not only in British newspapers such as the *Times*, *Guardian*, *Independent*, *Financial Times*, *Daily Mirror*, *Daily Mail*, and *Telegraph*, but also in *Le Monde*, *Die Zeit*, *Der Spiegel*, *Salzburg Kronen Zeitung*, *Globe & Mail*, *New York Times*, and *Los Angeles Times*. Writers and intellectuals around the globe publicly defended Rushdie's right to free speech. PEN International, the worldwide association of writers devoted to safeguarding free expression, organized a World Statement of Writers in Support of Rushdie that was signed by more than 1,000 and presented to governments and the United Nations on March 2, 1989.

Beyond drawing international opprobrium, Khomeini's legal ruling did more than offer a condemnation of the novel—or even demand a retraction or ban on the book, as British Muslim leaders had done. It imposed the death penalty. This incitement to bodily harm and violence directly transgressed British laws against murder. Indeed, because of his stature as a public literary figure and the nature of the ruling, the British state was forced to treat the death sentence as a credible threat and immediately provided Rushdie with state security protection.

Perhaps most significantly for the ensuing controversy, Khomeini addressed his verdict and judgment to "all valiant Muslims wherever they may be in the world."[7] He did not, that is, confine his audience to Muslims in Iran or other Islamic countries. While this aspect of the fatwa likely would have been glossed over by a Muslim audience, the effort to hail a global Muslim community resonated differently among British and European leaders. It drew their attention to a development that had gone largely unnoticed (or at least unremarked upon) for decades—namely, the substantial numbers of Muslim immigrants now settled in every major Western European country. The fatwa effectively summoned a global community of Muslims that crossed national borders and was potentially subject to an authority beyond any individual state. And it directed members of this community to violate the laws of many of the states in which they resided.

As we have seen, British Muslims had been objecting to the novel for months before Khomeini issued the fatwa, escalating their strategy for redress from letter writing to provocation (including staged burnings of the book) in an effort to get political leaders to respond to their offense and outrage. The Iranian cleric's ruling added two unique factors into the mix: the claim of extra-territorial authority and the prospect of violence on British soil, neither of which had been in play when local Muslims began protesting the book. Khomeini's shocking death warrant accomplished what the repeated appeals by local British Muslim leaders had not. It unleashed a torrent of responses from key representatives of the British government, public figures, and the media.[8]

The British Furor

Less than two weeks after the fatwa's broadcast, Home Secretary Douglas Hurd delivered a major speech to Muslim community leaders at the Birmingham Central Mosque. At the most basic level, this address sought to short-circuit the Ayatollah's efforts to exert religious authority over Muslims around the world and especially in Britain. Hurd enjoined British Muslims to heed the importance of "proper integration," highlighting the expectations for immigrants in the UK: observe the rule of law, respect freedom of speech, and tolerate alternative points of view. Above all, he warned: "None of us can choose to obey some laws and ignore others."[9] By stressing the fundamental principle of the rule of law, Hurd was attempting to uphold the sovereignty of the territorial state over British Muslims. This message was underscored by the editors of the *Financial Times*, who declared in an opinion piece the following day: "The central point in the speech" was "the law in Britain is above us all. It applies to everyone, whether Christian or Moslem or Sikh or Jew. No one is entitled to pick and choose which laws he or she obeys."[10] Muslim immigrants in Britain, in short, must not carry out the directives in Khomeini's fatwa because they contravened the laws of the United Kingdom.

By linking this lesson in "proper integration" to the rule of law, Hurd implied that the danger posed by an extra-territorial religious authority such as imam Khomeini was a problem unique to Muslim immigrants. It is worth noting that similar worries about native Catholics in Britain had endured for several hundred years after the Reformation and establishment of the Church of England.[11] In fact, questions about the reach of the Catholic Church and its continuing influence over Catholic Britons led British authorities to exclude Catholics from many public offices, including the House of Commons, until the Roman Catholic Relief Act of 1829. Nevertheless, British authorities responded to the fatwa as if doubt about loyalty to the state and its laws was specific to Muslims and Islam.

Concern about Khomeini's overreach and influence may ultimately have led Hurd to reassert British sovereignty and downplay the fact that local Muslims had expressed their offense in peaceful and law-abiding ways. Paradoxically, if the call to violence in the fatwa finally made government officials heed local upset over the Rushdie novel, it also led them to respond to British Muslims as if they were by definition part of the very global Muslim community that Khomeini had invoked and political leaders feared. Hurd's message treated British Muslims as if they belonged to a monolithic group that was willing to use force to defend Islam and the prophet—hence, the need to remind them of what proper integration looked like. Yet in the months leading up to the fatwa, the strategies that local Muslim leaders adopted were anything but violent. They organized public demonstrations, conducted letter-writing campaigns, and lobbied political representatives. Indeed, British Muslims employed forms of engagement firmly rooted in the liberal democratic protest tradition. It was only after months of frustration with the lack of public response or debate that they resorted to the more extreme tactic of symbolic book burning, which, in the wake of the fatwa, became the prime example of the British Muslim community's propensity to violence.

Most commentators, however, did not focus on Hurd's efforts to counter the global ambit of the fatwa. Instead, they emphasized his injunction that Muslim immigrants adhere to British expectations for integration. Home Office Minister of State John Patten stressed this point in an open letter to the British Muslim community published by the *Times* a few months later. This statement detailed more specifically what authorities meant when they urged immigrants to "be British." The "most important guiding principle," Patten declared, was "full participation in our society by Muslim and other ethnic minority groups." "Modern Britain has plenty of room for diversity and variety," he assured readers, but "there cannot be room for separation or segregation." Minority groups like Muslims "should be part of the mainstream of British life."[12] Indeed, Rushdie himself was precisely the kind of integrated immigrant that British authorities envisioned—well educated, successful, fully assimilated. By contrast, the Muslim community's reaction to *The Satanic Verses*—and particularly its request that the book officially be deemed blasphemous and banned—proved its isolation from mainstream British society or, at the very least, its failure to grasp the underpinnings of Britain's core liberal democratic principles.

Patten was quick to assure British Muslims that integration did not require them to "lay aside their faith, traditions or heritage," but it did presume putting down "new roots" that "must go deep."[13] Evidence of these new roots included "a fluent command of English," as well as "a clear understanding of British democratic processes, of its laws, the system of Government [sic] and the history that lies behind them." Even though Patten admitted that the "great majority of Muslims in this country" had "handled" their outrage at Rushdie in a "responsible way," his public letter suggested that British Muslims had somehow overstepped their place by assuming that the country's democratic processes and laws might be adapted and reshaped to address their specific concerns. He thus sought to clarify how the tenets of British liberal democracy worked: "We have, throughout the last few months, been guided by two principles: the freedom of speech, thought and expression; and the notion of the rule of law." Freedom of speech, moreover, "prevails for as long as no law is broken." According to Patten's assessment, British Muslims' desire to ban *The Satanic Verses* violated the "fundamental freedom on which democracy is built."[14]

While Patten cast his open letter as an attempt to instruct British Muslims on how to "be British," it had the effect of confirming the failure of Muslim immigrants to integrate into British society. Conservative commentators such as Michael Jones, political editor for the *Sunday Times*, praised the government for providing "a long overdue reassessment of the nature of British citizenship."[15] Patten's description of "the minimal meaning of being British," Jones declared, "is an important step forward. So, it may be judged, are his implicit warnings of the dangers of ethnic minorities spurning the entrenched, majority culture." For figures like Jones, the whole gamut of Muslim responses to Rushdie's novel—from outrage, to requests for an expansion of the blasphemy law, to the fatwa—constituted a rebuff of the "ground rules for the British way of life."[16]

This apparent refusal to embrace mainstream British culture and put down "deep" roots opened the door to questions about whether multiculturalism as a social model could work. Jones mocked the efforts of Labour Party deputy leader Roy Hattersley to empathize with Muslim upset as a "virtuoso display of logical gymnastics about the Rushdie affair" that attempted to "square the circles of fundamentalist bigotry."[17] But even before Whitehall's public demand that Muslim immigrants "be British," critics had raised the question about the "nature of the multi-cultural society to which this country is committed."[18] For the editorial board of the *Independent*, for instance, Khomeini's fatwa offered proof that "Islam is not a tolerant religion and makes no pretence of being so."[19] This display of intolerance mattered, they explained, because the reigning British model of multiculturalism—first set out by Labour Home Secretary Roy Jenkins in 1966—demanded an atmosphere of mutual tolerance and cultural pluralism on the presumption that "all manifestations of cultural diversity would be benign."[20] By this logic, "intolerant behaviour on the part of a minority" spelled the failure of liberal multiculturalism.[21]

Conservative journalist Barbara Amiel doubled down on this message in a column for the *Times*. The Rushdie brouhaha, she claimed in no uncertain terms, confirmed that Muslims are a people "whose entire moral ethos is illiberal and for whom tolerance is anathema."[22] How, then, "can a liberal democracy like our society continue to remain true to its principles when it contains a large number of people who are neither liberal nor democrats?"[23] To explain how Britain arrived at this predicament, Amiel offered a very specific interpretation of postwar history. In its effort to pursue a liberal society in which "people accept individual human beings without prejudice … on the basis of race, religion, colour or creed," Britain took in masses of immigrants and passed laws to protect them. But these laws—what Amiel described as part of the "race relations industry"—had a problematic effect on liberal society, limiting "the individual's freedom to say what he liked, write what he liked, employ whomever he wanted." The only antidote to this "disaster," Amiel argued, was to admit that "creating a multicultural society was in error." While "we can still have a multiracial society and we can certainly say to our citizens it doesn't matter where you come from," she concluded, we cannot go on saying "it doesn't matter where you are going. If we want one country, our citizens must be going in the same direction."[24] In terms of practical suggestions, moreover, Amiel proposed nothing short of dismantling the provisions associated with state multiculturalism—above all, rescinding the 1965 Race Relations Act that forbade discrimination on the basis of racial, ethnic, or religious background.

This portrait of postwar immigration and race relations was somewhat misleading. Amiel cast these "masses of immigrants" as foreigners bringing unwanted alien cultures to Britain. Yet the vast majority were actually British subjects from the Commonwealth, who had come to fill the postwar labor shortage and enjoyed the legal right to live and work in the United Kingdom. For conservative critics such as Amiel, the Race Relations Act and its subsequent amendments represented what we would now term "reverse discrimination": legislation meant to prevent discrimination on the basis of race or ethnicity was characterized as impeding one's liberty to rent to, employ, or serve some groups and not others.

At the time of its passage, it's worth noting, the 1965 Race Relations Act was part of a parliamentary compromise, worked out in the wake of the 1962

Commonwealth Immigrants Act.[25] The 1962 bill nominally imposed quotas on all non-skilled laborers coming from former British colonies, but its effect was to target non-whites. This effort raised the hackles of the Labour Party's left wing, which worried that the bill was racialist.[26] More pragmatic Labour leaders argued that the British people had a limited capacity for absorbing alien cultures, and if the government did not control the number of colonials and former colonials arriving in the UK, race relations would inevitably explode. The deal struck between Labour and Tory politicians represented the first effort to curb postwar migration from the so-called New Commonwealth, while also acknowledging that British subjects who had already settled in Britain ought to be integrated and protected from social discrimination. The logic of the compromise was neatly summed up by Hattersley, who in the mid-1960s was Junior Home Office Minister: "Integration without control is impossible, but control without integration is indefensible."[27] This strategy for managing immigration and its social consequences prioritized "racial harmony" and laid the groundwork for British multiculturalism over the next two decades.[28]

As a more open rejection of multiculturalism gained steam in the wake of the Rushdie affair, commentators from across the Atlantic took note. Dan Fisher, staff writer for the *Los Angeles Times*, observed that the heated controversy over *The Satanic Verses*—while global in scope—had divisive ramifications for Britain specifically. He declared that the "multicultural concept" was taking a "beating in Britain."[29] His assessment was based primarily on the backlash by conservatives, who wanted to replace this postwar experiment with an assimilationist approach. They sought to bolster the nation by demanding that immigrants "make peace with British culture and its values."[30] Together with local Muslim anger, the fatwa provided ample ammunition for those who were already disinclined toward multiculturalism to discredit it. But as Fisher pointed out, British conservatives had long been "uncomfortable with a multicultural concept that they believe weakens the national fiber."[31] They were merely taking advantage of the Rushdie affair to debunk what they perceived as the ascendant social model in Britain.

The Left's Retreat from Multiculturalism

Yet Fisher had an inkling that a major sea change was also taking place among left-of-center liberals. He mentioned in passing that the *New Statesman* magazine, "a consistent campaigner for minority rights, found itself deeply troubled by the implications of the angry British Muslim reaction to Rushdie's book."[32] Indeed, it was such leftist misgivings about multiculturalism, now being expressed in public, that marked the crucial shift in the British debate about immigrants triggered by the Rushdie affair. After all, the Labour Party had been vocal champions of an integrationist policy that promoted "equal opportunity, accompanied by cultural diversity, in an atmosphere of mutual tolerance."[33] This formulation, first articulated by Home Secretary Roy Jenkins in 1966, provided the guiding principles for a pluralistic British society based on the peaceful coexistence of different cultures.[34]

From the late 1960s through the 1980s, the Race Relations bills (1965, 1968, and 1976) that outlawed discrimination—together with the Local Government Act of 1966 that included a provision to extend central government funds to metropolitan areas with large numbers of immigrants—provided the legal scaffolding for managing diversity and constituted Britain's state policy of multiculturalism. This structure meant that mayors and town councils became important ground-level agents for shaping multiculturalism in practice. By and large, the strategy of local politicians was to identify ethnic minority leaders, who could act as conduits of information about their community and its concerns, as well as distributors of funding for immigrant associations.

A major beneficiary of these earmarked government funds was local educational authorities or school districts. As institutions where immigrants and white Britons came together, schools served as a key arena for grappling with diversity, initially through efforts to "remedy" the presumed deficits of ethnic minority children and later through initiatives to prepare all students "for life in a multi-racial society."[35] By the mid-1980s, British schools had largely embraced a multicultural curriculum that incorporated the contributions of immigrants and their cultures. Yet this apparent triumph did not go unchallenged. Between 1982 and 1984, Ray Honeyford, headmaster at an Asian-majority middle school in the city of Bradford, published a series of highly publicized articles condemning "the current educational orthodoxies connected with race" that promoted "cultural enrichment" at the expense of canonical English literature.[36] He openly railed against Asian and West Indian customs and values and claimed that the predominance of alien cultures threatened to degrade the British education system as a whole. When parents at his school publicly protested his comments as racist and demanded his dismissal, Honeyford was pushed into early retirement. But his critiques of multiculturalism paved the way for Margaret Thatcher's conservative government to pass the Education Reform Act of 1988, creating a national curriculum with standardized achievement metrics and requiring "broadly Christian" acts of worship in all schools.

The Rushdie affair, as we have seen, provided conservative Britons with another example of the problematic effects of alien cultures on their country. What was different was that the controversy also deeply unsettled those on the left who had been far more sympathetic to multiculturalism in Britain. The liberal left's new skepticism was articulated most explicitly and colorfully by the author Fay Weldon in a booklet for the Chatto *CounterBlasts* series entitled, *Sacred Cows: A Portrait of Britain, Post-Rushdie, Pre-Utopia*.[37] Weldon had established her literary reputation in the 1960s with fiction that unsettled traditional gender roles and disrupted male-centered narratives. By the late 1970s, she was a major feminist icon.[38] Describing herself as a "leftish humanist feminist," she offered this sardonic broadsheet as a defense of her friend Rushdie's right to free speech.[39] More importantly, perhaps, Weldon painted a distinctive picture of a center liberal and left-leaning British political culture—rooted in the so-called chattering classes—that was shaken by the fatwa's decree of capital punishment.

Weldon's tract, which appeared around the same time that Patten issued his open letter to British Muslims, depicted her own political awakening from "our agreeable and passive over-tolerance of everything and anything."[40] As she described it, her particular leftist feminist milieu had not bothered to engage seriously with the culture and customs of Muslim immigrants, "but instead murmured platitudes about 'great world religions' and thought Iran and Iraq were far-off places, whose troubles had nothing to do with us."[41] Local Muslim upset over Rushdie's novel—the rumblings of "'kill, kill, kill' from our own backstreets, and the crackle of pages burning"—managed to trouble a few in her circle, resulting in a "polite letter" or two to the newspapers.[42] But even as Weldon likened the burning of *The Satanic Verses* to the burning of witches in the middle ages, she satirized the typical leftist response: "A bit drastic, but we see their point. Their hearts are in the right place—it's just they're a bit primitive."[43] According to Weldon's account, it was Khomeini's fatwa, which dispatched "death squads after one of our own," that shook her out of her apathy and forced her to absorb the gravity of the threat.

In charting her own transformation from a well-meaning supporter of cultural tolerance and diversity to a skeptic of multiculturalism, Weldon conflated a foreign religious authority, who contravened the right of free speech by threatening death, with local British Muslims, who demonstrated their dislike of a book by burning it. Like Patten, she seemed to assume that Muslim immigrants in Britain were beholden to the Ayatollah or at least answerable for his dictates. Even as she described the escalation of her own concern, she treated

Muslim reactions to *The Satanic Verses* as if they were more or less the same—equal in weight, influence, and effect—and thus deserving of a blanket response.

In order to galvanize others in her social milieu, Weldon cast the repeated references by Labour politicians like Roy Hattersley to the "deep hurt of the Muslim community" as effectively making excuses for "rioting in the streets, book-burning, threats and intimidation."[44] The scales having fallen from her eyes, she boldly declared: "The Koran is food for no-thought. It is not a poem on which a society can be safely or sensibly based. It forbids change, interpretation, self-knowledge or even art, for fear of treading on Allah's creative toes."[45] The Iranian imam's harsh judgment for what she viewed as a mischievous work of fiction demonstrated clearly that Islam is not tolerant, but rather a vengeful and cruel religion.

Taking on the voice of a truth-teller, Weldon assailed the guilt of "white, middle class, prosperous" Britons like herself who "in the name of Freedom of Belief ... dwell contentedly (or thought we did) in our multicultural, multi-religious society" and dare not admit that this social model does not work.[46] The problem, as she saw it, was that "deep hurt and anger" were not so much a rejection of Rushdie's novel, but a repudiation of British culture, liberalism, and a society perceived by Muslim immigrants as morally rotten. To a certain extent, Weldon sympathized with this perception of British society in crisis, pointing to "the drunkards in the streets, the homeless, the purposelessness of our alienated youth."[47] She claimed to understand why Muslim parents might want to educate their children in religious schools and even admitted that Britain offered Muslims no real alternatives to "a retreat into fundamentalism."[48] Still, she insisted: "You cannot, should not, teach a primitive, fear-ridden religion, beat it into children, as the lesser of two evils."[49] The solution, according to Weldon, lay in acknowledging the failure of multiculturalism and insisting on a "uniculturalist policy" of assimilation. This approach would enable our children to "grow up with a sense of common identity—be they Afro-Caribbean, Asian or European in origin—not paralysed by confusion. Your God or mine? Your curry or my chips? Your sister on the hockey field, my brother down the mosque?"[50]

Continuing to uphold multiculturalism as the blueprint for British society, Weldon conceded, represented the path of least resistance—or at least seemed more convenient. It was "pleasanter, easier to be seen on the side of ethnic minorities, all in favour of the multi-cultural."[51] Yet she warned, "We have let ourselves be frightened by the labelling, the name-calling—racist, elitist, middle class—right out of the fray, and the religious extremists under this cover have rushed in to take over."[52] This worrisome development meant that British feminists could no longer ignore the fate of Muslim women who suffered "the wife-beatings, the intimidation, and the penalties for recalcitrance."[53] Weldon thus exhorted her fellow liberals to stop being "slaves to liberal orthodoxy." "Who is there left of us brave enough to state what we believe?" she prodded. "That, say, the Bible's a superior revelatory work to the Koran—or at any rate reveals a kinder, more interesting, less vengeful, less cruel God, one worth studying and worshipping?"[54] For Weldon, then, the Rushdie affair raised major doubts about the policy of multiculturalism and the unintended consequences of allowing illiberal and intolerant immigrants to establish themselves in Britain. This complication posed a threat to the core principles of liberal democracy and required a reassertion of the superiority of Western culture and civilization.

Sacred Cows offered one of the first articulations of the perils of multiculturalism from a left-of-center perspective. The tract operated on two levels. It simultaneously claimed to speak for and speak to a like-minded left, liberal, feminist audience: it sought to represent Weldon's collective "we" (precisely those in Britain who had traditionally been the most open to immigrants and cultural diversity) even as it gave them permission to admit the possibility that multiculturalism was a mistake. The key to this drastic rethinking was the conviction that Islam—in the form of book-burning and Khomeini's fatwa—was an intolerant religion that encouraged illiberal behaviors, from denying Rushdie's freedom of speech to forbidding images of God to controlling how women dressed.

In many ways, Weldon's conclusions about cultural diversity in Britain sounded a lot like those of conservative commentators. Both perspectives marshalled evidence from the Muslim response to *The Satanic Verses* to argue that Islam as a religion was intolerant and thus itself unable to accept or coexist with other cultures or ways of being. Both insisted that Britain must hold the line and defend liberal democracy by demanding that Muslim immigrants adhere to British values. Both declared that the days of allowing intolerant cultures to exist undisturbed and unchecked within society must now be over. This convergence marked a major departure for leftists, who had previously staunchly defended cultural pluralism as a legitimate and desired blueprint for society.

Weldon's arguments also anticipated—and set the very terms for—how Europeans would respond in the coming years and decades to what they perceived as an increasingly dire threat from Muslims settled in their countries. Eight months after Khomeini's fatwa, a controversy erupted in France over whether young girls should be forced to take off their headscarves in schools.[55] The heated debate, which came to be known as the headscarf affair, again highlighted the intractable presence of Muslims and raised questions about whether they were capable of integrating effectively into European societies. In this case, authorities interpreted the desire of Muslim girls to cover their heads at school as a violation of *laïcité* or secularism, a core principle of French republicanism that protects civic life from encroachment by religion. As with the Rushdie affair in Britain, the headscarf affair was understood as a challenge to the fundamental definitions of French citizenship. In both cases, the efforts to defend or maintain religious traditions—to claim their legitimacy in a European context—were identified as signs of Muslim obstinance, an unwillingness to accommodate European values and expectations.[56]

The French controversy, moreover, amplified Weldon's exhortation to Western feminists about the need to pay attention to the fate of Muslim women. Indeed, much of the French debate revolved around the deeper meaning of the headscarf, with most commentators across the political spectrum concluding that it symbolized the subjugation of women. As I have argued elsewhere, the treatment of women under Islam became the common cause that galvanized conservative defenders of a homogeneous Europe and traditionally left-leaning feminists.[57] "Saving Muslim women" served as a crucial rallying cry for both conservatives and liberals, even as the apparent fact that Muslim women required saving in the first place fueled the conviction that Islam itself could not be reconciled with Western liberal democracy.

Finally, in Weldon's arguments against multiculturalism and its embrace of cultural difference, we catch a glimpse of an emerging political logic among liberals and center-leftists that would become more pronounced over time. This logic framed the debate over the impact of immigrants on European society as a zero-sum choice. If the goal of *Sacred Cows* was to defend Rushdie's right of free speech and the fundamental principles of liberalism more generally, Weldon's conclusion was that these liberal-democratic values could only be protected by giving up multiculturalism. The argument went something like this: we cannot be tolerant of a culture that is itself intolerant. But this stance meant that critics such as Weldon were willing to cede the ground on one liberal value (cultural pluralism) in order to preserve another (freedom).[58] The deeply ironic and chilling implications of this choice only became clear several decades later, as the safeguarding of liberalism has become the basis for a distinctly illiberal turn across Europe and the United States.

Notes

1. For discussions of the global reach of the Rushdie affair, see especially Lisa Appignanesi and Sara Maitland, eds., *The Rushdie File* (Syracuse: Syracuse University Press, 1990) and Daniel Pipes, *The Rushdie Affair: The Novel, the Ayatollah, and the West* (New York: Birch Lane Press, 1990).
2. Bhikhu Parekh, "The Rushdie Affair and the British Press: Some Salutary Lessons," *Commission for Racial Equality* (1990), 3. Available online: https://citeseerx.ist.psu.edu/viewdoc/download?doi=10.1.1.178.6209&rep=rep1&type=pdf (accessed October 15, 2021).
3. Rushdie, at least according to Parekh, dismissed "the protesters as illiterate fanatics who had neither read nor understood the book and were only bent on suppressing a critical scrutiny of their cherished dogmas." Ibid.
4. According to Parekh, a London solicitor advised the group that such a tactic would be more effective if the national media had advance warning of the book burning. Ibid.
5. Ruhollah Al-Musavi Al-khomeini, "Fatwa against Salman Rushdie," *Iran Data Portal*, https://irandataportal.syr.edu/fatwa-against-salman-rushdie (accessed November 12, 2021).
6. Yaqub Zaki, "Rushdie's Real Crime," *The Times*, February 28, 1989, 14.
7. Khomeini, "Fatwa."
8. For analysis of the effect of the fatwa on the British debate over Rushdie, see Talal Asad, "Multiculturalism and British Identity in the Wake of the Rushdie Affair," *Politics and Society* 18, no. 4 (1990): 455–80; Aamir Mufti, "Reading the Rushdie Affair: An Essay on Islam and Politics," *Social Text* 21 (1991): 95–116; Peter Weller, *A Mirror for Our Times: "The Rushdie Affair" and the Future of Multiculturalism* (London: Continuum, 2009); Rita Chin, *The Crisis of Multiculturalism in Europe: A History* (Princeton: Princeton University Press, 2017), especially 178–91.
9. Stephen Goodwin, "Hurd Tells Muslims Not to Break Law over Rushdie Book," *The Independent*, February 25, 1989, 3.
10. "The Moslems in Britain," *The Financial Times*, February 25, 1989, Section I, 6.
11. Denis Gwynn, *The Struggle for Catholic Emancipation* (London: Longmans, 1928); J. H. Hexter, "The Protestant Revival and the Catholic Question in England, 1778–1829," *Journal of Modern History* 8, no. 3 (1936): 297–319.
12. John Patten, "The Muslim Community in Britain," *Times*, July 5, 1989, 13.
13. Ibid.
14. Ibid.
15. Martin Jones, "Ground Rules for the British Way of Life," *Sunday Times*, July 23, 1989, section B, 3.

16 Ibid.
17 Ibid.
18 "Limits to Mutual Tolerance," *The Independent*, February 18, 1989, 14.
19 Ibid.
20 Ibid.
21 Ibid.
22 Barbara Amiel, "A Blueprint for Disaster from the Best of Intentions," *Times*, February 24, 1989, 17.
23 Ibid.
24 Ibid.
25 Philip A. Sooben, "The Origins of the Race Relations Act," University of Warwick, CRER Research Papers in Ethnic Relations, no. 12, 1990; Zig Layton-Henry, *The Politics of Immigration* (Oxford: Blackwell, 1992), especially Chapters 2–4; Kathleen Paul, *Whitewashing Britain: Race and Citizenship in the Postwar Era* (Ithaca: Cornell University Press, 1997), 166–79; Randall Hansen, *Citizenship and Immigration in Post-War Britain* (Oxford: Oxford University Press, 2000), 100–52.
26 Hansen, 112–15, 130.
27 Quoted in Adrian Favell, *Philosophies of Integration: Immigration and the Idea of Citizenship in France and Britain* (Basingstoke: Palgrave, 2001), 104.
28 Multiculturalism is a notoriously tricky concept to pin down. For a recent overview, see Chin, *The Crisis of Multiculturalism in Europe*, 1–22. For discussions of multiculturalism in political theory, see Iris Marion Young, *Justice and the Politics of Difference* (Princeton: Princeton University Press, 1990); Charles Taylor, *Multiculturalism: Examining the Politics of Recognition*, ed. Amy Gutman (Princeton: Princeton University Press, 1994); Will Kymlicka, *Multicultural Citizenship: A Liberal Theory of Minority Rights* (Oxford: Clarendon Press, 1995); Amy Gutman, *Identity in Democracy* (Princeton: Princeton University Press, 2003). For an important discussion from a sociological perspective, see Stuart Hall, "Conclusion: The Multicultural Question" in *Un/settled Multiculturalisms: Diasporas, Entanglements, Transruptions*, ed. Barnor Hesse (London: Zed Books, 2000), 209–11.
29 Dan Fisher, "Multicultural Concept Takes Beating in Britain," *Los Angeles Times*, March 1, 1989, 10.
30 Ibid.
31 Ibid.
32 Ibid.
33 Quoted in E. J. B. Rose, *Colour and Citizenship: A Report on British Race Relations* (London: Oxford University Press, 1969), 25.
34 For a discussion of the development of British multiculturalism, see Chin, *The Crisis of Multiculturalism in Europe*, 240–54.

35 Swann Committee, *Education for All* (London: HMSO, 1985), 199. This report, led by Lord Michael Swann, rejected educational authorities' initial impulse to assimilate immigrant students and criticized the "problem-centered perception" of minority children. For a broader discussion of the Swann report, see Chin, *The Crisis of Multiculturalism in Europe*, 242–4; Favell, *Philosophies of Integration*, 126–32.
36 Ray Honeyford, "Education and Race: An Alternative View," *Salisbury Review* (Winter 1984): 30–2.
37 Fay Weldon, *Sacred Cows: A Portrait of Britain, Post-Rushdie, Pre-Utopia* (London: Chatto & Windus, 1989).
38 For more on Fay Weldon's career and reputation, see Mara Reisman and Fay Weldon, "An Interview with Fay Weldon," *Modern Language Studies* 37, no. 2 (2008): 32–49; Eden Ross Lipson, "The Life and Loves of Fay Weldon: A She-Writer's Subversive Style," *Lear's* (January 1990): 113–15; Jenny Newman, "'See Me as Sisyphus, But Having a Good Time': The Fiction of Fay Weldon" in *Contemporary British Women Writers*, ed. Robert E. Hosmer Jr. (New York: St. Martin's, 1993), 188–206.
39 Weldon, *Sacred Cows*, 4.
40 Ibid., 16.
41 Ibid., 7.
42 Ibid., 8.
43 Ibid., 9.
44 Ibid., 10.
45 Ibid., 6.
46 Ibid., 12, 20.
47 Ibid., 23.
48 Ibid., 30.
49 Ibid., 29–30.
50 Ibid., 32.
51 Ibid., 35.
52 Ibid., 36.
53 Ibid., 35.
54 Ibid., 33.
55 The most significant scholarly literature on the French headscarf affair includes: Joan Scott, *The Politics of the Veil* (Princeton: Princeton University Press, 2007); John R. Bowen, *Why the French Don't Like Headscarves: Islam, the State, and Public Space* (Princeton: Princeton University Press, 2008); Cécile Laborde, *Critical Republicanism: The Hijab Controversy and Political Philosophy* (Oxford: Oxford University Press, 2008); Christian Joppke, *Veil: Mirror of Identity* (Cambridge, UK: Polity Press, 2009).

56 Chin, *The Crisis of Multiculturalism in Europe*, 192–5.
57 See especially, Chin, *The Crisis of Multiculturalism in Europe*, Chapter 4.
58 I elaborate on this dynamic in Chin, *The Crisis of Multiculturalism in Europe*, 293–7; and more recently in Rita Chin, "Illiberalism and the Multicultural Backlash," in *Routledge Handbook of Illiberalism*, ed. András Sajó, Renáta Uitz, and Stephen Holmes (London: Routledge, 2021), 280–98.

3

Total Critique: *The Condition of Postmodernity* at the End of History

Don Mitchell

Late May 1989. While the world's gaze is focused on the dramatic events unfolding in Tiananmen Square, the residents and officials in the deindustrialized steelmaking city of Johnstown, Pennsylvania, could perhaps have been forgiven if their attention was elsewhere, focused inwards—and backwards—as they prepared for the centennial of the Great Johnstown Flood of May 31, 1889. Johnstowners were putting a lot of stock in the transformative effects marking this anniversary would have on their town. It had been a hard decade in Johnstown. Between 1980 and 1984, the number of steelworkers employed in the city's mills had been cut from more than 10,000 to about 2,000, unemployment had soared to more than 25 percent, and an epidemic of foreclosures had left a residential landscape pockmarked by abandoned homes, even as homelessness soared. AIDS had arrived with the devastation.[1]

The flood's centenary offered an opportunity to turn the town's fortunes around. In the wake of deindustrialization, politicians, local business owners, and remaining residents had scrambled to find new economic investment. With a large federal grant, for example, the city had sponsored the building of a Michael Graves-designed "world headquarters" for the regional shopping mall developer Crown America. With its postmodern flourishes and pastel coloring, the Crown America building stood in stark contrast to the rusting, hulking, largely empty steel mills and as a symbol for how the economy was changing. Around the turn of the twentieth century, Johnstown had been one of the high-tech wonders of the world, deploying more advanced steelmaking techniques than many of its global competitors. But its demise had been planned as early as the 1960s by its major corporations, Bethlehem Steel and US Steel, which were uninterested in making the investments required to address growing environmental problems and competition from new plants elsewhere. And their disinvestment only gained steam after the economic crises of the early 1970s.[2] Heavy industry was no longer Johnstown's future. Crown America was: a builder of malls, a builder of the postmodern, postindustrial economy.

And so was tourism, or so city officials hoped. "Come for the history. Stay for the fun." So read the official slogan of the Johnstown Flood Centennial. It was an odd, even desperate, slogan. More than 2,000 people had been killed in the flood. The flood itself had resulted from the negligent "improvement" of a dam on a branch of the Little Conemaugh River fifteen miles upstream from the city. Originally built to regulate water levels on the Pennsylvania Canal, the dam and lake had later been sold to a group of Pittsburgh investors who transformed the area into an exclusive playground for that city's industrial elite. When the dam burst just after three in the afternoon on May 31, 1889, it sent a wall of water cascading through the steeply incised valley of the Little Conemaugh. Picking up houses, barns, cows, horses, people, train cars, and telegraph poles as it went, the wall of water slammed into town about an hour later, ricocheting off the valley wall where the Little Conemaugh joined Stony Creek River and sloshing back across the valley floor. Eventually, the debris piled up against a strong stone bridge and caught fire, killing many who had survived the flood itself.[3]

The flood wiped out Johnstown's industrial infrastructure, offering fresh ground upon which a new high-tech industrial city could be built. In 1889, Johnstown remained a logical place to make steel. Appropriate and abundant resources were nearby, there was good rail access to growing markets, and America's borders were still open to Europe assuring a constant influx of fresh and needy workers. Built anew, Johnstown's mills outcompeted many of those in Pittsburgh and Youngstown. Johnstown's turn-of-the-century industrial future was bright. But its twentieth-century history was contentious. Johnstown was a center of militancy in the massive steel strikes of 1919 and 1937, despite interethnic rivalries and the importation of African American strike-breakers, which helped establish a pattern of racist deployment of labor by capital, deepen racial animosity, and forge white working-class solidarity. The steel companies' control over housing, stores, churches, and recreation was a source of great resentment among workers, which remained even when the companies began outsourcing their paternalism to government agencies like the Johnstown Public Housing Authority.[4] Class and racial struggle were rarely below the surface in Johnstown, even into the era of deindustrialization.[5]

This was not the history Johnstown officials hoped tourists would come for. That history was one of industrial ingenuity, community, and courage—in addition to 1889, devastating floods had struck in 1936 and 1977—and of the kind of resilience that always looked toward the new "morning in America" Ronald Reagan promised in his 1984 election campaign.[6] And it was a history that was going to be built right into the landscape. For the flood centenary was not just an occasion to mark an important event, it was the centerpiece of an ambitious plan to restart Johnstown's economy by selling its history. In anticipation of the centennial, the Johnstown Flood Museum remade itself into an institution "attempting to assist the community in using its historic resources for revitalization and economic development," in the words of one of its directors, and shifted from focusing on the flood alone to "document[ing] the city" as a whole.[7] With support from the National Park Service and Bethlehem Steel, museum officials, planners, and politicians launched an ambitious plan to remake the whole of the city's landscape into an industrial heritage museum, with heritage serving as "a springboard to further develop the city."[8] The idea was to retain the steel mill facades and eventually convert the interiors of some of them into "living museums" where a simulacra of steelmaking would entertain and inform visitors. Planners hoped to attract as many as 200,000 visitors a year by emphasizing the city's heroic industrial history and its reputation for being a "city of survivors." Nowhere was there mention of Johnstown's contentious labor history. Contention was considered unsellable (though this too was contentious, with some officials at the museum arguing for a more realistic view of the town's history).[9]

Even if many of the plans fell through, Johnstowners had pinned a lot on the promise that heritage could be leveraged to create a place in the new postindustrial American economy, and while their struggles were surely not of the word-historical scale of the students and workers occupying Tiananmen halfway around the world, they were just as indicative of the wrenching transformation of the political-economic and geopolitical global order at the end of the 1980s. And Johnstown's landscape showed it. While some big, industrial mill buildings were preserved, others were knocked down and postmodern headquarters for shopping mall builders erected in their stead. The aesthetic shift matched the economic shift. The hulking steel mills represented the history; Michael Graves' playfully designed Crown America building represented the fun—and the future—people might just stay for.

I

China's wrenching transformation into a state-capitalist powerhouse and the struggles it unleashed—like Tiananmen in May and June 1989—captured the world's attention. Johnstown's simultaneous effort to keep from becoming merely a liberal-capitalist backwater likely did not, probably not even that of the geographer David Harvey. Harvey had recently written insightfully about the similar wrenching transformation of Baltimore, three hours to the southeast, where Bethlehem Steel was also a dominant presence and where the forces of deindustrialization had been equally devastating in recent years. Baltimore had been Harvey's hometown since 1969. From his earliest days there, the city's deindustrialization, racial struggles, deepening poverty, and experiments in new modes of urban development and governance had been a primary touchstone for his geographical rethinking of Marx's theory of capitalism.[10]

But by May 1989, Harvey had been away from Baltimore for two years, having moved back to his native England to take up the Halford Mackinder Chair of Geography at Oxford. On April 24, 1989, while Chinese Communist Party General Secretary Li Ping and high-ranking Beijing officials met to adopt a hardline position against the Tiananmen protestors, David Harvey was in Stockholm to receive the Swedish Society of Anthropology and Geography's Andreas Retzius Medal in Gold from King Carl XVI Gustav and present a lecture on the transformation of urban governance from "managerialism" to "entrepreneurialism."[11] Based in part on his understanding of Baltimore—where the "transition point" from managerialism to entrepreneurialism could "be dated exactly" to the 1979 passage of a referendum allowing for the public-private redevelopment of the Inner Harbor—this paper was destined to become one of the most cited works of Harvey's long career.[12] Few other works of the time explained so clearly why cities around the world were undergoing the kind of shift experienced in Baltimore and Johnstown, and what this portended for the broader culture of "late capitalism."

It certainly helps explain much of what was afoot in Johnstown, as civic leaders there saw its now-abandoned industrial landscape, together with its history, inner-city property ripe for redevelopment, and land on the outskirts suitable for attracting back-office and other low-wage service industries as its only real assets in what was now clearly a competition for inward investment. And it helps explain why the grandiose plans for heritage development failed and why, by the turn of the twenty-first century, Crown America had gotten out of the mall-building business and become only a real estate-investment and hotel-holding company:

> How many successful convention centres, sports stadia, disney-worlds [sic] and spectacular shopping malls can there be? Success is often short-lived or rendered moot by parallel or alternative innovations ... elsewhere. Local coalitions have no option, given the coercive laws of competition, except to keep ahead of the game thus engendering leap-frogging innovations in life styles, cultural forms ... even institutional and political forms if they are to survive. The result is a stimulating if often destructive maelstrom of urban-based cultural, political, production and consumption innovations.[13]

In Johnstown, the result was definitely destructive; it is questionable how stimulating it was. Nonetheless, it is the next sentences in Harvey's Retzius lecture that resonate most strongly not only in formerly industrialized places like Baltimore and Johnstown, but with the general tenor of the times—a decade into the Thatcher-Reagan-Xiaoping era, four years after Mikhail Gorbachev first publicly uttered the word "perestroika," and three after the "Big Bang" financial reforms in London that freed capital to stalk the globe in search of rent—which seemed to be increasingly defined by a cultural as well as economic dispensation:

> It is at this point that we can identify an albeit subterranean but nonetheless vital connection between the rise of urban entrepreneurialism and the post-modern penchant for design of urban fragments rather than comprehensive urban planning, for ephemerality and eclecticism of style rather than the search for enduring values, for quotation and fiction rather than invention and function, and, finally, for medium over message and image over substance.[14]

As the Society of Architectural Historians writes about Johnstown's Crown America Building: despite its Tuscan coloring, its four-story square-pillared porte-cochère, its monumental Doric rotunda, its brown granite from South Dakota, and its massive rooftop arcade—all architecturally anomalous for the region, not to mention stylistically incoherent—the "building's unusual silhouette fits well within the context of downtown Johnstown, primarily because Graves kept the edifice in scale with its surroundings, even though some of its individual parts are on a monumental scale."[15] As Harvey made clear in his lecture, such playfully incoherent styling fit exactly the fragmented real estate surface of the postindustrial, postmodern city.

David Harvey was already something of a superstar in the small world of academic geography (the Retzius Medal is sometimes called geography's Nobel) and the somewhat larger world of Marxist political economy. His breakthrough into the latter had come seven years earlier with the publication of *The Limits to Capital*, still one of the most remarkable works of spatial political-economy available.[16] In *Limits*, Harvey had set out to rework Marx's theories of capital circulation and accumulation by placing geographical space at their center. It's a complex book that operates at the level of capital's general logic and therefore only rarely examines its specific effects, except insofar as they reflect back on that logic. It is more like the Marx of *Grundrisse* than the Marx of the first volume of *Capital*, much less the *Eighteenth Brumaire*.

But a concern with the historical and cultural unfolding of the logic of capital was hardly foreign to Harvey. During the 1980s, he had written a series of essays not only about the transformation of Baltimore, but also about the remaking of Haussmann's Paris, the building of Sacré Coeur in the wake of the Paris Commune's defeat in 1871, and the shifting experience of space and time in the early twentieth century.[17] Yet Harvey's Retzius lecture hinted at a project of significantly different scope and object: nothing less than a full synthesis of economic with cultural theory that would account for why political economies were shifting the way they were and why they so often took forms like they did in Johnstown, where economic crises were reimagined through heritage, the mobilizing of images, the courting of tourists, the fragmentation of urban space, and the building of architectural confections like the Crown America building. Why was the economy in crisis anyway? How should such a thoroughgoing and widespread economic transformation—often understood to be from industrial to postindustrial, notwithstanding the rise of China as an industrial powerhouse based in the hyper-exploitation of an increasingly feminized workforce[18]—really be understood? Why did the surface appearances of such transformation take the form they did and why did so many people—economists as well as artists, politicians as well as philosophers, Eurocrats as well as Eurocommunists—embrace the kind of "creative destruction" this transformation entailed?

"Creative destruction" was often deadly, after all. Harvey had ended *Limits* with a dystopian view of total nuclear annihilation (not an uncommon worry at the beginning of the 1980s) as a particularly perverse result of capital's frequent need to devalue its existing landscapes—destroy them just as they were being destroyed in Johnstown, but even more violently—to prepare the ground for a new round of capital accumulation. Why had creative destruction, together with the disruption of whole ways of life it entailed, become such an object of celebration rather than an object of concerted, oppositional struggle? Why, Harvey wondered, had there been a "sea-change" not only in political-economic, but also in cultural practices around the world "since about 1972?"

After the festivities in Stockholm, as protesters in Tiananmen were gaining confidence in their occupation following a series of missteps by Li Ping and his associates between April 24 and April 26, and as Johnstowners planned for their centenary commemoration as well as for a highly uncertain future, Harvey returned to Oxford to put the finishing touches on his next book, *The Condition of Postmodernity*, due to be published in the autumn, in which he set out to answer exactly these questions.

II

There has been a sea-change in cultural as well as in political-economic practices since around 1972.

This sea-change is bound up with the emergence of new dominant ways in which we experience space and time.

While simultaneity in the shifting dimensions of time and space is no proof of necessary or causal connection, strong a priori grounds can be adduced for the proposition that there is some kind of necessary relation between the rise of postmodernist cultural forms, the emergence of more flexible modes of capital accumulation, and a new round of "time-space compression" in the organization of capitalism.

But these changes, when set against the basic rules of capitalistic accumulation, appear more as shifts in surface appearance rather than as signs of the emergence of some entirely new postcapitalist or even postindustrial society.[19]

This, announced David Harvey, was "the argument" of *The Condition of Postmodernity*, the basic outline of the case he would make over the ensuing 350 pages. For Harvey, postmodernity was "not so much ... a set of ideas, but ... a historical condition that required elucidation" and as a condition it was rooted in shifting material structures and processes, not just habits of thought.[20] He sought to explore this condition and expose its roots, subjecting both to a unified, total critique. Such a project was hardly fashionable. Postmodernism stood, "incredulous" before "metanarratives" like those offered by Marxism and Marxists like Harvey, as Jean-François Lyotard put it in *The Postmodern Condition*.[21] In Terry Eagleton's somewhat mocking words, postmodernism was "the process of waking from the nightmare of modernity, with its manipulative reason and fetish of the totality, into the laid-back pluralism of the post-modern, the heterogenous range of lifestyles and language games which has renounced the nostalgic urge to totalize and legitimate itself."[22] Harvey was interested in this laid-back pluralism, this incredulity before metanarratives, this proliferating range of lifestyles, only to the degree they were symptomatic of something deeper, something structural beneath the surface and the play that postmodernism valued so highly. Harvey's project in *Condition* was thus unfashionable, but for him it was necessary, given how hegemonic postmodernist thinking had become in universities, the worlds of art and culture, and even in popular discourse.

He particularly thought that much of what passed as postmodern critique of modernism was based in a range of faulty or incomplete assumptions about the nature of modernism. As Harvey argued in the first part of *Condition*, modernity comprised the dialectical entanglement, and the constant struggle for primacy, between the fixed, stable, determinant, universal, deep, rational, and sure, on the one hand, and the transient, fleeting, indeterminant, local, partial, surficial, irrational, and unsure, on the other. Modern industrial capitalism had given rise to the grand plans of Le Corbusier and Daniel Burnham; yet equally in industrial capitalism "all that is solid melts into air," as Marx and Engels so famously put it. The bourgeois revolution was a permanent revolution. Next to Burnham's Chicago World's Fair's "White City" stood the Midway Plaissance; it was not very far from the Corbusien towers of Manhattan's Stuyvesant Town to the squatted tenements and contested streets of the Lower East Side. There was always a dialectic between the permanent and fleeting, rational and irrational, solid and effervescent, and the great art, literature, music, and philosophy from the mid-eighteenth century forward found its subject in—or in reaction to—this dialectic.[23] Certainly, modernist architecture, for example, hewed to the side of the universal, while the romantic arts-and-crafts movement leaned more toward the local (though rooting it in an imagined, stable, universal, relation to a benevolent nature), but both of these arose out of the same economic and cultural milieu, a milieu defined by capitalism's incessant transformation of the world around us. Each tried to capture, and some sought to corral, its wild, constantly modernizing tendencies. By contrast, postmodernism stuck only to one side—the side of the fleeting, indeterminant, local, and irrational—and sought, in Harvey's view, to make a virtue out of what it did not even realize was a necessity.

The Condition of Postmodernity is divided into four parts. The first part seeks to describe the "sea-change." Harvey works contrapuntally through literature (Jonathan Raban's *Soft City*, Goethe's *Faust*, and the broad reorientation of literary sensibilities associated with Woolf, Lawrence, Proust, and Joyce), art (Cindy Sherman's self-portraits, Rivera's murals, and a complex lineage of painters from Manet to Rauschenberg), architecture (Le Corbusier and Burnham, but also postmodernist pioneers and icons like Philip Johnson, Aldo Rossi, and Charles Moore), and philosophy (from Rousseau through Kant, Hegel, and Marx to Foucault, Lyotard, Derrida, and Rorty), to say nothing of a whole raft of social and cultural critics, to lay out the case that there has been a significant shift in the "structure of feeling" in western capitalist society, while showing how this shift had its roots in the earlier modernism. Postmodernism was not as *sui generis* as many of its proponents liked to claim.

If postmodernism grew out of modernism, and if it represented a significant shift in modernism's structure of feeling, then Harvey wanted to show what was at the root of the shift. The second part of *Condition* was thus dedicated to making the case that the shift in the structure of feeling was tightly bound to a shift in the dominant capitalist "regime of accumulation" and its associated "mode of social and political regulation." On the one hand, the logic of capitalist growth and the dynamics of competition require "creative destruction"—constant innovation and transformation. On the other hand, a relatively stable set of social relations and governing forms are required to, if not harmonize, then coordinate the larger social formation with the imperatives of capitalist growth. In the early decades of capitalism's industrialization, the regime of accumulation relied on a kind of hyper-exploitation of the working class, colonial plunder and slave labor for raw materials, the expansion of the economy in "absolute space" (that is, new geographical territories), and, finally, growth in luxury consumption sufficient to meet growing industrial output. The mode of regulation was significantly laissez-faire, tempered by overt class struggle and by the autocracy required for running the colonies. Together both the regime of accumulation and the mode of regulation were highly crisis-prone.

With the European colonial powers' "Scramble for Africa" coming to a head in the 1884 Berlin Conference, capitalist expansion into absolute geographical space could no longer be counted on as a central part of the regime of accumulation. Now space, for both colonial plunder and capitalist expansion, could only be divided and re-divided among the capitalist, imperial powers, a fact noted by both the British Liberal geopolitician Halford Mackinder (for whom Harvey's Oxford chair was named) in 1905 and Lenin in 1917.[24] This induced a significant and long-term crisis in what economists call "effective demand," which was expressed on the ground as a series of more-or-less intensive crises of over-accumulation, where over-accumulated commodities, labor, financial capital, and fixed capital (machinery, buildings) lay idle side-by-side.

Johnstown's rebuilding after the 1889 flood positioned it at a leading edge of this new—or rather still-in-formation—regime of accumulation, and the violent strike of 1919, with its extensive use of African American strike-breakers, was but one step in the long-term making of a new associated mode of regulation. The crucial earlier step had been taken five years before in Dearborn, Michigan, when Henry Ford introduced the five-dollar, eight-hour workday. Coupled with new innovations in the detailed division of labor—the so-called Taylorism that so thoroughly advanced what Marx called the "real subsumption" of labor by capital—and Ford's insistence on inserting his managers and ministers into every aspect of his workers' lives, the five-dollar day remade the capital-labor bargain (that is, the regime of accumulation and its associated mode of regulation) significantly enough by the early 1920s that Antonio Gramsci was calling the result "Fordism."

As Harvey details, Fordism did not really become dominant until after the Second World War, that is, until after the deep, multiple crises of the Depression, the long season of labor unrest that accompanied it, the centralized industrial planning that the war required, and the seemingly ready-made intellectual justifications and policy prescriptions that Keynes' theories offered.[25] When Fordism did become hegemonic, it was premised on several key factors that set it apart from the previous regime: in key industries, worker wage increases were pegged to productivity gains, wages were set high enough that workers could become the source of "effective demand"; the significant, effective devaluing of labor-power through the subsidizing of social reproduction (bread subsidies, public housing and mortgage guarantees, state-funded infrastructure development, heavily subsidized education through the tertiary level, and so forth); and a globally coordinated monetary policy to undergird all this.

The Fordist-Keynesian postwar capitalist regime was remarkably stable for three decades, promoting steady economic growth, massively expanded consumption, and the rapid growth of the middle and professional classes. The Cold War and Communist revolution in China played their part too, with capitalist states (and many capitalists) anxious to moderate class struggle and to broaden access to the levers of power as a counter to the socialist and communist militancy in the west that had marked the Depression and still lay just below the surface of most capitalist states. This too was the era of "high" or "heroic" modernism, evident not only in the soaring internationalist skyscrapers and massive urban redevelopment projects that marked western cities, but also by rapid advances in medical technology, aerospace engineering, and food processing (among other things). Despite roiling red scares, stalemated wars in Korea and Indochina, growing demands for independence in colonial lands, and mass civil rights movements in the US, South Africa, and elsewhere, it was a time of optimism.

Yet by the early 1960s, as Harvey details, the Keynesian-Fordist system was beginning to fray. Global markets in durable goods were becoming saturated, profit-rates were falling, and the mounting fiscal problems in the United States could only be addressed "at the price of an acceleration in inflation, which began to undermine the role of the dollar as a stable international reserve currency."[26] The crisis came in stages: the abandonment of the gold standard in 1971, the OPEC embargo of 1973, the associated deep recession that lasted until 1975, resumed rapid inflation, and the second OPEC embargo in 1979, all of which induced a massive remaking of fiscal policy (and common sense as Keynesianism was shown the door) as well as, of course, a massive industrial restructuring across the industrialized capitalist world. Places like Johnstown, so central to the making of the Fordist world and whose blast furnaces were the epitome of the Promethean heroism of modernity, bore the brunt.

Like other radical political economists (and many mainstream ones), Harvey argued that the new regime of accumulation that was beginning to form out of these crises was "marked by a direct confrontation with the rigidities of Fordism."[27] The new regime was thus one of "flexible accumulation" which entailed not only breaking down mass-production systems to allow for more flexible small-batch production highly responsive to changing consumer demand (and the growing power of the advertising and retailing industries), but a breaking down of the unions with their enforced work-rules, job-security protections, demands for higher pay and secure pensions, set hours of work, free weekends, and paid vacations. In their place came more "flexible," "agile" work and the growing expectation that a stable career with a single employer was a thing of the past. Self-employment, subcontracting, a return of "sweating out": all these marked a new, flexible labor regime imagined to be appropriate to the new regime of flexible accumulation.

But what marked the new regime of accumulation most of all was intense, unrelenting pressure to increase turnover time in capitalist production—essentially the speed at which capital invested in production yields new, surplus capital. Yet, and this is crucial not only for the regime of accumulation and mode of regulation but especially for the cultural forms they helped engender, accelerated turnover time in production required accelerated turnover time in consumption. Harvey argued that flexible accumulation had halved the "half-life" of many consumer products, assuring they had to be replaced within a year or two, rather than once or twice a decade.[28] Flexible accumulation demanded a sped-up life. This speed-up was accompanied—driven—by the rising importance of finance capital and its various exotic investment vehicles which sped up the circulation time of capital by deploying ever-increasing amounts of debt, or fictitious capital (value that circulates "ahead of itself," which is to say debt premised on the production of future value). Such conditions promoted ephemerality, disposability, surface transformation (stylistic changes even as underlying components remain the same), and speed, and with this a remarkable restructuring of supply chains so that production could become more "nimble," more seemingly postindustrial, maybe even poststructural. For Harvey, the thoroughgoing remaking of the regime of accumulation was the root of the shift in the structure of feeling and the increased valorization of the ephemeral, fluid, transient side of modernism. It just made good economic sense.

Though Harvey questioned whether this new flexible regime was here to stay or merely a transition to something else (in the summer of 1989, the full contours of the new regime were simply not yet visible; the term "neoliberalism" was yet to gain general currency), he also argued that shifts that had already occurred had been sufficient to radically transform our understanding and experience of space and time. This is the theme of the third part of *Condition*. As with his arguments concerning the roots of postmodernity as a structure of feeling, and because time and space are "sources of social power" (to quote a chapter title), Harvey sought to show how our experiences of time and space are shaped by the structure of the capitalist political economy. The sense (and indeed reality) of "time-space compression," which is the sense (and reality) of living in an ever-shrinking world (just consider how much transatlantic travel quickened between, say 1820, when it took months, and 1970, when the Concorde could do it in three hours), was tightly linked to capital's demand that turnover and circulation times be reduced as much as possible. "The annihilation of space by time," Marx called it, and this process radically remade the relationships among absolute space, relative space (for example, the relative "closeness" of Europe and the Americas given supersonic transport), and relational space (the space defined by the internalization of social relations).

Condition's third part examines these shifting relationships through a complex and fascinating foray into the philosophies and social theories of space and time (as well as how they have been understood in physics), but the thrust of the argument is that "the uses and meanings of space and time [have] shifted with the transition from Fordism to flexible accumulation."[29] Under flexible accumulation, relative and relational space become vital components of production (absolute space remains important too, but becomes subordinate).

If Fordism promoted a certain homogeneity ("you can get a Model T in any colour you want as long as it is black"), and if the crisis of Fordism was "a crisis of spatial and temporal form"[30] among all the other things it was, then flexible accumulation demanded a differentiation of space, and especially its "pulverization," and it required a new spatial acuity on the part of capital:

> If capitalists become increasingly sensitive to the differentiated qualities of which the world's geography is composed, then it is possible for the peoples and the powers that command those spaces to alter them in such a way as to be more rather than less attractive to highly mobile capital. Local ruling elites can, for example, implement strategies of local labour control, of skill enhancement, of infrastructural provision, of tax policy, state regulation, and so on, in order to attract development within their particular space.[31]

They, like the planners in Johnstown, need to remake the absolute spaces that define their relative place in the global political economy. This is unavoidable, for "space can only be conquered through the production of space,"[32] including investment in the built environment—"long-term investments of slow turnover time" that have the ultimate goal of "accelerat[ing] the turnover time of the mass of capitals"[33]—"and it is only in this context that we can better situate the striving ... for cities to forge a distinctive image and create an atmosphere of tradition that will act as a lure to both capital and people 'of the right sort.'"[34] Come for the history. Stay for the fun. "Heightened inter-place competition," Harvey summarizes, "should lead to the production of more variegated spaces within the increasing homogeneity of international exchange. But to the degree this competition opens up cities to systems of accumulation, it ends up producing what [M. Christine] Boyer calls 'recursive' and 'serial' monotony."[35] If Johnstown's Crown America Building is the hatchback model of Graves' Portlandia Building built a couple of years earlier, Denver's Public Library of a decade later is the SUV of this particular production line. No longer does the Model T have to be black. But underneath its new pastel colors, it is still a Model T.

The experience of space and time, and especially of its compression, is, however, more than just this; it is a socially defining fact of life, and thus finds its expression in the literature, art, and cinema of its time. As in the first part of the book, then, Harvey embarks on a tour through the shifting territories of art, cartography, and literature, before ending this part with an analysis of the structure and aesthetics of two "postmodern" films, Wim Wenders' *Wings of Desire* and Ridley Scott's *Blade Runner* suggesting that though different, both films show that the current age is beset by "a crisis of representation in cultural forms" generated by "the experience of time-space compression" and the "turn to more flexible modes of accumulation" requiring the creation of "new ways of thinking and feeling." The point, for Harvey, was that "any trajectory out of the condition of postmodernity had to embrace exactly such a process."[36]

The final part of *Condition* is one such—quite sly—embrace. Over the course of nine short chapters that form something like a collage of ideas, conclusions, and bold assertions, Harvey insists on the new necessity of meta-theory. "Meta-theory," he argues, "is not a statement of total truth but an attempt to come to terms with the historical and geographical truths that characterize capitalism both in general and in its present form."[37] In its present form, the base of economic relations does not determine the superstructure of cultural production and the structure of feeling in the "last instance" (as per Engels and Althusser). Rather, "the odd thing about postmodern cultural production is how much sheer profit-seeking is dominant in the first instance."[38] However, and this is crucial to Harvey's whole argument, precisely why and how that is the case—as well as what it might mean—can only be understood through understanding capitalism as a "totality of political-economic and cultural-ideological processes in which oppositions and interpenetrations of the modern and postmodern, flexible and Fordist, are continually structuring each other."[39] It requires a fully historical-geographical-materialist analysis that can understand the "real geographies of social action" and their associated cultural forms.[40] Come for the history (and geography). Stay for the fundamental insights into the postmodern condition and the conditions that will allow for its undoing.

III

The Condition of Postmodernity was hardly greeted with universal acclaim. Though many readers appreciated both the scope of its cultural critique and the depth of its political-economic analyses, others were put off by exactly these same features of the book. For them, it was too totalizing in its critique, too seamless, too oblivious to just what postmodernism was making clear: this kind of analysis was not just totalizing, but essentially totalitarian.

Maybe *Condition* just suffered from bad timing. It was published on November 1. On November 9, the Berlin Wall was torn down—even it was transient—and as it came down, history itself came to an end, or so we were told. Who had a need for linearity, for progress, for a search for roots, for a history other than heritage, when time itself was now at a standstill. And, by now fully discredited, there was just no need for Marxism. It would have been immediately tossed in the ashbin of history if there still was history. With Marxism vanquished, a new era of freedom and liberalism was being born and the gloating of its ideologues could not have been any smugger. Tiananmen had already shown that Communism could never be anything other than tyranny. Leipzig, Prague, Budapest, Berlin, and eventually Bucharest showed that tyranny could be defeated. Out of the gray, standardized, bureaucratized, ineluctably modern socialist rubble would arise new, fragmented, diverse, playful, colorful landscape open for exploration by newly liberated postmodern subjects. Harvey may have thought there was a need for a total critique of actually existing capitalism, but it seemed as if the world did not. Why read Harvey, when you could read Fukuyama?[41]

One reason, of course, was that innumerable cities across Eastern Europe were very soon going to have the rug pulled out from under them, just like in Johnstown, as factory after factory was shuttered in what proved to be perhaps the most rapid and thorough-going industrial restructuring in modern world history, condemning millions of workers and their families to a new kind of economic and existential insecurity as capital came in to colonize all this freshly available absolute geographical space, to remake it in its own image, to construct an even more fully global regime of flexible accumulation. As history came to an end, and a new geographical dispensation seemed to be at hand, the ground was also prepared—both at the level of everyday structures of feeling and in the precincts of postmodernist theory—"for the re-emergence of charismatic politics."[42] But that was still in the (near) future.

Another reason for *Condition*'s sometimes chilly reception was the simultaneous publication of Edward Soja's *Postmodern Geographies*.[43] Like Harvey, Soja sought to understand the shifting importance of space under postmodernism and to link it to capitalism's restructuring. But Soja was friendlier to philosophers Harvey deeply criticized (Foucault especially), and more open to the value of anti-foundationalism in much postmodern theorizing. It did not take long for *Postmodern Geographies* to win the hearts and minds of practitioners of (the relatively new field of) cultural studies. While Soja's cultural theory carried with it an aura of appropriate complexity, his political-economic theory was more easily digestible than Harvey's. Similarly, architectural theorists also quickly latched onto Soja's account, finding his approach to geographical space more amenable than Harvey's to architecture's then-current concerns and obsessions (for example with the kind of speed and ephemerality Harvey critiqued).

A third reason critics objected to *Condition* was that Harvey seemed to hew too closely to the grand narratives of the grand men of art and cultural criticism (like T. J. Clark and Frederick Jameson), and especially that he ignored "the persistent presence of feminism in postmodernism" as the urban and art theorist Rosalyn Deutsche put it.[44] Aiming at the very heart of Harvey's arguments (and his prominence as a theorist of urban space), Deutsche suggested that "it would be a shame if urban studies intervened in cultural theory" in a way that ensured "nonsubordinated feminism would ... be equated with political escapism and feminist contributions ... rejected as evasions of urban reality."[45] Harvey's project was masculinist to the hilt, "a phallocentric" effort to "unify all cultural events, all social relation, and all political practices by locating their origins in a single foundation." In addition, Harvey persistently misrecognized and misrepresented both theorists and arguments, while his brand of materialism represented an outmoded Marxism incapable of understanding the materiality of representation. Finally, women were presented in the figures in the book primarily as sexualized objects.[46]

Deutsche's criticisms were amplified by the prominent Marxist-feminist geographer Doreen Massey. She charged Harvey (and Soja) with not just ignoring, but actively denying the salience of feminism. Though *Condition* was a "magnificent achievement," Massey identified three symptomatic problems in Harvey's account: a too-limited and unaware reading of postmodern cinema (unaware particularly of the feminist literature on the films he examined); a use of images—from art to advertising—of naked women to illustrate points about the different representational strategies of modernism and postmodernism (evincing again an unawareness of feminist literature and contributing to the objectification of women); and an ignorance of "the other spaces of modernism"—women's spaces and not just the male-dominated spaces of the public sphere. Beyond these, however, Harvey's primary sin was to constantly subordinate all aspects of identity to a politics of class. Massey acknowledged that Harvey recognized a range of subject positions as vital to any reinvigorated progressive politics, but argued that he always asserted class as separate and superior:

> [E]ven while he recognizes the need to construct alliances in the search for unity, Harvey forces everyone into one mould: "The very possibility of a genuine rainbow coalition defines a unified politics which inevitably speaks the tacit language of class, because this is precisely what defines the common experience within the differences." Any on-the-ground experience of trying to build alliances

would demonstrate the inadequacy of this view. There is here no understanding of the need to recognize conflicts ... and complexity ... as unities which are articulations of genuine and often contradictory differences.⁴⁷

Deutsche's and Massey's critiques launched vigorous debate about Harvey's book, but especially about his project. One result was that for the next decade, *Condition* was more deployed than drawn on. Those opposed to the presence of a strong Marxism in the spatial and cultural disciplines and in favor of a wider cultural turn held up *Condition* as exhibit A of what they were fighting against, and the critiques of Deutsche and Massey of what they were fighting for (whether they accepted the radical feminism of the two or not). Those seeking to preserve at least some space for historical materialism in the post-Tiananmen, post-Berlin 1990s hailed it for just how fruitful Marxist analysis could still be.

IV

In the centennial summer between Tiananmen and Berlin, such academic debates were likely of little importance to Johnstowners, who were preoccupied with festivals, commemorations, and, for many, the hunt for gainful employment, no matter how "flexible." Many left town to seek work elsewhere. A few, relying on their Fordist pensions and whatever other forms of income they could muster, opened a replica museum-factory in Bethlehem's old Franklin Works, wagering (unlike the Flood Museum planners) that a more accurate, more authentic history could draw in visitors and money. Some back-office jobs (insurance paperwork and the like) arrived in Johnstown's suburbs. In the increasingly abandoned downtown, however, it was not long before typical jobs were like those at the various dollar stores opening up in abandoned store-fronts: feminized and with variable and insecure working hours, no job security or benefits (beyond help with applying for food stamps), productivity targets determined by larger, suburban franchises, and management strategies consisting primarily of sowing distrust among employees and between them and customers.⁴⁸ By the turn of the twenty-fist century, matters of gender in places like Johnstown had not become subordinated to matters of class, as Massey worried Harvey's theorizations thought they did, but had become matters of class.

Throughout the 1990s and into the new century, while postmodernists and other social theorists continued to play down its importance, capitalists and their ideologues oversaw a remarkable return of class. As David Harvey argued some years later—once the new regime of accumulation and mode of regulation had solidified into what we now recognize as neoliberalism—the neoliberal revolution was substantively a reassertion of class power, and a retaking of the wealth that Fordist Keynesianism had sought to at least partially redistribute (if for no other reason than to spur effective demand).[49] As class resurged as a dominant social process shaping contemporary political economy, as the assault on stable conditions for labor grew in intensity, as inequality became the defining trait of post-Cold War globalization, the importance of images, heritage, and the rest that seemed to mark postmodernism hardly faded. Indeed, they intensified as more and more of the economy was dedicated to so-called immaterial commodities.[50]

But, curiously, discourses of postmodernism did fade, though fade is not quite the right word. Intense struggles over the value of the concept and the politics of it intensified in the early 1990s, sparked in part by Harvey's book.[51] But then they lost steam. Rather than being convinced by better modes of explanation, many of those enraptured by postmodernism simply found new ways to express their passions without having to utter the word (as with, for example, "assemblage theory," which hyper-valorizes the contingent and anti-foundational and denies the salience of explanatory, historical logic). Indeed, it could be argued that postmodernism as a discourse became a victim of its own ideologies: a fleeting, contingent, playful passion with no necessary foundation in the world it celebrated, and thus easy to abandon when the next shiny new fad came along. By the time of the Great Recession, recourse to "postmodernism" as a means of coming to terms with what was going on was hardly to be found. The Great Recession was neither a crisis nor an effect of postmodern thought, postmodern practices, or any kind of postmodern condition. It was a crisis of capitalism in its flexible, financialized, neoliberal form. And there was precious little that was playful about it or anything that has followed.

The year 1989 was indeed a pivotal one for the "sea-change" Harvey set out to analyze. And while he clearly did not see the full scope of the change that was afoot as he finished correcting his proofs for *Condition*—the only references to the Berlin Wall in the book are in his analysis of *Wings of Desire*, and China figures hardly at all—he did turn out to be completely right when he argued that what so many celebrated as a new postmodern condition was really only "shifts in surface appearance rather than … signs of the emergence of some entirely new postcapitalistic or even postindustrial society."[52]

Notes

1. Jack Metzger, "Plant Shutdowns and Worker Response: The Case of Johnstown, PA," *Socialist Review* 10 (1980): 9–49; Jack Metzger, "Johnstown, PA: Ordeal of a Union Town," *Dissent* 32 (1985): 160–3.
2. Karl Berger, ed., *Johnstown: The Story of a Unique Valley* (Johnstown: Johnstown Flood Museum, 1985).
3. David McCullough, *The Johnstown Flood* (New York: Simon and Schuster, 1968).
4. Don Mitchell, "Public Housing in Single-industry Towns: Changing Landscapes of Paternalism," in *Place/Culture/Representation*, ed. James Duncan and David Ley (London: Routledge, 1993), 110–27.
5. Metzger, "Johnstown."
6. Don Mitchell, "Heritage, Landscape, and the Production of Community: Consensus History and Its Alternatives in Johnstown, Pennsylvania," *Pennsylvania History* 59 (1992): 198–226.
7. "The New Johnstown Flood Museum to Play a New Role in the Community," *Centennial Reports* 3 (1989): 6.
8. Margie Fusco, "Johnstown Flood Centennial Project Is Unique," *Centennial Reports* 2 (1998): 3.
9. John Brant, "Unemployment: The Theme Park," *New York Times*, January 28, 1996.
10. Among many other works, see the essays in David Harvey, *The Urban Experience* (Baltimore: Johns Hopkins University Press, 1989).
11. David Harvey, "From Managerialism to Entrepreneurialism: The Transformation of Urban Governance in Late Capitalism," *Geografiska Annaler* 71, B (1989): 3–17.
12. Ibid., 7.
13. Ibid., 12.
14. Ibid., 12–13.
15. Lu Donnelly et al., "Crown America Building," *Society of Architectural Historians SAH Archipedia*. Available online: https://sah-archipedia.org/buildings/PA-01-CA20 (accessed October 14, 2021).
16. David Harvey, *The Limits to Capital* (Oxford: Blackwell, 1982).
17. Harvey, *Urban experience*; the Paris essays were later collected in David Harvey, *Paris: The Capital of Modernity* (London: Routledge, 2005).
18. See Melissa Wright, *Disposable Women and Other Myths of Global Capitalism* (New York: Routledge, 2005).
19. David Harvey, *The Condition of Postmodernity* (Oxford: Blackwell, 1989), vi.
20. Ibid., x.
21. Jean-François Lyotard, *The Postmodern Condition: A Report on Knowledge* (Manchester: Manchester University Press, 1984).

22 Terry Eagleton, "Awaking from Modernity," *Times Literary Supplement*, February 28, 1987.
23 Marshall Berman, *All That Is Solid Melts into Air* (New York: Simon and Schuster, 1982).
24 Neil Smith, *Uneven Development: Nature, Capital, and the Production of Space* (Oxford: Blackwell, 1990).
25 Harvey, *Condition*, 126–40.
26 Ibid., 141.
27 Ibid., 147.
28 Ibid., 156.
29 Ibid., 284.
30 Ibid., 196.
31 Ibid., 295.
32 Ibid., 258.
33 Ibid.
34 Ibid., 295.
35 Ibid.
36 Ibid., 322.
37 Ibid., 355.
38 Ibid., 336.
39 Ibid., 339.
40 Ibid., 355.
41 Francis Fukuyama, "The End of History?" *The National Interest* 16 (1989): 3–18.
42 Harvey, *Condition*, 350.
43 Edward Soja, *Postmodern Geographies* (Oxford: Blackwell, 1989).
44 Rosalyn Deutsche, *Evictions* (Cambridge, MA: MIT Press, 1996).
45 Deutsche, *Evictions*, 201.
46 Ibid., 203.
47 Doreen Massey, "Flexible Sexism," *Environment and Planning* D, no. 9 (1991): 55–6.
48 Tracy Vargas, *Dollar Store Economy*, PhD dissertation, Syracuse University, 2018.
49 David Harvey, *A Brief History of Neoliberalism* (New York: Oxford University Press, 2005).
50 See Don Mitchell, "Revolution and the Critique of Human Geography: Prospects for the Right to the City after 50 Years," *Geografiska Annaler* 100, B (2018): 2–11.
51 See, for example, the essays collected in Claudia Minca, ed., *Postmodern Geography: Theory and Praxis* (Oxford: Blackwell, 2001).
52 Harvey, *Condition*, vi.

4

Beyond Binaries: Stuart Hall and the History of Science

Michell Chresfield

The commercial opens in a brightly lit home where we see an African American woman identified as "Lyn" reflecting on the importance of ancestry DNA testing. "I didn't know where I was from ethnically," Lyn proclaims to the camera with an enthusiastic smile. And so, Lyn, like thousands of other "root-seekers," sought out ancestry testing in order to unlock the mystery. After results indicated that Lyn was "26 percent Nigerian," Lyn tells the camera "I'm just trying to learn as much as I can about *my* culture."[1] To signify the importance of her newfound ethnicity, the camera then cuts to Lyn wearing a *gele*, a traditional Nigerian headwrap that can be worn in everyday settings, though they are primarily worn during special occasions in Nigerian culture. Holding back tears, Lyn stares into the camera explaining the significance of first placing the *gele* on her head. "I put the *gele* on my head and I looked in the mirror," she said, "and I was trying not to cry, because it's a hat, but it's the most important hat I've ever owned." Premiering in the spring of 2017 under the tagline "Discover the story only your DNA can tell," this commercial illustrates the promise of ancestry DNA testing for black Americans seeking to connect with a history obscured by the displacement of slavery.[2]

The ethnicity showcased in this commercial is one that can be claimed, commercialized, and fashioned: first through the process of DNA test-taking, and later through the purchasing and wearing of a *gele*. It is important to note that this flexible approach to identity isn't limited to Lyn: it is in fact the entire notion underpinning the practice of ancestry DNA testing, as root-seekers from all backgrounds utilize this service to uncover a past which allows them to refashion identities in the present. Companies like 23AndMe and Ancestry have now aired dozens of commercials highlighting the supposed mutability of ethnicity. In one striking example from Ancestry, a man who previously understood his heritage to be German speaks about the surprise of discovering his Scottish ancestry, having now decided to trade in his lederhosen for a kilt.[3] There is also the commercial from 23andMe, which aired during the World Cup in the summer of 2018, touting ancestry DNA testing for its ability to help viewers decide which country to support. The commercial ends with young soccer fans wearing the soccer jerseys of their newly discovered ancestral homes.[4]

As of 2017, the ancestry DNA industry has amassed over $117 million in revenue, with expectations that it will top $611 million by 2026.[5] While scholars have devoted significant attention to detailing how white consumers engage with ancestry DNA testing, scholars are only now beginning to grapple more fully with how ancestry DNA testing impacts the identity formation of black Americans like Lyn Johnson.[6] As a people impacted by trans-Atlantic slavery and therefore lacking in documentary records and other forms of remembering available to those of European heritage, ancestry DNA testing has been particularly path-breaking for the black diaspora, especially as it has engendered new biosocial identities. For instance, African Americans have used these tests to create new cultural communities, establish health agendas, and make reparative claims on the US government for the horrors of slavery. Though these new communities are largely imagined, they nevertheless become concretized as participants draw on traditions, language, and other cultural markers of inclusion. And yet, the import of DNA testing does not lie merely in its usefulness for the past. It also heavily influences the ways in which participants see and think about themselves in the present. In this way ancestry DNA testing is both politically and psychically important to the modern black experience. This is not to suggest that ancestry DNA testing is without faults. As Lyn's commercial suggests, ancestry testing promotes notions of biological essentialism, suggesting that one's identity is immutable and fixed, while also suggesting that identity can be casual and shifting, thus allowing consumers to create new ethnicities where they did not previously exist.

While the "new ethnicities" of today are not necessarily the ones that Stuart Hall envisioned when he released his ground-breaking article of that title in 1989, Hall's ability to foresee a move away from essentialized notions of race and the concomitant embrace of identity's contingent nature is of great relevance to our current moment.[7] A giant in the field of cultural studies, Stuart Hall has been described as "black Britain's leading theorist of black Britain," though the compliment hardly encapsulates the significance of Hall's scholarship.[8] One of the most important contributors to Marxist theory, as well as the author of ground-breaking studies on culture and policing, Hall's career exemplifies the intellectual nuance that is at the center of "New Ethnicities." Hall's theoretical explorations of race and identity help us to better understand the black diasporic experience writ large as he takes up such themes as placelessness, cultural unity, and the meaning of blackness.

Hall's "New Ethnicities" was inspired by his interest in black British film and the ways in which it highlighted the fracturing of essentialized black identity taking place in 1980s Britain. As someone interested in exploring identity, film made sense for Hall who saw filmmakers as the practitioners of the ideas he wrote about.[9] The ideas that would become "New Ethnicities" began as a paper delivered at the first annual Caribbean Film Festival, held in Martinique in 1988. The essay that resulted, released through the Institute of Contemporary Art's *Black Film British Cinema* collection, was a part of a move to recognize the diversity of black representation on display in such films as *My Beautiful Launderette* (1985) and *The Passion of Remembrance* (1986). It was in this art that the black British public, as well as cultural critics, sought to work through what was authentic and inauthentic about these representations, what Hall describes as "the politics of representation."[10]

The release of "New Ethnicities" also coincided with a growing global preoccupation with multiculturalism, a topic Rita Chin takes up in this volume. Opinion polls from the likes of *ABC News* and the *Washington Post* suggested increasing socialization between the white and black populations, as well as a narrowing gap in black achievement.[11] So too did the 1980s mark important if not symbolic firsts in black political progress. The 1989 election of David Dinkins, New York City's first black mayor, elicited declarations that the US's race problem had ended, a refrain that would be echoed almost twenty years later with the election of the country's first black president. Similarly, the founding of the Organization for Multiethnic Americans in 1988, and its challenge to the US census's practice of monoracial identification, all signaled a new dawn of ethno-racial politics.

Though absent in Hall's analysis, scientific advancement, more specifically DNA testing, also flourished in the 1980s after Alec Jeffrey's 1984 development of a DNA profiling process. What began as a method of forensic analysis in criminal cases would go on to complicate understandings of race, ethnicity, and the self for decades to come. Given Hall's interest in the arts and social relationships, it is perhaps unsurprising that his article would not include any mention of science. Fields as diverse as anthropology and genetics were historically used to reify race and identity: as a result, the late twentieth century was marked by efforts, largely led by feminist theorists, to establish the social construction of race, a theme that Hall confronts head on in "New Ethnicities."

In what follows, I explore how the contemporary discourse around science and ancestry DNA testing has contributed to the development of new ethnicities. At the forefront of Hall's critique of ethnicity was the need to grapple with the ancestral past, an opportunity made possible by the proliferation of ancestry DNA companies like 23andMe and Ancestry. In Britain, an estimated 4.7 million people have had their ancestry tested, while the number in the US stands at around 26 million as of 2019.[12] Together these numbers underscore Hall's contention that, in the development of new ethnicities, "there can, therefore be no 'simple return' or 'recovery' of the ancestral past which is not reexperienced through the categories of the present," and which "are not transformed by the technologies and identities of the present."[13] As such, this chapter sets out to uncover how the technologies, political contexts, and identities of the present are leading to new ethnicities. Though interested in the ways in which Hall's prediction has been borne out, this chapter is chiefly concerned with the mechanisms and contexts that have elicited new discussions around race, ethnicity, and the meaning of identity.

Essentialism in Science and Society

Black culture is stunningly complex and diverse, marked by myriad social formulations, intellectual orientations, and artistic expressions. Despite this, both black history and culture are often reduced to a static experience. This tendency is most clearly on display within the racial science of the eighteenth and nineteenth centuries, during which black people were defined by purportedly essential and unifying characteristics such as thick skin, an immunity to pain, or skulls that were smaller than their white counterparts. Such ideas not only served to justify slavery by advancing a fictitious argument that black people were better suited to such conditions, but the belief in innate racial differences would also go on to buttress 100 years of Jim Crow segregation. And this essentialist thinking endures. A 2016 study of white medical residents found that a proportion believed that black patients experienced pain less intensely than whites.[14] So too have black people battled the unfortunate tendency of having individual observations of character, often negative, extrapolated onto the entire racial group. And yet, racial science and racist stereotype represent a significant though incomplete picture of the overall essentializing of black identities. We must also account for the ways in which black communities have participated in the gatekeeping of black identity through the development of cultural standards meant to differentiate authentic versus inauthentic blackness.

Scholars like Michael Eric Dyson have traced the development of essentializing black political projects to the mid-nineteenth century as manumitted and fugitive slaves acquiring literacy and public voice used the umbrella of racial unity as a means of consolidating cultural resources in order to offset the divisive effects of slavery.[15] Once emancipated, black leaders relied on a politics of respectability that would proscribe certain forms of behavior as a strategy to guard against racist assumptions about black intelligence, beauty, and worth. In effect, black political essentialism has promoted the idea of a unifying history of slavery and dispossession that obscures the multiethnic histories of the enslaved and their descendants. As Dyson astutely observes, "the quest for racial unity has represented largely the desperate attempt to replace a cultural uprooting that should have never occurred with a racial unanimity that never existed."[16] Though imagined and symbolic, the unitary idea of the black community is politically important, having served as the lynchpin of modern black freedom struggles.

Stuart Hall wrote "New Ethnicities" while trying to grapple with the British iteration of this racial unity narrative and its implications for the meaning of black identity. While the term "black" has, in the US context, traditionally referred to people of African or Caribbean descent, in the British context it has a more complicated history. In the UK, the concept of "political blackness" has functioned as an umbrella term referring to any groups facing discrimination on account of skin color. In essence, the concept of political blackness allowed black Caribbean, African, and South Asian communities an organizing identity through which to promote greater racial equality in Britain. According to Hall, the development of political blackness signals that "Black is not a question of pigmentation ... [It] is a historical category, a political category, a cultural category."[17] In her study of the history of blackness in Britain, sociologist Claire Alexander posits that this history is best characterized by two distinct phases. The first spans the 1960s to the mid-1980s and is characterized by the development of political blackness, as migrants from former British colonies including Africa, the Caribbean, and South Asia formed political coalitions through their shared experiences of racial discrimination. The second phase, stretching from the mid-1980s to the 2000s, witnessed the dissolution of this invented unity, as culture and ethnicity emerged as central aspects of state-sponsored multiculturalism, and political cohesion became harder to sustain amid rising religious and socioeconomic tensions between Asian and Afro-Caribbean constituencies.[18]

Hall published "New Ethnicities" during what he described as the "conjuncture" between these two phases.

By the 1980s, Hall was devoting more of his time to understanding the contours of identity, particularly as it related to race and ethnicity, an interest borne out in his desire to grapple with those parts of identity that are felt and experienced, and those that are structural and political.[19] This core tension between the personal and political is precisely why ancestry DNA testing has represented such an important and controversial development in contemporary debates over identity. Racial and ethnic identity are at once externally ascribed and internally adopted. Therefore, identity always straddles the line between the personal and political. Ancestry DNA testing, vested as it is in the notion of objectivity and infallibility, functions as a powerful new tool in the adjudication of identity, especially when there is disagreement between inward identity and outside ascription.

For his part, Hall uses "New Ethnicities" to think through the theoretical aspects of this tension, particularly its impact on black political formation. Utilizing black film, a genre that has historically resisted the negative stereotyping of black people through the elevation of countervailing positive representations, Hall argues that black British cinema's emphasis on a unitary black identity mirrors what is taking place within the broader community. In calling for an end to "the innocent notion of an essential black subject," Hall pushes for a new representational politics that recognizes "the extraordinary diversity of subjective positions, social experiences, and cultural identities which compose the category 'black.'"[20] Once we move away from an essentialized notion of blackness and naturalized notions of difference, Hall argues, our cultural commitment to the concept of race is weakened. Thus, the new ethnicities that Hall proposed "acknowledge the place of history, language, and culture in the construction of subjectivity and identity, as well as the fact that all discourse is placed, positioned, situated, and all knowledge is contextual."[21] In other words, unitary racial and ethnic identities, as well as the unitary political projects they supposedly made possible, were untenable fictions. This is not to say that Hall did not understand the impetus for such movements. He described these unitary projects as necessary fictions, evoking what Gayatri Chakravorty Spivak calls "strategic essentialism," the use of essentialized identities for the promotion of emancipatory politics.[22] Going beyond Spivak, however, Hall argues that true emancipatory politics are only fully realized through an identity politics that does not subsume other identities—notably gender, sexuality, disability, and class—but recognizes that "the central issues of race always appear historically in articulation, in a formation, with other categories and divisions and are constantly crossed and recrossed."[23]

The debate over representation politics was not limited to Britain. In fact, African Americans also spent much of 1989 grappling with the implications of new ethnic identities. During a 1988 press conference to announce a new political agenda for black Americans, Jesse Jackson, heading a coalition of seventy-five activist groups, announced that black people now preferred to be called "African Americans."[24] Jackson and other black American leaders would work throughout 1989 to encourage the uptake of this new ethnonym—first amongst black Americans generally ambivalent to the term, and later amongst major press bodies and the wider public.[25] While 1988 would not have been the first time that the public heard the term "African American"—the earliest mention of the term dates to 1782, and the closely related term "Afro-American" gained popularity in the 1960s—this press conference marked a significant turning point in black American identity politics as the debate surrounding the use of "African American" sparked important new conversations about the meaning and function of ethnicity.[26]

Where the use of "Black" in the 1970s helped to develop racial pride, the 1988 move to "African American" was meant to deliver a similar cultural pride by granting black Americans an ethnic identity. According to Jackson, "to be called African Americans has cultural integrity. It puts us in our proper historical context. Every ethnic group in this country has a reference to some land base, some historical cultural base. African Americans have hit that level of cultural maturity."[27] As Jackson's comments suggest, this new nomenclature was political as well as cultural.

By adopting this new hyphenated identity specifically rooted in Africa, black Americans were now able to reclaim political and cultural connections lost through the displacement of the slave trade. Ben Martin has argued that the move to "African American" was a natural response to black Americans' growing recognition that the US state used ethnicity as a means of distributing rights and benefits.[28] Though Martin was specifically referring to affirmative action, it is worth noting that "African American" is introduced just as the debate on reparations gained new energy. In 1989, Congressman John Conyers of Michigan introduced HR 40, a bill to create a commission to study reparations. Though the measure was unsuccessful at the time, Conyers reintroduced the bill every year during his almost two-decade tenure.[29] Thus, not only did "African American" function as an ethnic marker evoking a particular history of displacement and loss linking black American identity to the African continent and the sins of slavery, it provided black Americans with a unifying identity through which to justify redress for this particular history.

Though Jackson hoped that this new ethnicity would root black Americans, like other hyphenated Americans, to a cultural and territorial home, the term itself embodies the difficulty of that project. The term "African American" does not link black Americans to a specific African state, but to a continent with 54 states, 3,000 ethnic groups, and 2,100 languages. Furthermore, such a link would be almost impossible for a significant proportion of black Americans who lack the documentary evidence of their specific ethnic origins. Black Americans were not the only ones pursuing new ethnic identities: this trend also extended to the white majority. Polish, Italian, Irish, and Scandinavian ethnicity took on new importance in this period as did the importance of multiracial identity politics writ large. By 1990, more than 2 million children were reported as belonging to a race different from either one or both parents, and this trend further increased with the introduction of "check all that apply" options.[30] Scholars have offered several theories on what has driven this rise in new ethnicities: some have argued that it is the result of a globalized capitalist society that privileges choice over real experience, while others have voiced concern about the ways in which these new ethnic identities, especially as exercised amongst members of the white majority, are attempts to distance themselves from the guilt and responsibility of white privilege.[31] But with ethnic and racial identity appearing ever more porous and socially constructed, what is the role of evidence? And who gets to make these determinations?

New Ethnicities Now

Direct-to-consumer (DTC) genetic ancestry testing has promised to lend reliability and scientific certainty to our modern questions of identity. Emerging at the turn of the twenty-first century, DTC genetic ancestry testing has powerfully reshaped how Americans engage genealogy, one of the most popular American pastimes. As well as generating websites, television shows, and a booming tourist industry, genetic ancestry testing has precipitated a new "roots phenomenon" in which people around the globe attempt to understand the genetic basis of their individual family histories.[32]

People are always searching for identity, and direct-to-consumer DNA testing companies have successfully capitalized on this desire to sell their products. Though ancestry DNA testing did not become commercially available until

2012, it now represents a ubiquitous part of our culture. When the United States soccer team failed to qualify for the World Cup in 2018, 23andMe partnered with Fox Sports to roll out a marketing campaign in which they offered to help users determine which qualifying team they could root for based on their genetic profiles.[33] More recently, Ancestry DNA partnered with Spotify to provide a genetics-based playlist under the headline, "if you could listen to your DNA, what would it sound like?"[34] While these examples may seem absurd, they are hardly innocuous, as each takes advantage of the popular belief that there is something both measurable and immutable in our genetic material. These examples also elucidate how such companies actively sell a past meant to inform the present. This was exactly the case when, in September 2018, a previously white-identifying man petitioned to become a minority business owner after a 2010 test showed he had 4 percent African ancestry.[35]

Commercial ancestry-DNA testing is an outgrowth of anthropological genetics, which is interested in tracking and preserving ancient genetic markers. There are two types of common tests: lineage-based tests focusing on mitochondrial (mt-DNA) and Y-chromosome DNA, and autosomal tests using Ancestry Informative Markers, or AIMs, to determine biogeographical ancestry. Sometimes likened to "paternity testing writ large," both tests are focused on finding historical ancestry rather than immediate relatives though, as this alternative name suggests, genetic ancestry testing invariably raises questions about familial linkages and belonging. For some, ancestry testing is a salve for missing or broken familial connections. For others, testing is the first step in establishing a familial relationship, especially as many commercial companies provide databases allowing their customers to find close genetic matches, given that the participating parties have granted permission.[36] This diversity of user motivations highlights some of the stakes involved in ancestry testing, as consumers grapple with how familial and genetic ways of knowing inform their identity.

Both mt-DNA and y-DNA tests focus on genetic material that passes through the ancestral line virtually unchanged. Therefore, it is very useful in reconstructing maternal and paternal lines in ways that are also regionally specific. The major disadvantage of these tests is that they focus on a single maternal or paternal line, thereby neglecting a vast majority of those ancestors contributing to an individual's overall genetic profile. In contrast, autosomal testing is better designed to distinguish amongst genetic frequencies at the population level, whether through national or continental frequencies. Yet the reliability of autosomal testing is significantly impacted by the geographic dispersion of autosomal markers and the size of the genetic reference population used, both of which can significantly impact results. Though ancestry DNA testing was designed to present population-level information, this has not prevented companies and consumers from thinking about test results in ways that are very individualized, promoting what scholars have called personalized genetic histories.[37]

While it is difficult to speak of commercial DNA testing without mentioning the large corporations like 23andMe and Ancestry, both of which specialize in autosomal testing, there are a surprising array of boutique firms focusing on specific populations. For example, DNA Fingerprint sponsored a 2010 y-DNA project focusing on the Melungeons, a geographically diffuse population whose ancestors were believed to have comprised free black people, white colonial settlers, and Native Americans. DNA Fingerprint now claims to have the largest repository of Melungeon DNA. For $99, customers can have their own DNA tested against this reference population and if results indicate a significant probability of Melungeon heritage, they also have the option to pay an extra $25 for a certificate attesting to this fact.[38]

Many of the targeted ancestry DNA projects are not exclusively commercial. They also often support academic research seeking to understand human migratory history. For example, researchers framed the Melungeon project as an academic study of the Melungeons' racial history, though participants were well aware of the project's commercial ties. In other instances, however, these links are more concealed. The Genographic Project, sponsored by the National Geographic Society, IBM, and the Waitt Family Foundation, is a research project that began in 2005 and seeks to use comparative genetic analysis to reconstruct human history.[39] Much of the collected data, drawn from so-called isolated and indigenous populations, has been used to provide reference populations (the base-line data used to approximate ancestral matches) for commercial enterprises like the Houston-based Family Tree DNA. In addition to commercial enterprises using genetic data gathered under academic auspices, a longstanding concern of indigenous communities, the recent past has seen law enforcement agencies subpoena companies to obtain the DNA of potential suspects.[40] A 2018 study of white Americans and their involvement in ancestry testing estimates that, based on contemporary uptake, within fifteen years 90 percent of white Americans will be identifiable through the DNA contained in commercial repositories.[41] The porousness between commercial and scholarly enterprises, and the implications of this slippage for donor privacy, is just one reason that ancestry DNA testing has proven so controversial.

More recent scholarship has done an excellent job of unpacking other concerns surrounding ancestry DNA testing. In addition to limited reference populations for non-Europeans—a significant issue in terms of gauging the accuracy of a particular test—critics also point out that these reference populations are based on present-day geopolitical formations and not those that would have existed historically.[42] All of these issues are muted or completely absent, however, in the advertising materials released by ancestry DNA companies. Instead, they tout their reliability and capacity to connect customers to their past. So, too, have critics raised concerns about the ways in which ancestry DNA testing reifies biological notions of race. This last line of argument represents perhaps the most robust critique of ancestry DNA testing. Scholars, such as Troy Duster, Jenny Reardon, and others, have argued that despite the industry's reliance on ideas of interconnectedness and diversity, ancestry DNA companies reinforce notions of natural difference through their marketing, data collection, and analysis of genetic material. As such, DNA testing is best understood as a form of "racecraft," in which race is made and remade in the modern world.[43] However, as Alondra Nelson so powerfully argues in her benchmark work, *The Social Life of DNA*, an exclusive focus on the limits of ancestry DNA testing obscures the equally important task of understanding how consumers use ancestry DNA testing, specifically in terms of the social and political projects that testing makes possible.[44] Thus, a turn to the ways in which ancestry DNA testing has facilitated new ethnic identities elucidates how both self- and collective identities have shifted in light of so-called genetic answers.

In terms of those populations most impacted by the turn to DNA, studies of black Americans have received little attention. Scholars have devoted much more lip service and column space to investigating DNA's impact on the construction of white ethnic identities. This is perhaps unsurprising given the fact that the industry's customer base is predominantly white-European. However, black Americans represent an important customer base for ancestry testing because of their unique history vis-à-vis the slave trade. Most black Americans descended from slavery would find it difficult to trace their ancestors back more than six generations before hitting what genealogists call "the brick wall" of slavery, a euphemism pointing to the fact that enslaved Africans receive only scant attention in the documentary record.[45] In fact, the federal government did not fully enumerate black Americans until the 1850 census, a full 230 years after the first Africans arrived on the shores of Virginia.[46]

Thus, those black Americans turning to ancestry DNA testing are in search of a past that was not only taken from them but is unrecoverable by conventional means. Gina Paige, cofounder of African Ancestry, the first black-owned ancestry DNA company, summarizes this point vividly by referring to black Americans as "the original victims of identity theft."[47] To this end, ancestry DNA testing is part of a larger reconciliatory project that promises to right a historical injustice. African Ancestry was founded by Paige and geneticist Rick Kittles in 2003 and utilizes mt-DNA and y-DNA testing to make geographic ancestral determinations. Kittles, then co-director of the molecular genetics unit at Howard University, began pursuing commercial ancestry DNA testing after working on the African Burial Ground Project, a federally funded initiative to study the remains of enslaved Africans found in New York City. Kittles worked to match the genetic material collected from the remains to reference populations in Africa.[48] It was during this time that Kittles became interested in what this technology might do for black Americans writ large.[49]

Describing its mission as "helping people connect with their ancestry prior to the Atlantic slave trade," African Ancestry exemplifies the ways in which ancestry testing capitalizes on the feelings of fragmentation and discontinuity felt by its customers. Moreover, by touting its access to one of "the world's largest databases of African DNA," the company promises customers a reliable result. And with a retail price of $299, one can imagine that customers are expecting a certain level of scientific certainty. Test results not only list the percentages of DNA from each African state, but users also get a list of associated ethnic tribes, and a certificate of ancestry. However, the most striking aspect of African Ancestry's marketing campaign is the way in which it positions ancestry DNA testing as a key to unlocking a hidden aspect of identity, providing information that, once known, legitimizes the cultural performance of these identities.[50]

African Ancestry began offering testing in 2003: the company pioneered new territory in the genetic ancestry industry with the launch of its African Ancestry Family Reunion Program in 2019. Marketed as an immersive experience allowing customers to return to their homeland, the company offers all-inclusive travel packages to the country matching customers' DNA profile. Current itineraries include Sierra Leone, Senegal, Nigeria, Ghana, Cameroon, and Burkina Faso.[51] Paige describes these trips as "a birthright journey for people to learn the country, learn the history, the cultures, the traditions from the people who lived there that they have distant ancestry connections to."[52] As such, African Ancestry privileges ethnicity rather than the generic link to Africa the motherland.

African Ancestry's family reunion program is not the first attempt to make genetic ancestry testing a tool of tourism. In 2007, the Ghanaian government proposed the use of a gene map as part of a tourism campaign called the Joseph

Project, established to commemorate the fiftieth anniversary of the nation's independence. Though the gene map never materialized, the plan was to collect DNA samples from across Central and West Africa in order "to establish for every returnee/pilgrim interested, a personal report on his/her antecedents: to be able to organize visits to the villages of the ancestors."[53] Thus the groundwork was already established when Diallo Sumbry, partnership director for African Ancestry and Ghana's first African American tourism director, helped to facilitate African Ancestry's inaugural reunion trip. The trip was planned to coincide with Ghana's Year of Return, a program of events commemorating the 400th anniversary of the arrival of enslaved Africans in Virginia. In a press conference announcing the initiative, which formally launched in September 2018, Ghanaian President Nana Akufo-Addo described the Year of Return as a "landmark spiritual and birth-right journey."[54] Though links between the US and Ghana were a central aspect of the Year of Return program, the initiative was also geared toward what Akufo-Addo described as the "global African diaspora."[55] As such, the number of African descended people from the UK, South Africa, and Liberia also increased in this period.[56] Yet, Ghana's project was not just about reconstituting a diasporic connection. The development of political and economic connections, especially with black Americans, was also central to the Year of Return program: Ghana raised $1.9 billion in revenue.

Ghana's Year of Return marks the latest iteration of diasporic reunification. Finding some of its earliest articulations in the work of W. E. B. DuBois and the Pan-African Congress, historical reunification projects were undergirded by a commitment to decolonization, advancing economic opportunity for native Africans, and creating political cohesion between African descended people and their diasporic kin. While these interests persist in some circles, modern reunification projects such as those facilitated by African Ancestry set themselves apart by seeking to lend these political projects greater legitimacy by capitalizing on the imprimatur of science. Such was the case when African Ancestry organized an "ancestry reveal" for 126 black Americans, and the company disclosed their genetic ancestry results for the first time. These results were then officially certified when Akufo-Addo extended Ghanaian citizenship to the newly identified Ghanaians.[57] As this example makes clear, genetic ancestry represents an important new avenue in the formation of transnational black identities. Considering that African diasporic peoples often experience feelings of "statelessness," or might otherwise be positioned outside of the national body politic in which they reside, the ability to establish new national identities can function as a subversive act. On the other hand, the new national identities made possible through ancestry DNA testing, tethered as they are to colonial understandings of identity as that which is rooted in biology, serve to reify the very bounds of nationality ancestry DNA testing seeks to upset.

Roots tourism in Ghana has a long history dating back informally to the presidency of Kwame Nkrumah who encouraged diasporic Africans to return and help build the new nation. As "the first African colony south of the Sahara to gain its independence," Ghana is often imagined, popularly and commercially, as "the gateway to the homeland."[58] In this way, Ghana represents a stand-in for Africa as a whole. The more formal origins of roots tourism took shape during the 1990s, as President Jerry Rawlings developed a bustling heritage tourism industry centered on the transatlantic slave trade and Pan-African identity. Ghana's many castles and coastal forts, central historical monuments of the Trans-Atlantic slave trade, were integral aspects of this tourism market. Those taking part in heritage trips have described them as a cathartic and healing step in making peace with the historical legacies of slavery.[59] Though heritage trips may represent opportunities for national reclamation for black Americans and other diasporic peoples, they also signal the ways in which imagined ideas of Africa are commodified for (American) diasporic consumption. Heritage tourism also places the matter of the unitary black subject into sharp relief. While some native Africans welcome the cultural and economic investment from their diasporic kin, others are critical of this project and refute the notion that these people could ever become true Africans.[60]

As the contemporary debate surrounding the ADOS community makes clear, the African diaspora continues to work through the links between blackness, identity, and belonging. An acronym for American Descendants of Slavery, ADOS is primarily an online community advocating for economic reparations. However, members of the ADOS community argue that reparations should be limited to those Americans able to trace their ancestry to enslaved Africans brought to the United States, as opposed to black America as a whole. Having first spread as a hashtag in 2016, ADOS gained significant attention during the 2020 presidential election cycle as ADOS community leaders like Yvette Carnell and Antonio Moore criticized presidential candidates they accused of ignoring the interests of American descendants of slaves. The ADOS movement has garnered criticism from the liberal left in particular, which accuses the movement of dividing black Americans, of promoting anti-immigrant ideas, and of circulating misinformation surrounding the 2020 election.[61] While more research is needed before we can gain a fuller picture of ADOS's ideological stance, it is abundantly clear that by calling attention to the heterogeneity of black American life, the ADOS movement underscores the fiction of black experience as a unitary phenomenon.

One of ADOS's principal aims is to highlight the disparities that exist between black people who immigrated voluntarily, and those whose ancestors were subjected to forced migration. According to a 2007 study published in the *American Journal of Education*, despite representing only 13 percent of the black population in America, black immigrants and their children comprised 41 percent of black first-year students at Ivy League institutions. Similarly, a 2015 report from the Pew Research Centre found that black immigrants have a median income that is $10,000 higher than their US-born counterparts.[62] Although none of these studies suggest that black immigrant populations have it easy, or that all are doing well, this data underscores the precarious socioeconomic conditions of black Americans; especially as the wealth gap between white and black Americans, a longstanding indicator of racial progress, continues to widen.

The ADOS movement likewise addresses an important hurdle facing the reparations movement—the question of how to determine which black Americans are eligible for economic redress. When lawyer/activist Deadria Farmer-Paellman led a class-action lawsuit against Aetna, CSX, and Fleet Brothers—three companies with historical ties to the slave trade—her initial suit was dismissed after the judge ruled that it was impossible to conclusively identify the descendants of those enslaved people exploited by the three companies. Using testing services from African Ancestry, Farmer-Paellman refiled her case, this time presenting the court with what she viewed as definitive proof establishing her clients' claims to redress.[63] Though her case was not successful, the suit illustrates the political projects that ancestry DNA testing makes possible for black American descendants of slavery.

Yet economic redress is only the first part of the ADOS agenda. According to the website of the ADOS Advocacy Foundation, reparations as envisioned by ADOS also require that the federal government recognize ADOS as an ethnic category, thereby acknowledging the particular history and identity of ADOS people as having persisted through phases of American racism. Not only are ADOS supporters seeking census enumeration that is separate and distinct from black immigrants, they also want future governmental studies to disaggregate the ADOS population so that the government can develop specifically targeted programs that will address its needs.[64]

The 2020 census represented the first opportunity for black respondents to list their specific country of origin: the ADOS movement, it seems, has made an important first step in realizing its goals. Yet ADOS activist Tariq Nasheed encapsulates the feelings of a large contingent of ADOS supporters when he states, "every other group when they get here goes out of their way to say, 'I'm Jamaican.' 'I'm Nigerian.' 'I'm from Somalia.' But when we decide to say, 'OK. We are a distinct ethnic group,' people look at that as negative."[65] Although the ADOS movement uses ethnicity to advance a political project that is, in certain ways, in keeping with the spirit of Hall's "New Ethnicities," the movement is also guilty of swapping one set of essentialisms for another. We might also rightly wonder if the ADOS label reinforces US colonial nationalism through its insistence on a distinctly American identity. Either way, like the heritage tours marketed through African Ancestry, the ADOS movement raises important questions about the degree to which identity should be defined by African heritage, or by other experiential markers like slavery or racial discrimination.

Conclusion

In June 2020, the Associated Press—a standard bearer of style and usage guidelines—announced that it would update its stylebook to capitalize "black." Inspired by the racial uprising that began in the aftermath of George Floyd's murder, the Associated Press explained its move as a step toward recognizing the cultural identity of black Americans. Other media and corporate bodies would follow this effort to rhetorically affirm their commitment to black politics by affording black communities the respect of a capital B.

In the long history of debates on blackness and terminology it would seem that "Black is back," though one would be hard pressed to make the case that it ever left. Even as Jessie Jackson implored members of the media to take up the term "African American," many remained wedded to "black"—sometimes written as "Black"—celebrating the term as a positive holdover from the consciousness-raising period which established that "Black Is Beautiful" and "Black Power" is emancipatory. Geneva Smitherman has described this 1970s moment as a "semantic inversion," when that which was considered "bad was turned on its head and made good, as the celebration of 'Black'—Black culture, Black skin color, the Black experience—became a rallying cry for unity, empowerment, and self-definition."[66]

There are echoes of this same sentiment in our more recent embrace of Black with a capital B, yet what stands out in this latest chapter of the racial name game is the extent to which "Black" is used to assuage some of the tensions surrounding geography and nation highlighted in the African Ancestry and ADOS Project.

For supporters like Lori Tharps, a leading voice in the capitalization movement, Black underscores a shared cultural identity that is unbound to a unified geographic identity; thus, it is accommodating to a range of diasporic identities.[67]

And so here we return to a politics of blackness, though it is not the same blackness as outlined by Hall in 1989. Thanks to feminist activism, LGBTQI advocacy, class uprisings, and black people's own willingness to confront the limitations of the "essential black subject," black identity politics is more fraught but also more nuanced than ever before. As the example of ancestry DNA testing makes clear, for some, blackness is real and sometimes even genetic. For others, it is rooted in a particular relationship to injustice, while still other groups root blackness in a specific geographical context. In all these examples, however, blackness is never stable. It is always shifting, and always operating subjectively, informed by individual choice as well as the power systems in which we all operate. Thus, only in recognizing the changing contours of blackness can we come to fully adopt new ethnicities and the political projects that they make possible.

Notes

1 Emphasis Lyn's Jonathan Black, "Newport News Woman Lands National Commercial," *Newport News Daily Press*, April 27, 2017. https://www.dailypress.com/life/dp-fea-newport-news-woman-ancestry-0430-20170429-story.html (accessed October 15, 2021).

2 Ancestry, "Lyn Discovers Her Ethnicity" [TV commercial] https://www.ispot.tv/ad/wK8r/ancestrydna-lyn-discovers-her-ethnicity-discoveries (accessed October 15, 2021).

3 Ancestry, "Kyle Traded in His Lederhosen for a Kilt," December 9, 2015 [TV commercial] https://www.youtube.com/watch?v=Yfz2KJQvH-0 (accessed October 15, 2021).

4 "Root for Your Roots with 23andMe," April 6, 2018 [TV commercial] https://www.ispot.tv/ad/wv29/23andme-fox-root-for-your-roots.

5 Credence Research, "Direct-to-Consumer (DTC) Genetic Testing Market Future Prospects and Competitive Analysis, 2018–2026," *Credence Research*, no. 57820-02-18, 2018.

6 For some recent examples of scholarship, see Sarah Abel and Hannes Schroeder, "From Country Marks to DNA Markers: The Genomic Turn in the Reconstruction of African Identities," *Current Anthropology* 61, no. 22 (October 2020): S198–S209; Alondra Nelson and J. W. Hwang, "Roots and Revelation: Genetic Ancestry Testing

and the Youtube Generation," in *Race after the Internet*, ed. L. Nakamura and P. Chow-White (New York: Routledge, 2013), 277–96.
7   Stuart Hall, "New Ethnicities," in *Critical Ideologies in Cultural Studies*, ed. David Morley and Chen Kuan-Hsing (New York: Routledge, 1996), 444.
8   Maya Jaggi, "Prophet at the Margins," *The Guardian*, July 8, 2000. Available online: https://www.theguardian.com/books/2000/jul/08/society (accessed October 15, 2021).
9   Ibid.
10 Hall, "New Ethnicities," 444.
11 John Brennan, "Race Relations in the 80s: A Polling Review," *The Public Perspective* (January/February 1990): 1–2.
12 Antonio Regalado, "More than 26 Million People Have Taken an at-Home Ancestry Test," *MIT Technology Review*, February 11, 2019. Available online: https://www.technologyreview.com/2019/02/11/103446/more-than-26-million-people-have-taken-an-at-home-ancestry-test/ (accessed October 15, 2021); "Instafam': Ancestry Reveals Boom in DNA Testing as Brits Hunt for Real Connections," *PR Newswire*, April 25, 2019. Available online: https://www.prnewswire.co.uk/news-releases/-instafam-ancestry-reveals-boom-in-dna-testing-as-brits-hunt-for-real-connections-842510678.html (accessed October 15, 2021).
13 Hall, "New Ethnicities," 449.
14 Kelly M. Hoffman, Sophie Trawalter, Jordan R. Axt, and M. Norman Oliver, "Racial Bias in Pain Assessment and Treatment Recommendations, and False Beliefs about Biological Differences between Blacks and Whites," *Proceedings of the National Academy of Sciences* 113 (April 2016): 4296–301.
15 Michael Eric Dyson, "Essentialism and the Complexities of Racial Identity," in *Multiculturalism: A Critical Reader*, ed. David Theo Goldberg (Oxford: Blackwell Publishers, 1994), 218.
16 Ibid., 220.
17 Stuart Hall, "Old and New Identities, Old and New Ethnicities," in *Theories of Race and Racism*, ed. John Solomon and Les Black (London: Routledge, 2000), 149.
18 Claire Alexander, "Breaking Black: The Death of Ethnic and Racial Studies in Britain," *Ethnic and Racial Studies* 41, no. 6 (2017): 1038.
19 Phil Cohen, "Both Sides of the Line: Stuart Hall and 'New Ethnicities' Then and Now," *New Formations* 96 (2019): 147–59.
20 Hall, "New Ethnicities," 444.
21 Ibid., 447.
22 Gayatri C. Spivak, "Subaltern Studies: Deconstructing Historiography," in *In Other Worlds: Essays in Cultural Politics*, ed. G. C. Spivak (New York: Methuen, 1987), 197–221.
23 Hall, "New Ethnicities," 444.

24 "Leaders Say Blacks Want to Be Called 'African-Americans,'" *Associated Press*, December 21, 1988.
25 Ben L. Martin, "From Negro to Black to African American: The Power of Names and Naming," *Political Science Quarterly* 106, no. 1 (1991): 83–5.
26 Fred Shapiro, "The Origin of the Term 'African American,'" *Yale Alumni Magazine*, January/February 2016. Available online: https://yalealumnimagazine.com/articles/4216-the-origin-of-african-american (accessed February 13, 2022).
27 "Leaders Say Blacks Want to be Called 'African Americans,'" *Associated Press*, December 20, 1988.Available online:https://apnews.com/article/089fc3ab25b86e14deeefae3adb7a5ad (accessed February 13, 2022).
28 Martin, "From Negro to Black to African American," 86.
29 John Conyers, "The Commission to Study Reparation Proposals," in *When Sorry Isn't Enough*, ed. Roy Brooks (New York: New York University Press, 1999), 367–70.
30 ESRI, "Trends in the US Multiracial Population from 1990–2000," *ESRI White Paper* (November 2005), 2. Available online: https://www.esri.com/content/dam/esrisites/sitecore-archive/Files/Pdfs/library/whitepapers/pdfs/trends-in-multiracial-population.pdf (accessed October 15, 2021).
31 Matthew Jacobson, *Roots Too: White Ethnic Revival in Post-Civil Rights America* (Cambridge, MA: Harvard University Press, 2006), 21.
32 Alondra Nelson, *The Social Life of DNA: Race, Reparations, and Reconciliation after the Genome* (Boston: Beacon Press, 2016), 4–5.
33 Chris Matyszczyk, "23andMe Wants You to Find a New World Cup Team in Your Blood," *CNET*, April 5, 2018.
34 "If You Could Listen to Your DNA, What Would It Sound Like?" https://www.ancestry.com/cs/spotify.
35 Though the application was successful at the state level, it failed at the federal level due to Taylor's inability to prove that his minority status or his race had caused him social or economic hardship. See Antonia Foori Nazan, "A DNA Test Said a Man Was 4% Black, Now He Wants to Qualify as a Minority Business Owner," *The Washington Post*, September 25, 2018; Selena Hill, "White Entrepreneur Insists He's a Minority Business Owner Based on DNA Results," *Black Enterprise*, September 23, 2013.
36 Dena S. Davis, "The Changing Face of 'Misidentified Paternity,'" *Journal of Medicine and Philosophy* 32 (2007): 368.
37 Mark D. Shriver and R. Kittles, "Genetic Ancestry and the Search for Personalized Genetic Histories," *Nature Reviews Genetics* 5 (2004): 611–18.
38 "Melungeon DNA and Databases," *DNA Consultants*, https://dnaconsultants.com/melungeon-dna-database-and-studies/
39 Marianne Sommer, "DNA and Cultures of Remembrance: Anthropological Genetics, Biohistories and Biosocialities," *BioSocieties* 5 (2010): 368.

40 See Jenny Reardon and Kim Tallbear, "'Your DNA Is Our History': Genomics, Anthropology, and the Construction of Whiteness as Property," *Current Anthropology* 53, no. 5 (2010): 233–45; Reardon, "The Democratic, Anti-Racist Genome? Technoscience at the Limits of Liberalism," *Science as Culture* 21, no. 1 (2012): 25–47.

41 Yaniv Erlich et. al., "Identity Inference of Genomic Data Using Long-range Familial Searches," *Science* 362, no. 6415 (November 2018): 690–4. Available online: https://pubmed.ncbi.nlm.nih.gov/30309907/ (accessed October 15, 2021).

42 See Deborah Bolnick, "Individual Ancestry Inference and the Reification of Race," in *Revisiting Race in the Genomic Age*, ed. Barbara Koenig, Sandra Soo-Jin Lee, and Sarah S. Richardson (New Brunswick, NJ: Rutgers University Press, 2008), 70–87; Abram Gabriel, "A Biologist's Perspective on DNA and Race in the Genomics Era," in *Genetics and the Unsettled Past: The Collision of DNA, Race, and History*, ed. Keith Wailoo, Alondra Nelson, and Catherine Lee (New Brunswick, NJ: Rutgers University Press, 2012), 43–66.

43 See Troy Duster, *Backdoor to Eugenics* (New York: Routledge, 2003); Stephan Palmié, "Genomics, Divination, 'Racecraft,'" *American Ethnologist* 34, no. 2 (2007): 205–22; Jenny Reardon, "The Democratic, Anti-Racist Genome? Technoscience at the Limits of Liberalism," *Science as Culture* 21, no. 1 (2012): 25–47.

44 Nelson, *The Social Life of DNA*, 18.

45 Katherine Scott Sturdevant, "Walls Tumbling Down: Teaching Black Family History and Genealogy in Social History Context," *Black History Bulletin* 83 (2020): 30.

46 Although free black Americans were included in the 1790 census, they were lumped into the general category of "all other free persons of color," a designation that failed to distinguish blacks from Native Americans. The 1790 census also included enslaved Africans but only as a statistical population listed under the enslaver. See "African Americans and the Federal Census, 1790–1930," National Archives and Records Administration, July 2012. https://www.archives.gov/files/research/census/african-american/census-1790-1930.pdf (accessed October 15, 2021).

47 Mohammed Awal, "Tracing Our Family Roots Not a Novelty, It's a Necessity: African Ancestry President," *Face2Face Africa*, December 27, 2019. https://face2faceafrica.com/article/tracing-our-family-roots-not-a-novelty-its-a-necessity-africanancestry-president (accessed October 15, 2021).

48 Sam Fulwood Iii, "His DNA Promise Doesn't Deliver," *Los Angeles Times*, May 29, 2000. Available online: https://www.latimes.com/archives/la-xpm-2000-may-29-mn-35219-story.html (accessed October 15, 2021).

49 Ibid.

50   Outlined on their webpage titled "The Process," African Ancestry describes the fourth step of the testing process as "Exploring your Ancestry," stating "Now that you know where you're from, you can study the people and country, travel, adopt a new name, or incorporate new traditions into your family." https://shop.africanancestry.com/pages/the-process (accessed October 15, 2021).
51   "African Ancestry Family Reunions: Now That You Know, It's Time to Go Home!" https://travel.africanancestry.com/ (accessed October 15, 2021).
52   Awal, "Tracing Our Family Roots Not a Novelty."
53   "The Ghana Joseph Project," https://www.africa-ata.org/gh9.htm
54   Ibid.
55   Ibid.
56   "African Diaspora: Did Ghana's Year of Return Attract Foreign Visitors?" *BBC News*, January 30, 2020. Available online: https://www.bbc.com/news/world-africa-51191409 (accessed October 15, 2021).
57   Katharina Schramm, "Diasporic Citizenship under Debate: Law, Body, and Soul," *Current Anthropology* 61, no. 22 (October 2020): S210–S219.
58   https://www.africa-ata.org/gh9.htm
59   Bayo Holsey, "Transatlantic Dreaming: Slavery, Tourism, and Diasporic Encounters," in *Routes of Remembrance: Refashioning the Atlantic Slave Trade in Ghana*, ed. Fran Markowitz and Anders H. Stefanson (Chicago: Chicago University Press, 2004), 144–60.
60   Schramm, "Diasporic Citizenship," S213.
61   Because ADOS exists as an online community, it is difficult to determine if some of the more problematic examples of ADOS activism emerge from the community itself or from individuals wishing to appropriate the ADOS hashtag for more incendiary purposes. On the controversies surrounding ADOS, see Samara Lynn, "Controversial Group ADOS Divides Black Americans in Fight for Economic Equality," *ABC News*, January 19, 2020. Available online: https://abcnews.go.com/US/controversial-group-ados-divides-black-americans-fight-economic/story?id=66832680 (accessed October 15, 2021).
62   Douglas S. Massey, Margarita Mooney, Kimberly C. Torres, and Camille Z. Charles, "Black Immigrants and Black Natives Attending Selective Colleges and Universities in the United States," *American Journal of Education* 113, no. 2 (February 2007): 243–71; Monica Anderson, "A Rising Share of the US Black Population Is Foreign Born," *Pew Research Center*, April 9, 2015, https://www.pewresearch.org/social-trends/2015/04/09/chapter-1-statistical-portrait-of-the-u-s-black-immigrant-population/ (accessed October 15, 2021).
63   Nelson, *Social Life of DNA*, 121–6.
64   ADOS Advocacy Foundation, "The Roadmap: Reparations Agenda," https://adosfoundation.org/reparations (accessed October 15, 2021).

65 Farah Stockman, "'We're Self-Interested': The Growing Identity Debate in Black America," *New York Times*, November 13, 2019. Available online: https://www.nytimes.com/2019/11/08/us/slavery-black-immigrants-ados.html (accessed October 15, 2021).

66 Geneva Smitherman, *Talkin That Talk: Language, Culture, and Education in African America* (New York: Routledge, 1999), 47–9.

67 Lori L. Tharps, "Opinion: The Case for Black with a Capital B," *New York Times*, November 18, 2014. Available online: https://www.nytimes.com/2014/11/19/opinion/the-case-for-black-with-a-capital-b.html (accessed October 15, 2021).

5

Intersectionality as Heuristic: A Conversation

Phanuel Antwi and Amira Ismail

With her 1989 *University of Chicago Legal Forum* article "Demarginalizing the Intersection of Race and Sex: A Black Feminist Critique of Antidiscrimination Doctrine, Feminist Theory and Antiracist Politics," Kimberlé Crenshaw reconceptualized the multiple oppressions facing Black women with her widely influential coinage of "intersectionality."[1] Highlighting how "the tendency to treat race and gender as mutually exclusive categories of experience and analysis" marginalizes, distorts, and erases Black women's multidimensional experiences, Crenshaw's landmark essay indicated that those experiences comprised "more than the sum of racism and sexism."[2] In antidiscrimination doctrine—which Crenshaw analyzes through the lens of three Title VII cases involving Black women plaintiffs—discrimination against Black women went unaddressed because legal discourse and precedent focused singly on either sex-based or racial discrimination.[3] In *DeGraffenreid vs. General Motors*, for instance, the plaintiffs' assertion of gender discrimination on the part of their employer was denied by the courts because white women were not discriminated against in the same way. Hence, the court asserted, gender discrimination did not take place and, furthermore, Black women "should not be allowed to combine statutory remedies to create a new 'super-remedy' which would give them relief beyond what the drafters of the relevant statutes intended."[4] For Crenshaw, this uncritical acceptance of a status quo that does not see how forms of discrimination may intersect—and the effects and consequences of such compound discrimination—extended to feminist theory and antiracist politics: feminist theory for privileging the experiences of white women and ignoring those of Black women; antiracist politics for marginalizing Black women's concerns in favor of the broader struggle for racial justice. In the conversation below, artist, poet, and literary scholar Phanuel Antwi and International Relations scholar and community advocate Amira Ismail consider intersectionality and the legacy of Crenshaw's article, from the term's recent (and sometimes problematic) ubiquity to the power it retains for Black women today. In contemplating whether "Demarginalizing the Intersection" was transformative, or reflected the values of its moment, Antwi and Ismail draw attention to ambiguities that are characteristic of many texts of 1989.

Part One

Phanuel Antwi (PA): This is not going to be a conversation where I am the expert.[5] I am interested in thinking with you: I think it's rare to get to have a conversation with a fellow Black person in the academy, so I am going to enjoy this!

Amira Ismail (AI): Definitely! I went all through my undergraduate degree without having one Black professor, lecturer, or seminar lead. And this topic means so much to me because it was my introduction to feminism, so for me it's a big part of my identity.

PA: Fantastic. I love that already!

AI: The first question is about 1989 as a moment, as a transitional year, that's what this whole collection is about. Of course, this framework—intersectionality—comes from Kimberlé Crenshaw in 1989. When I think about it, the thing that was emphasized to me about 1989 as a history student was the Berlin Wall, the Cold War ending, Perestroika and Glasnost. But Kimberlé Crenshaw always stood out, especially in terms of my personal history with feminism: 1989 was also a transitional year because I think intersectionality created a certain tension in highlighting what liberal feminism was trying to do but failed to do. So first I want to look at 1989, when this term comes into existence. What are your thoughts on the year 1989? What's so special about that year?

PA: Let's talk about it as key date in the sense of the convergence it allows. You know Raymond Williams's idea of keywords, right?[6] We can think of 1989 in terms of key dates, how they become key moments where we are forced to think globally about the ways in which the interdependence of geopolitical relations becomes more clear to us.[7] Key dates are when we are forced to rethink notions of borders and nation-states, forced to contend with the choreographies between colonial empires and how they trickle into the micro-levels of our everyday lives. So, we have this kind of syncopation of our geopolitical life that we are also living in our daily lives. The micro and the macro begin to dance with one another. When we attend to such dates, we are in a transitional moment, as you are saying, an interregnum.

We are in the space where we know that something is about to come up, to burst. But it's also a moment that we can only see retrospectively. So, 1989 is an anachronistic date, in that we feel the fervor of that moment, but we begin retroactively to mark it as a significant year, returning, when we've had the privilege of time, to think about its consequences for us.

AI: Yes, when you're far removed from a point in history, it's easier to amplify the specificity and significance of the political thought it produced. And I think it's easy to romanticize such moments as well.

PA: I think we narrate different years into history in different ways. Of course, historians have taught us a lot about periodization and its significance, and I think that this book reveals both the value of periodization and the limits of a given periodization. Or maybe it reveals how we end up creating what we think is important about a year. One context we might keep in mind here for our conversation about Crenshaw's article is that in 1989 we are hardly done with civil rights movements—we are still in their wake. So many different things converge.

AI: But when you think about the year 1989, it wasn't necessarily transformational because of Crenshaw's theory. I don't know whether we agree on this, but it seems to me that intersectionality only came to the fore within popular discourse in the last decade or so, when it is used colloquially and applied heuristically. The term intersectionality wasn't part of a widespread, popular vernacular even in relation to feminism. It has only gained traction recently.

PA: One thing I want to do is differentiate between what Kimberlé Crenshaw wrote and what the term has become, which is now something of an industry in its own right. It has become almost a form of arithmetic—a mode of thinking through identity that I really struggle with. I have a beef with how this concept has been taken up. I sometimes say to students "we are not using 'intersectionality' any longer," because it has become an alibi to avoid thinking through histories. It becomes a substitute for thinking. And it also becomes a way for some not to be implicated in the struggle, because they occupy multiple identitarian positions. And then this framework—this epistemological framework—is instrumentalized as a method for acquiring power. Framed this way, the term loses the kind of possibilities that it introduced into practice, into history.

AI: Like a pie chart of identities.

PA: Very much so. And it becomes a discourse we get stuck in. I'm not interested in that. Let's of course have a conversation about the history of gender, about the history of race. About why, for example, Stuart Hall had difficulties with the ways that E. P. Thompson emphasized class in a manner that dismissed work done by racialized Black folks who wrote about class as produced through race. Intersectionality helps us think through such things, but it is sometimes taken up in a way that adds race and other structures of power in a kind of mathematical manner. I struggle with how folks have turned to this mode of aggregation to make sense of our identities.

AI: Yes, this is something that makes intersectionality difficult to talk about because the paradigm encourages thinking in terms of an aggregation of identities.

PA: When Crenshaw was thinking about this, she was thinking about Black women in the juridical structure. And yet its application has no structural grounding to it. It moves us away from thinking about the structural concerns that make lives disposable, make lives not able to be accounted for, and so there is this disjuncture between the impetus to develop this framework and how it's actually mobilized. It becomes autonomous—me and my intersections—as opposed to how we think about the structural implications of this concept, and how we think about it in terms of struggle. If we are willing to think about intersectionality in terms of struggle, we see its limits and then that takes us to conversations around solidarity and then we are forced to think about the limits of solidarity. We think about the betrayals that are part of solidarity, and so it moves us away from the autonomous subject.

AI: Do you think that the term intersectionality has given Black women specifically the subjectivity to self-identify? Don't you think there's power in that?

PA: Well, I'm talking to a Black woman—talk to me! [Laughs]

AI: [Laughing] Yeah, there's that very pivotal idea of being able to name your injustices, which gives you power and gives you the language with which you can actually address them. Crenshaw has said that she cared, like you mentioned, more about the structural issues that this theory uncovers. Because once you address that, you can think about identity and the way you self-identify a lot more. For me there was a dichotomy between the two because I'm of a generation where intersectionality is at the tip of our tongues and it explains everything away. So I wonder, especially with the last two years we've had, in a time where injustice is still completely rife and institutional: how much work has the theory done? For me it hasn't done a lot in terms of changing structural inequalities, but I think it's given young Black women like me a language to identify with. When I'm thinking about feminism, that's the language I go to. I did English literature at school, and I was looking at Maya Angelou and she's talking about a completely different existence than someone like Angela Carter, whose feminism doesn't fully make sense to me. It hints at parts of my identity, but someone like Angelou gets it completely. I'm also from a diaspora, so that's another conversation about what my identity is as a Black woman. That's where I come at intersectionality: a framework to talk about something that's gone wrong.

PA: Interesting! I'm also from a diaspora and I'm struck with that thinking about intersectionality and diaspora. I'm of Ghanaian descent, so I'll invoke the word *Sankofa*, or maybe some folks might prefer the Benjaminian "angel of history" who is looking back but also being pulled forward by the force of history. *Sankofa* is the bird who is constantly looking back and so I think about both Benjamin and this Akan concept together.

AI: That's poetic, and very ancestral as well. Which I think is where intersectionality lives for Black feminists—it's an ancestral term at this point.

PA: Your response about what it has made possible for young Black women is something I think is fantastic. It's given language; it's given visibility; it's given a sense of agency to be able to articulate one's self-fashioning.

AI: I was thinking about Patricia Hill Collins and the way she says that when we think about Black women and Black intellectual thought for women, first of all we need to identify what that is.[8] And that's what intersectionality is for me. It's that language and that's a starting point. For me it's about the framework itself: where it's gone, where it's traveled, and how it's conceived by other people.

PA: Fantastic. The term travels across space and also across time. And it feels like folks are committed to this term collapsing space and time. They want it to do the work that it did in '89 when Crenshaw invoked it, while we are in a completely different political moment right now. Even when it emerged, there was sort of a limit where the activist organizers of the period were already in tune with that politics. So it becomes a theory about systems—it becomes a theory about looking for legibility within systems. It was looking for entry into these oppressive structures.

AI: I think we both agree that, whilst we might accept the tenets of specific—especially great—Black scholars, we don't have to agree with everything. I think activists often think you need to die on the hill that you started on, and I think that allows for no growth to take place. I feel like that's why the term hasn't grown.

PA: Exactly. I was having this conversation with Denise [Ferreira da Silva] the other day, and this is something that she taught me about what intersectionality named and made.[9] Because sometimes we need to name the injustices in order for us to work on them. So, in 1989, intersectionality named a limited way of seeing certain marginalized folks. In the twenty-first century, is that what we need to be doing? This is, for me, where transporting intersectionality into this moment is not useful, because we've got other modes of thinking about this moment. If we want to transport it, if we want to render it portable across time, we have to think through what we need to do to it in order for it to attend to our needs of this moment.

Furthermore, many Black folks, particularly Black feminists, are not interested in being "included," to invoke [Sara] Ahmed's language.[10] Mere inclusion is not what we are seeking. We are seeking a dismantling of the very structures—including cognitive structures—that make meaning of us. And so, while intersectionality is making us legible within these spaces— and I'm not going to say that it hasn't enabled folks! And sometimes that's the entry point that we need to begin politics—I sometimes worry about its ability to move us into the world that we want without bringing with us the same limiting logics that informed that heuristic.

AI: As you were saying about language as an entry point: after that it loses, to a certain extent, its utility for the people that it was created for, but it's a trigger point for anyone outside of that marginalized group. So, especially for white, liberal feminists—if they want to include you in that space, that language is invoked instantly. But inclusion is often tokenistic. When I think about Black feminism, it's about dismantling structures, it's not about upholding them. It's not about even using the language that the spaces have created. It's about coming up with your own intellectual property and your own spaces.

PA: Crenshaw's term was responding to the infrastructures of the 1980s and before. What is the infrastructure of today that we are responding to? That we need to actually think through? And for folks for whom that term is helpful, how do you amend it to now, as opposed to thinking that the term in itself is enough?

AI: Taking it out of the space where it signifies representation and identity and bringing it back to its original use as a tool is a start.

PA: One of the things that it did for feminism is to insist that feminism has many preoccupations, not simply gender—And I don't like the phrase "not simply gender." Feminism's preoccupation with gender is everything!—but it was drawing attention to the fact that we can think about feminism as a juridical space as well. And I think that was a very, very useful intervention into political theory and also into the environment of 1989. It allowed us to contend with a different worldmaking that centered feminist concerns, and to make it absolutely clear that as an analytic, it was interested in multiple areas and that its concerns about gender were also concerns about capital, were also concerns about reproduction, were also concerns about the environment. So, in that sense, if that's what we are taking with us, then yes, I'm there with it. Where Crenshaw was reminding folks that feminism, at large, is concerned about these other supposedly "politically charged" issues, then yes, intersectionality is where I want to be working. The minute it becomes about the aggregation of the personal, and only about that, that's when, for me, it ceases to be useful.

AI: I think you would enjoy the work of Mikki Kendall, like *Hood Feminism*, and also Lola Olufemi's *Feminism Interrupted*, because they're both Black feminists, one from the UK and one from America, and that's the way they think about intersectionality.[11] It's a call to action to these multiple social injustices. It's unifying these different identities to give them more strength.

PA: One of the things that I've learned from feminists that I hold onto is that when we think of identities as personal—as "me, me, me"—we lose the power of thinking about identity epistemologically. Epistemology is the study of knowledge and knowledge is constantly limited. And if we are to remember that our identities are also knowledge-forming systems, then that position as an epistemological ground is also not complete. And so, with intersectionality, if we are willing to think about it in those modalities, it means then that there's a cocreation where one cannot wield it as an "arsenal" to shut down someone else, but rather everyone is mobilizing in a moment when one is opening to and actually working with others. But that's not how we understand it now—we often wield it as a weapon—and for me that makes it not a very liberating and decolonizing resource.

AI: I think once it's something that's constructed and not something that you use as a call for social protest, then I think you divide its applicability and you take away its power because you decided to use it in the structures already in place instead of creating a different space.

PA: Precisely that. Your statement is haunting me, though—it will modulate how I teach intersectionality now—about how it is such a good entry point particularly for young Black women who need language.

Part Two

PA: Maybe I'll use this occasion to think about the date, 1989, which is what has brought us here. One of the things we've acknowledged is how intersectionality comes out of a specific moment but there's a portability to it, in terms of time and geography. Also it has shifted from being an analysis of structure that was trying to understand Black women's particular experiences as they pertain to labor. One of the cases Crenshaw used was a lawsuit against General Motors. "Demarginalizing the Intersection" is from 1989, and yet the cases that she mobilizes are all cases that arose from Title VII in the United States, the Civil Rights legislation from 1964. So, I'm interested in your question about different settings. Intersectionality arcs back to a different moment, 1964, to think about this discrimination act, this Title VII Act, and we are now arcing forward at the same time.

I also want to think about my setting for doing this work, which is Canada. Here, I want to bring in two contexts. One is the Montreal massacre of December 6, 1989, when fourteen women—engineering students—were killed at a polytechnic university.[12] There's an anti-feminist politics of that moment that I want to bring to bear here.[13] Secondly, I want to bring in the Kanesatake resistance, or Mohawk resistance. The Oka Crisis (or the Mohawk Movement) was a seventy-eight-day standoff between Mohawk land defenders—or protesters (it depends on who's talking)—and Quebec police officers, the RCMP [Royal Canadian Mounted Police], and the Canadian Army. These land defenders and protesters were refusing a proposal to expand a golf course and to develop townhouses on disputed land that included burial grounds. Though the standoff happened in 1990, the golf course expansion began in 1989 when the Mayor of Oka announced his plan which impinged on an ancestral cemetery. It was in 1989 that the Mohawk Resistance Movement galvanized. This was the atmosphere in Canada in 1989. I mention this as a way to think about intersectionality— to get us to think about how it's not about simply a compounding issue. Rather, this was a moment when we were being asked to think about politics in quite complex, messy ways. We can think about identity, we can think about gender and race, which are part of the heuristic, but we have to think about them in relation to structure, in relation to epistemology, and in relation to these different kinds of systems of power and violence.

When we mobilize intersectionality now, it becomes quite tricky in terms of thinking about politics, and about how we might hack intersectionality. The setting sometimes gets to determine how it is actualized. We must ask, what are the histories in this moment? What is being attended here that requires that kind of analytical structure to make sense of it? That's what I'm thinking about in terms of hacking intersectionality, and in terms of the different settings and how we mobilize it within them. It becomes for me a very ineffective tool if we think of it as a general theory—as an ungrounded theory—because one of the things that Crenshaw is really committed to is a bottom-up analysis. Each time it is grounded in place and in history, intersectionality allows for movement and it allows us to think about ways to recast—this is the language in the article—and rethink the kinds of systems that are discriminating against folks. In this conversation, you've helped me realign my thinking on that.

AI: I have so many questions about just what you've said, because the way you are talking about the date and the setting—that's not a definition of the theory or any other event but it's more about the tensions before and the tensions after and how certain social and political dimensions are recalibrated.

There are so many questions about intersectionality itself. Has it reworked the way we think about patriarchy? Has it reworked the way we think about gender norms? And the way families work in all these different social dimensions? I want to say "reworked," but I feel like it recalibrates the language people use when they talk about it. As we've said, it doesn't provide any answers, but it provides a modality to think through different multidimensional intersections of identity, the tensions between different social groups and parties about how to unpack something that's so complicated because it's so multidimensional. In work that I do, I'm always trying to think about who's not at the table, who's not here, and then I feel like I'm still failing somebody.

PA: I like many things about what you are highlighting here. Particularly, I want us to think about what you mean by intersectionality providing not answers, but rather modality to think through. And if we considered intersectionality less—as you are saying—as a tool for justice, a tool or a method or process, but rather consider it as a moment of thinking, as an analytical structure, we might be able to focus on intersectionality, as Crenshaw says, as a challenge to "the dominant way of thinking about discrimination." I'm struck by this idea of challenging the dominant way of thinking.

I'm interested in that because it becomes an epistemological structure, and it also becomes a site of thought and, because she situated it in an argument within Title VII, which is about employment discrimination, intersectionality then is about labor. It's getting us to think about productive and reproductive labor. Intersectionality becomes a site to think about reproductive labor and it makes thinking a reproductive act. It gets us to reconsider, maybe, the sites that she's mobilizing—the sites that she wants to get us to think through which are the courts, civil rights thinking, and also feminist theory. These are the different sites that she's thinking about, and then there's this reproductive labor in rethinking these different environments that I find really invaluable. So, I want to think of thinking as a reproductive labor.

AI: So, when you say reproductive thinking, I'm thinking about where the burden lies in producing political thought for Black women, because Crenshaw says: "Black women are theoretically erased," and I am considering her mode of thinking here. In producing this piece of work, how does she combat that theoretical erasure? How does she add a stepping stone to overcoming this barrier of erasure? The self-valuation of Black women has so long been predominantly in the hands of the dominant society, the white dominant society. So the way she's reclaiming this is really interesting to me because the burden is shifted—it's not in the hands of Black men, it's not in the hands of white women, but it's shifted toward Black women, and it gives them a sense of agency.

PA: I'm thinking of when she turns to Sojourner Truth's "Ain't I a Woman" speech …

AI: Crenshaw said, "by using her own life to reveal the contradictions between the ideological myth of womanhood and the reality of Black woman's experience, Truth's oratory provided a powerful rebuttal to the claim that women were categorically weaker than men," and before that Crenshaw talks about how Black women are seen as hybrid; you're never purely a woman, you're never purely Black.[14] So it's an unknown space, I guess, because you haven't been given those structural, social tools, or political tools to formally actualize your existence in the public space. Black women have carved and claimed their own space and continue to do so to this day. I remember reading "Ain't I a Woman," when I was in the second year of my history degree, because that was the first time I got to choose what I wanted to research. I'd never really looked at Sojourner Truth. What I found really interesting was the way her speech was written, and kept changing, depending on who was writing it. The way the language completely changes when a white man writes it, and it's completely different when they tried to make her seem a bit more palatable to the white women she's presenting the speech to, so I found it very interesting how her own words were being used in different ways to how she probably presented them, and how they were taken away from her, even though the speech is centered on reclaiming agency.

PA: Absolutely. I like that you noted the language switch and particularly what I've noticed is that there's also a grammar in her speech that I see shifting depending on which version I'm reading. In the one Crenshaw cites, the quotation is

> "Look at my arm. I have ploughed and planted and gathered into barns, and no men could head me. And ain't I a woman? I could work as much and eat as much as a man—when I could get it—and bear the lash as well. And ain't I a woman? I have born thirteen children

and seen most of them sold into slavery, and when I cried out with my mother's grief none but Jesus heard me. And ain't I a woman?"[15] I find the interrogation—the "ain't I a woman?"—such an agential question. It is not interested in telling you that "I am a woman," but it is asking you, "am I not?"

AI: It is turning the question back around at the audience by asking "how can you not see me as a woman?"

PA: Exactly. It's an interrogation. And intersectionality is an interrogation of a dominant system. It's less about "let's resolve it" and more about "let's interrogate what makes this the way that we organize our social lives." There is such an agential quality to that kind of interrogation. What I like about it is that it doesn't presume to know, if interrogated, what it will become, so what it becomes then is a collective project if we are willing to take it upon ourselves. It offers us the kind of tools to interrogate that system—the dominant system of thinking—as it was in its initial emergence, which was to challenge the dominant way of thinking about discrimination. So, we can inherit that method of interrogation to bear on systems of oppression.

AI: It makes you think through the narrow ways you think about certain intersections and certain multidimensional identities. I think you're right, and I didn't really think about intersectionality that way. The most common appeals to intersectionality now are often those who are trying to be socially liberal as a way to protect themselves.

PA: The reason I'm interested in intersectionality as a system of thought—as an exercise in thinking, perhaps—is that Black women's intellectual work is not elevated. As we are seeing, intersectionality is everywhere. It's almost part of the weather around us now, particularly organizational weather in any space you go to. But I think that Crenshaw has offered a way of thinking about what the concept of intersectionality is asking you to do. It's asking us to actually change, asking us to think. The court functioned as an ideological apparatus. So she was challenging how the courts were making sense of Black women's claims. Intersectionality is challenging that ideology, that dominant thinking, that is protected or that is offered by the court system, and also by feminist theory at that moment, and also by social movements. Crenshaw's interested in the ideological ways that we organize society—even the civil rights movements, where folks in those movements would find Black women's interests dangerous. She reminds us in the essay how often those movements wanted us to go along with what they were saying as opposed to supporting the interests that Black women expressed. She's challenging these different spaces of ideology that privilege either race or gender, or the exclusion of the distinct positions that Black women occupy.

AI: Yes, especially the idea that Black women's interests are dangerous. As you said, Black women's intellectual thought is often undervalued—I sometimes wonder whether it is because Black women's political and social thought is fed through their personal experiences that people miss the richness those experiences can give to thought. We undervalue that as a society because we have tried to dehumanize thought, to separate ourselves from what we're thinking.

PA: You've got me thinking—rethinking—going back to that essay and reengaging with it. Sometimes I'm just so fed up with this framework. But your idea that Black women's political thought is perhaps undervalued because it is often rooted in the personal and the experiential haunts me to return to the essay and think about it. One thing that she does really well in this essay is to render experience as a philosophical question. It becomes a philosophical and juridical question, rather than only an individual question. We often domesticate experience; yet, we know enough feminists, particularly feminists of the 1960s, '70s, '80s, who taught us that the personal is political. So we know this is also the context she's working from. The personal is political, and the political is also intellectual, because there were political movements that were there to change systems.

This is the context—one of the contexts—within which Crenshaw is working. So when you say that the relationship between thought and experience is seen, sadly, as the space of the rational, and experience is received as that of the body, there's this duality that is sometimes still in our work. And in the example that she's offered us, we are being forced to think about the phenomenological aspects of experience—how these experiences actually shape the world and shape systems of thought. So, yes, we can think of intersectionality as embodied thought if one wants to go there, and we can also receive it as a political philosophy. If we recast it within these modalities we might see it for what it is, but also we might recast it as a complicated site of meaning making. So, these are ways of thinking about your question, about your statement, about how perhaps experience is undervalued, because these political thoughts come from experience. And we've got scholars, like [Frantz] Fanon and others, who have really pushed for that. But again, that was a Black man, right? Your point is really quite a fascinating one to go back to.

AI: It is interesting that you bring up the idea of rationality. It leads me to consider the model of the rational man and how it contrasts with the value we have placed on personal experience in the academy. The former is very much present in the public sphere, whereas the latter is a more interior experience that has been relegated to the private sphere. I wonder if it's devalued because that private space has been domesticated for so long. When you link that with gender, and when you connect that with spaces that women traditionally haven't been able to enter—especially Black women—when you are segregated from political thought even though your whole experience is political, that's very interesting to me. I mean, there's no bridge between the two, and I think you just have to wreck the whole separation of these two spaces. I don't see the way you can bridge the two.

When you mention Fanon, for example, that's someone who's done so much work on the personal experience, on the psychological experiences of Black people.[16] Because he's a Black man, maybe that hasn't been platformed as much. How can we value and nurture personal experiences more in intellectual thought? When you read someone like Audre Lorde, the interior is the center. It comes first, and it is the home of powerful political protest. Where does intersectionality as a mode of thinking move to once we understand that personal experiences are a rich center for political thought to take place in?

PA: Maybe it's also significant that in thinking about intersectionality she arcs back to Title VII. The 1960s was a moment in which feminists were highlighting that "the personal is political." The reason her theory, when it came out in 1989, was significant for me is that the kind of work that made the personal political was work that was done by feminism and feminist analysis. Crenshaw, from this analysis, made it possible to rethink ideas about institutions, about economics. And then she's saying "okay, this is all possible but let's remember that feminism has also excluded this."

AI: What you're saying about marginalized groups being excluded from academic spaces, excluded from academia, is that they've done the movement work, the social work, the political work, and I find it interesting how Crenshaw's work stands on the shoulders of that.

PA: Precisely! I'm thinking of folks like Chandra Mohanty, who was doing loads of work about transnational feminism in the '60s and '70s and onwards, and even Angela Davis—there's so many folks who were organizing and thinking and refusing, particularly, the global North idea. Many were interested in questions and ideas affecting people in the global South, thinking about Indigenous Peoples.

PA: There's something here that maybe is quite obvious to both of us, but that maybe needs to be pointed out: intersectionality is a Black feminist knowledge.

AI: That is its home. You can apply it to different spaces, but intersectionality was made with Black women in mind.

PA: Yes, intersectionality is Black feminist knowledge, and not simply a feminist project. Oftentimes, it is seen as the product of feminism, and thus becomes universalized, which then moves it away completely from Black women, and it also sometimes feels post-racial. But intersectionality is Black feminist knowledge.

AI: My favorite part is that last sentence where Crenshaw writes "when they enter, we all enter." That was such a powerful statement to end with because it's so aspirational. At the beginning, when we were thinking about 1989, we were really thinking about transformation. But she's actually been going back to that the whole time—it's this idea of bringing that ancestry, that political thought, that social thought, with you as you go along. It's not something that you leave behind you, but it's something you take with you as you move forward. It can be burdensome. It takes a lot of work and energy to contend with past experience, present experience, and future experience, but there's so much richness within that. We can find a connection with Crenshaw's words because she is talking about things that still matter so much to women I know, to people I know.

Notes

1   Kimberlé Crenshaw, "Demarginalizing the Intersection of Race and Sex: A Black Feminist Critique of Antidiscrimination Doctrine, Feminist Theory and Antiracist Politics," *University of Chicago Legal Forum* 1, no. 8 (1989): 139–67.
2   Crenshaw, "Demarginalizing the Intersection," 139, 140.
3   Title VII of the Civil Rights Act of 1964 prohibits employment discrimination based on race, color, religion, sex, or national origin: https://www.eeoc.gov/statutes/title-vii-civil-rights-act-1964 (accessed December 6, 2021).
4   Crenshaw, "Demarginalizing the Intersection," 141.
5   This conversation took place in two installments over Zoom, recorded in September and October 2021. It has been edited for clarity.
6   Raymond Williams, *Keywords: A Vocabulary of Culture and Society* (London: Croom Helm, 1976).
7   Phanuel Antwi and Ronald Cummings, "1865: The Disenchantment of Empire," *1865: The Disenchantment of Empire.* Special Issue of *Cultural Dynamics* 31, no. 3 (2019): 161–79.
8   Patricia Hill Collins, *Black Feminist Thought: Knowledge, Consciousness and the Politics of Empowerment* (1990; London: Routledge, 2009).
9   See Denise Ferreira da Silva, *Unpayable Debt* (Cambridge, MA: MIT Press, 2022); Phanuel Antwi and Denise Ferreira da Silva, "Toward the End of Time,"

in *Saturation: Race and the Circulation of Value*, ed. C. Riley Snorton and Hentlyle Yapp (Cambridge, MA: MIT Press, 2020), 141–53.

10 See Sara Ahmed, *On Being Included: Racism and Diversity in Institutional Life* (Durham, NC: Duke University Press, 2012).

11 Mikki Kendall, *Hood Feminism: Notes from the Women That a Movement Forgot* (New York: Penguin, 2021); Lola Olufemi, *Feminism Interrupted: Disrupting Power* (London: Pluto Press, 2020).

12 On the afternoon of December 6, 1989, Marc Lépine murdered fourteen women—thirteen engineering students and a nursing student—at Montreal's École Polytechnique. In his suicide note, Lépine wrote: "I have decided to send the feminists, who have always ruined my life, to their Maker." Peter Langman, "Mark Lépine's Suicide Note," www.schoolshooters.info (July 29, 2014).

13 Lépine wrote: "The feminists have always enraged me. They want to keep the advantages of women … while seizing for themselves those of men." Ibid.

14 Kimberlé Crenshaw, "Demarginalizing the Intersection of Race and Sex: A Black Feminist Critique of Antidiscrimination Doctrine, Feminist Theory and Antiracist Politics," *University of Chicago Legal Forum* 1, no. 8 (1989): 139–67.

15 Ibid., 153.

16 See Frantz Fanon, *Black Skin, White Masks* (New York: Grove Press, 1967).

Part Two

Culture and Politics

6

The New Concerned Intellectuals and Civil Society: Democracy Movements in Taiwan

Song-Chuan Chen

In the spring of 1989, when student protests took place in Tiananmen Square, I was a sixteen-year-old student attending a polytechnic vocational high school on the outskirts of Taipei. A few classmates and I went with a teacher, on the evening of June 3, to the city center to join a vigil at the Chiang Kai-Shek Memorial Hall, an event to support the students in Beijing. Attended by over 10,000 people—the majority university and high school students like us—the vigil was planned as a night of joint singing with our Beijing counterparts over a telephone line. On the list were songs such as "Roar! The Yellow River," "Descendants of Dragon," and "Wound of History," the lyrics of which were imbued with constructed memories of Chinese history, ones supposedly resonant on both sides of the Taiwan Strait.

The joint singing was scheduled to begin at 10 p.m., but when the hour came, the telephone failed to connect. The line was only restored a few minutes past eleven o'clock, and news came that the army had entered the vicinity of Tiananmen Square. The telephone line to Beijing did not bring a crescendo of emotional connection between the two Chinas, but instead served as a frantic live broadcast of the bloodshed taking place. The anticipated chorus from Beijing was replaced by the sound of the machineguns of the People's Liberation Amy firing on protesters and citizens.[1]

What happened that night around Tiananmen is well documented: it is estimated that between several hundred and several thousand people were massacred.[2] But looking back at 1989, for the Taiwanese, is a complicated process. Only later did I realize that, while we were concerned about what happened in China, very little about Taiwan, where we lived, was taught to us in school. Taiwan's history textbooks, instead, mostly narrated China's alleged 5,000 years of glorious history. As students, we were told to believe that one day we would go back to rule over the whole of mainland China. A democratic culture and the identity of being Taiwanese—as opposed to being Chinese—were, nonetheless, fast-growing in those years.

Three decades after the Tiananmen massacre, Taiwan has been hailed as a beacon of democracy in Asia, categorized in the "Democracy Index 2021" as a "full democracy," ranked number eight, ahead of the United Kingdom (18), France (22), and the United States (26). In sharp contrast, China is under the category of "authoritarian," ranked 148 of 167 countries listed in the Index. What has not been fulfilled in China has been achieved in Taiwan.[3] Focusing on democracy movements in Taiwan, this chapter attempts to probe why Taiwan succeeded where China failed.

In the years following the Tiananmen massacre, researchers in the West questioned China's democratic future. Samuel P. Huntington took an absolutist view, arguing that democracy has "little resonance" in Confucian China.[4] Other political scientists took a more nuanced approach to chart alternative futures for China. Taking Western democracies as a model, explicitly or implicitly, political scientists often argued that economic development would eventually lead to China's political transformation.[5] Analysis became more complicated when focus was drawn to the role of civil society, with some scholars questioning if China has ever had such a thing, and others doubting the usefulness of this category in understanding China's historical conditions.[6] Taiwan's success as a country with a Chinese culture throws into question assertions of fundamental difference, like Huntington's. This chapter foregrounds the role of intellectuals in establishing Taiwan's civil society and safeguarding its democratic transformation. The intellectuals of Taiwan were "new concerned intellectuals" who reimagined state-society relations by first reinventing their own role within them.

Knowledge traditions of both China and the West were drawn upon by Taiwanese intellectuals to reconceptualize Taiwan's politics. Their imagination of Western democracy centering on the Chinese term *minzu* (literally "government by the people," 民主) was crucial in bringing about a transformation. Involved in a great deal of reading, writing, publication, and organization of societies as their brand of political activism, intellectuals in the second half of the twentieth century propelled a democracy movement on the island. The pen, or writing brush, as the traditional Chinese saying goes, is a weapon that possesses a transformational power that must not be underestimated.

In this chapter, I contextualize 1989 as a moment of change—when Taiwan was turning toward an embrace of liberal democracy that China did not take up—and of continuity, when intellectuals and their textual culture played an important ongoing role in public discourse about just what democracy means. Taiwan's very embrace of liberal democratic politics is itself strong refutation to the notion that Chinese values and Western democratic ideas are inherently incompatible. In what follows, I first consider the history of intellectuals' influence in China, before turning to intellectuals in Taiwan since the Second World War, and intellectual activism in Taiwan after Martial Law. Along the way, I focus on the self-immolation of journalist Cheng Nan-jung (1947–89, 鄭南榕), who lit a fire under Taiwan's politics in 1989 and in so doing exemplifies the most radical of the new concerned intellectuals. Other protests were launched by new concerned intellectuals who possessed comparably radical ideas to Cheng, but who had less diehard temperaments. They negotiated with the political power holders—Chiang junior and his Nationalist Party—and mobilized a Cold War international environment to their advantage. By focusing on intellectuals, this article is not arguing that knowledge elites were the sole agents of Taiwan's democratic transformation. Rather, it draws attention to the specific Chinese historical context in which intellectuals were given a unique role that empowered them to take political action that shaped state and society.

Intellectual Activism

After Western imperial invasions shook a declining imperial China to its core, traditional intellectuals experienced what historian Hao Chang has called a crisis in search of a new China.[7] This crisis is best symbolized by the abolition of the Civil Service Examination in 1905, which formally ended a tradition more than one and a half millennia long in which intellectuals were made to serve the imperial state, a state with Confucianism upheld as its formal ideology. Reform and revolution were called upon to save China and chart a course in a world where Western civilization had great gravitational pull. The intellectuals needed to first reinvent their intellectual traditions, however.[8] It was out of this context that new concerned intellectuals first emerged.

The introduction of Western knowledge in these years can be traced to the Christian missionary schools and Chinese overseas students of the second half of the nineteenth century. By the beginning of the twentieth century, the influx of Western ideas gathered such momentum that a torrent of change resulted in politics, economy, society, and values.⁹ Intellectual transformation in this context was, literally, text based. Written Chinese characters changed from classical to colloquial forms, making written text closer to spoken Mandarin. This measure was intended to imitate the colloquialization of Latin, which allegedly democratized European languages and cultures and freed up energy for modernization. Western Romantic and Enlightenment texts were translated into Chinese and eagerly consumed by the reading public.¹⁰ In this conscious and intentional process, Western knowledge metamorphosed to become the new heritage and reference point for China's rejuvenated intellectuals, just as much as their traditional bases of knowledge had been. Where once traditional Chinese intellectuals were educated and socialized using Confucian-based texts, Taoist writings, and Buddhist and Legalist classics, intellectuals now referred—not without resistance and internal contradiction—to a hybrid body of knowledge from two worlds—an information pool which was neither Chinese, nor Western, but both. The writings of Yu Kwang-chung (1928–2017, 余光中)—who reimagined traditional China in the newly invented genre of modern Chinese poetry—are an illustration, as was his desire to be buried at Poets' Corner in Westminster Abbey.¹¹

The term "intellectual" is a compromise that this article uses to catch the English meaning of the term, its Chinese translation *zhishifenzi* (知識分子), and an old Chinese term *dushuren* (讀書人)—literally "book-reading people." Only a cocktail of meanings containing all three can capture the identity of the new concerned intellectuals. "Book-reading people," defined against the illiterate or semi-literate common people, were associated with the Civil Service Examination through which, after the mid-sixth century, the governing elite of dynastic China was selected. The term referred to students who prepared for the examination, and also the failed candidates who became clerks, teachers, street scripters, litigation masters, and other literary professionals. Above all, "book-reading people" were the system's graduates who assumed the role of scholar-officials running the country.

In its colloquial, modern use, the term refers broadly to the university-educated population that includes public intellectuals, academics, schoolteachers, university students, and other professionals. This new meaning of "book reading people" is not dissimilar to Edward Said's that defines intellectuals as urban professionals.¹² Crucially, however, the self- and social expectations of the West and East differed. The new Sinophone intellectuals inherited from the Chinese tradition the idea that they had a right and duty to speak truth to power that made them the new *concerned* intellectuals.

The new concerned intellectuals' unique position to act as the conscience of the nation (*lianxin*, 良心) reflects ideal Confucian moral politics, especially in its Neo-Confucian form from the late imperial era between the fourteenth and nineteenth centuries. Moralistic education equipped them for, and entitled them to, a seat at the political table to speak to the rulers on behalf of the people. This relationship between being intellectuals and serving the state—and thus society—was well expressed in the Confucian *Analects*: "The official, having discharged all his duties, should devote his leisure to learning; the student, having completed his learning, should apply himself to be an official."[13] Learning and officialdom were closely intertwined, and the ideal intellectuals would crave neither fame nor wealth. As scholar-official Fan Zhongyan (989–1052, 范仲淹) of the Song dynasty (960–1279) most famously put it, the intellectual always held the social duty to "be the first to bear the world's hardship, and the last to enjoy its comfort."[14]

The social contract of the intellectual as society's conscience was accepted as a norm by commoners and emperors alike, although the latter kept their absolute divine power. Scholars such as those of the Donglin school of the late Ming (1368–1644) dynasty were known for their dissidence against what they saw as corrupt politics. Their leader Gu Xiancheng (1550–1612, 顧憲成) put the following couplets on the door of their academy, showing how they regarded their duty of being concerned intellectuals: "Sounds of the wind, rain and reading into the ears; Matters of family, nation, and the world concerned the heart."[15]

In times of crisis, like the late Ming, the late Qing (1644–1911), and the Republican era (1911–49), intellectuals were expected to act. The words of Donglin scholars, together with Fan's and the quote from *The Analects*, were widely circulated and recited by the intellectual community in the early twentieth century as a reminder of its role in charting a path for the crisis-ridden world. Referencing the Confucian textual tradition reflected the new concerned intellectuals' inheritance of their unique social position. Jeffrey N. Wasserstrom explains how the expectation of taking the world on their shoulders, and their self-image as political actors, informed student protests of the twentieth century.[16]

Journal publication was a major means through which the new intellectuals formed societies for gathering the like-minded and exchanging ideas during the Republican era. *New Youth* (*Xin Qingnian*, 新青年), one of the earliest and best-known journals, took a radical position and was at the forefront of introducing Western knowledge to China. Its editor Chen Duxiu (1879–1942) was responsible for coining the term Mr. Democracy (*Dexiansheng*, 德先生)

that together with Mr. Science (*Saixiansheng*, 賽先生) became the two principal Western ideas that the new intellectuals privileged.[17]

Chen, a typical new concerned intellectual, was educated in the Confucian classics, passing the county level of the Civil Service Examination a decade prior to its abolition. At eighteen years of age, and much like his peers, he attended a new-style school learning French and shipbuilding, headed to Japan for further Western-style learning, and eventually converted to communism. Chen emerged as a key leader of a New Culture Movement aimed at inventing a new intellectualism for a new China.[18] By actively shaping a new tradition that combined the knowledge systems of both worlds, these intellectuals intended to kick-start a transformation of the country. Despite their ideological differences, curricula in schools and universities in both Taiwan and China were written by the new intellectuals of this era, making the campus an institution of the new intellectualism.

Challenging the Undemocratic State

The new concerned intellectuals of postwar Taiwan inherited this new tradition. Together with other agents of political transformation, such as the local social elite, they played what they saw as their prescribed role in forcing the state to adopt their Western-inspired democratic agenda. Their democratic inspirations were pivotal to Taiwan's political transformation, especially regarding fostering an effective opposition party and a civil society through which they forced the power holders on the island country to democratize politics, while Cold War international pressures helped their cause.

The effective opposition was born out of an ethnic identity of being Taiwanese that can be traced back to the Japanese period (1895–1945). In resisting Japan's colonization, which climaxed in the 1920s when Japan tried to "Japanize" Taiwanese people under their rule, a Taiwanese identity came into being. In reality, the early Taiwanese were mostly descended from immigrants from China's Fujian province, who had settled on the island since the seventeenth century. The Qing imperial state came to set up a prefecture in 1874, and then a province in 1885, formally colonizing the island.[19] A decade later, Taiwan was ceded to Japan after the Qing lost the First Sino-Japanese War (1894–5).

When Japan was defeated in 1945, following the Second World War, Taiwan returned to China, which had become a Republic in 1911. The insensitive rule, arrogant attitudes, corruption, and harsh policies of the Republic of China's officials on assuming control over Taiwan caused anger and protest, culminating in riots and widespread violence on February 28, 1947, or, as it became known, the "228 Incident." Two years later, Taiwan witnessed the entire government of the Republic of China descending on the island in the form of Chiang Kai-shek's Nationalist Party, which lost the civil war and its control over mainland China to the Communists. Chiang brutally ruled Taiwan over the following two decades, partly in fear of communist infiltration.[20]

Challenges to Chiang's tight political control came first from mainland intellectuals who followed the government to the island and brought with them the new intellectual tradition. In the late 1950s, in his journal *Free China*, Lei Chen (1897–1979, 雷震) voiced concerns about the absence of political freedom arguing that an "opposition party is the key for solving all problems."[21] On May 4, 1960, Lei formed the Chinese Democratic Party to challenge Chiang's one-party system. Chiang put Lei and his cofounders under house arrest, ending this first intellectual activist upsurge.[22]

A decade later another attempt to challenge to the Nationalist Party's authoritarianism came from Pen Ming-min (1923–, 彭明敏), a Taiwanese Political Science professor from National Taiwan University. Pen criticized Chiang's unrealistic policy of attempting to recover the mainland and, like Lei, advocated political freedom. Taiwanese intellectuals like Pen distrusted Chiang as much as they had distrusted the Japanese, and believed democracy could only be fulfilled by building a national Taiwanese state. In 1964, Pen and a few likeminded Taiwanese intellectuals published the "Declaration of Formosan Self-salvation." For this, Pen ended up in exile in the United States.[23]

Journal publications in Taiwan were, as during the Republican period in mainland China, the means for concerned intellectuals to take collective action, spreading their ideas and garnering support. Lei's *Free China* followed this tradition. In 1971, Chang Chun-hung (1938–, 張俊宏) founded a journal advocating Taiwanese identity and democratization. He called it *Daxue* (大學), which is both the Chinese word for "university" and the title of the Confucian classic, *The Great Learning*. *Daxue*'s English title is *The Intellectual*.[24] The symbolism in the title spelt out the dual East and West traditions of the new intellectuals with the university campus as their institution. Chang and the exiled Pen both belonged to this new group of concerned intellectuals who saw themselves as being Taiwanese, as opposed to being Chinese. An umbrella organization, World United Formosans for Independence, was formed in 1970 in Tokyo, uniting their radical comrades, including those living in the Americas, Europe, and Japan.[25]

The growth of this radical Taiwanese identity took place in a Cold War international environment in which Chiang Kai-shek's Republic of China on the island of Taiwan was becoming isolated. Chiang's Taiwan had played a key role as a buffer zone containing communism in the 1950s and 1960s. Since Taiwan's strategic position was valued, it was Chiang's "China" that took a permanent seat in the all-important Security Council of the United Nations. This arrangement became untenable, however, after the Sino-Soviet split of the mid-1960s. Seeing the importance of joining forces with communist China in its rivalry with Soviet Russia, the United States stopped blocking communist China from joining the UN. In 1971, Taiwan left the UN, before it was expelled. President Nixon then visited China in 1972. Taiwan's international standing was dealt another blow when President Carter announced the normalization of China–US relations in 1978. However, the United States maintained its commitment to the island's defense and economy through the Taiwan Relations Act (1979), propping up the island country's precarious existence as an autonomous state.

Taiwan's existential crisis was not faced by Chiang Kai-shek, who died in 1975, but by his son Chiang Ching-kuo (1910–88, 蔣經國). Chiang junior became prime minister in the year Nixon visited China, and then became president in the year Carter announced the normalization of US–China relations. The harsh international environment, and the fact that Taiwan belonged to the Western camp of the Cold War, albeit on the margins, helped the cause of democracy. The more Taiwan was marginalized by the new US–China relationship, the more it needed to appear to be following democratic norms to gain the formal and informal commitment of the US to its defense against communist China. Chiang junior's tolerant approach to political dissidence was born of these circumstances. Under his leadership, Taiwan's politics transitioned "from hard to soft authoritarianism."[26]

Domestic political conditions helped, too. The Nationalist Party had a formal commitment to electoral politics going back to the founding of the republic when the first general elections were held in 1912.[27] During the ensuing two decades of the warlord era, and the decade of Japanese invasion, the electoral system was put on hold. But in 1946, after the end of the Second World War, general elections again took place. Throughout its exile on Taiwan, the Nationalist Party was committed to electoral politics, even though the process was not free from manipulation. Shelley Rigger describes this as the Nationalist Party's "mobilizational authoritarianism."[28]

The flawed electoral system was, nevertheless, used by opponents to break the Nationalists' political monopoly, especially for positions in the Legislative

Yuan—Taiwan's parliament. Taiwanese business elites Huang Hsin-chieh (1928–99, 黃信介) and Kang Ning-hsiang (1938–, 康寧祥) entered the Legislative Yuan in the early 1970s, where they urged Chiang junior to open up Taiwan's politics. Chiang invited them for private conversation in which they educated him about Taiwanese identity.[29]

The major challenge to the Nationalists' political monopoly came from Taiwanese intellectual activists. They launched many-pronged assaults on the Nationalist Party through demonstrations in the streets, and the formation of political societies, an opposition party, and the publication of politically charged journals and books. The most well-known event of this period was a demonstration held in the southern city of Kaosiung in 1979 that came to be known as the "Formosa Incident." The demonstration, organized by *Formosa Magazine*, the major organ of the Taiwanese new concerned intellectuals in the late 1970s, ended with the arrest of its major leaders. The ensuing trial and reports by media in the West put pressure on Chiang junior's government to handle the matter with care. The arrested leaders, mostly intellectuals, and the attorneys who defended them would become the leading political figures of the 1990s and 2000s.[30]

The Taiwanese intellectuals' political activism culminated in the formation of the Democratic Progressive Party (DPP) in 1986, though doing so was illegal under Taiwan's martial law, which dated from 1949. Chiang junior did not stop the party's creation, however, and in fact lifted martial law the next year, the year before his death. By the late 1980s, Taiwan was noticeably transformed, and so were its intellectuals. In the late 1950s, figures like Lei and Peng voiced their dissatisfaction with politics under the senior Chiang knowing they could face jail and even death. They did so following the age-old tradition of intellectual self-sacrifice in the speaking of truth to power. The launch of Lei's Chinese Democratic Party on May 4, 1960—in reference to the May Fourth Movement when the first major student demonstrations broke out in 1919 in protest against the Treaty of Versailles—and the 1979 march in Kaosiung on International Human Rights Day show the political symbolisms at work. The "May Fourth Spirit" of the New Cultural Movement formed the ultimate symbol of the new concerned intellectuals who brought about social change through their combination of writing and activism. Taiwanese intellectuals' gradual abandonment of this symbol in favor of Human Rights was a deliberate act of rejecting "Chineseness" in an attempt to emphasize Taiwanese identity.

In their political activism, both the mainlanders and Taiwanese nevertheless tapped into intellectual traditions of both West and East. That their transformation was intertwined with the state followed the same pattern of early twentieth-century China, except that they were not crippled by warlords and Japanese invasion, and thus had a better chance of success. In the 1970s, the influence of mainland intellectuals like Lei diminished, while Taiwanese identity like Pen's intensified. By taking an independent democratic Taiwan as their responsibility, the new concerned intellectuals of 1980s Taiwan developed a well-articulated identity as the descendants of immigrants who first came to Taiwan in the seventeenth century, and experienced Japan's, and then the Nationalist Party's, colonization. Their independent Taiwanese democratic identity was, in these years, imagined, advocated, and made.

Over My Dead Body

When martial law was lifted in 1987, Taiwan's society was far from fully free. The Nationalist Party's entanglement with institutions and instruments of state would take a further three decades to sort out.[31] Such was the context in which, in 1989, journalist Cheng Nan-jung (known as Nylon Cheng) took the extreme action of self-immolation for the cause of democracy. Cheng embodied a newly articulated Taiwanese identity: his martyrdom would be translated into multiple forms of political activism including a publication, his widow's election success, a museum, and a foundation for championing democracy.

Crucially, in lifting martial law, Chiang junior did not abolish its legal instrument, the "Temporary Provisions against the Communist Rebellion" (1948–91), which legitimized the state intrusion in people's everyday lives that created legal chaos and confusion in the post-martial law era. The Taiwan Garrison Command, or TGC (1945–92), that controlled publications and censorship, for instance, was one institution buttressed by these Temporary Provisions. The right to form political parties and to free publications guaranteed by the constitution were—in theory—allowed, but the TGC still had the statutory duty to censor publications and make arrests. Moreover, civil officials retained the habit of reacting to most issues as they had under martial law. Society, likewise, did not yet fully comprehend the meaning of lifting the martial law.[32] The intellectuals needed to break these constraints in order for their political activism to recast the state as a democratic institution. Cheng's drastic action—self-immolation—shook society and was the intellectuals' call to arms.

In his youth, Cheng attended an academically prestigious high school, then the National Taiwan University to study philosophy. As Taiwan faced international isolation, university campuses in the 1980s became more than ever incubators of concerned Taiwanese intellectuals who, in the parlance of the time, "worried about the nation and the people (*youguo youmi*, 憂國憂民)." Although Cheng's father came from mainland China during the Second World War, he grew up in his mother's Taiwanese community and Cheng identified as Taiwanese. His sense of dual heritage was not uncommon, and it informed his belief in advocating not just for Taiwanese independence but also for the reconciliation of all groups—mainlanders, Taiwanese, and the indigenous Austronesian people who had lived on the island before the Chinese—together into a new social whole.[33]

As a young concerned intellectual, Cheng was influenced by the mainland philosopher Yin Haiguang (1919–69, 殷海光), who was put under house arrest for his part in Lei's Chinese Democratic Party in 1960. Each time he visited Yin, Cheng walked past the surveillance personnel stationed outside Yin's house. For Cheng's safety, Yin eventually turned him away. The intellectual relationship between Cheng and Yin represents a connection between the earlier period and the 1980s, in which mainlander and Taiwanese intellectuals started to go their separate ways, with the identity of being Taiwanese gradually foregrounded in the island's politics.

Cheng's intellectual activism saw him devote the mid-1980s to the publication of the political journal *The Freedom Era Weekly* (*shidai zhouka*, 時代周刊), which exposed government corruption and advocated democratic Taiwanese identity. The journal became a commercial success, meeting a need among the population to challenge the status quo. Not content with this alone, Cheng involved himself in other forms of political resistance, organizing a demonstration in 1986 which added to the social pressures that forced the lifting of martial law the following year.

Commemorating the February 28, 1947, incident was Cheng's next activism. The fact that that day happened to be his birthday and that, in 1986 when he was jailed for provocative journal articles his prisoner number was "2280," added to the pathos. Responding partly to this private symbolism, Cheng took advantage of the incident's fortieth anniversary to form the "Association for Advocating the 228 Peace Day." By giving talks and staging commemorations across Taiwan's major cities, likeminded intellectuals drew attention to the suppressed side of Taiwan's history, accentuating the incident in the narrative of Taiwanese identity.[34] They recast the history of Chiang's Nationalist Party retreating to Taiwan as a colonization even more brutal than the Japanese occupation which preceded it.

The lifting of martial law in 1987 and the death of Chiang junior the following year only heightened Cheng's desire to challenge the regime. On December 1,

1988, Human Rights Day, Cheng's *Freedom Era Weekly* published "The Draft of the Constitution of the Taiwan Republic," openly advocating independence. This went too far for the government of the Republic of China on Taiwan, which still imagined itself to be the legitimate government of mainland China. A month later, on January 21, 1989, Cheng received a court summons charging him with treason, to which he responded, in English, "over my dead body."[35]

Over the following seventy-one days, Cheng's wife, Yeh Chu-lan (1949–), together with friends and relatives, attempted in vain to talk Cheng out of his determined resistance, while Cheng barricaded himself inside his office in anticipation of arrest. The day of reckoning came on April 7, when police broke into the office building, fortified by iron gates. Locked inside with three barrels of petrol and a lighter, Cheng set himself on fire.

Yeh and fellow activists were prepared. Cheng's charred body was draped with a flag emblazoned with the phrase "New Nation Movement." A photo shows Yeh and Cheng's comrades standing next to the body with poignant and anguished expressions. Photos like this along with others of Cheng and his family were published in a memorial booklet containing ten articles spelling out Cheng's life goal of an independent democratic Taiwan. Cheng's comrades knew well that the articles and photos would powerfully reinforce Taiwanese identity in the minds of readers.

Figure 6.1 Yeh and comrades with Cheng's charred body beneath the flag. Courtesy Hsieh San-tai, 謝三泰.

Years later, Yeh described how, when the news of Cheng's self-immolation came, she calmly changed out of the business suit that she wore as an executive in an advertising company and put on comfortable clothes and a pair of trainers, ready for "fighting battles."[36] Her anger was aimed directly at the political system that made her husband sacrifice his life. She told their daughter that her "father abandoned us for his great love of Taiwan," a quintessential discourse of self-sacrifice for the state that can be traced back to dynastic China through the May Fourth generation. Yeh expressed that she possessed inside her a great amount of *qi*, a word that means both "energy" and "anger."[37]

For two days before the funeral on May 19, Cheng's charred body was open for public viewing. The phrase "New Nation Movement" on the flag that covered the remains framed the meaning of Cheng's death, allowing no other interpretation. In a gesture of defiance, and leaving police and intelligence officers stunned, the funeral procession moved along the roads around the Presidential Office Building at the center of Taipei's political district. Some 40,000 people attended. Since the dead and their families have special rights and power in Chinese culture, agents of the state did not dare to intervene.

When the funeral procession stopped in front of the Presidential Office Building, Chan I-hua (1957–89), who had worked in Cheng's publishing company and was active in the independence and labor movements, also set himself on fire. On his burning body, Chan flew a banner: "Born Taiwanese, died a soul of Taiwan," directly referencing the romantic attitude of the New Nation Movement. A booklet commemorating Chan was published soon after, defining his action as that of a national martyr echoing and amplifying Cheng's clarion call.[38] Word of the two self-immolations spread in the media, while discontent spread across Taiwan. The Nationalist government attempted with no avail to recast the deaths as the macabre performance of political thugs. In response, and to show their solidarity with the independence movement, many members of the public set up shrines.[39]

By coincidence, an election for the Legislative Yuan was due that year. Yeh stood and won a seat on the strength of being Cheng's widow, starting her career as a politician, and working within the system—rather than from without as her husband had done—to make Taiwan a democratic country. Shelley Rigger argues that the elections of 1989 were "the watershed elections" in Taiwan's road to full democracy. The DPP, the opposition party established two years earlier and for which Yeh stood, gained an unshakable foothold in Taiwanese politics thereafter.[40]

Figure 6.2 Front cover of *The Freedom Era Weekly* (May 21, 1989) showing Chan's self-immolation. Courtesy of Cheng Nan-jung Liberty Foundation.

Knowing full well the meaning and textual power of his martyrdom, Cheng's diary referenced his planned self-immolation by quoting the eighth-century poet Du Fu (712–70, 杜甫): "Somewhere, ages and ages hence, honored you will be; Albeit after your lonesome death in time." For his Western reference, Cheng cited Socrates: "When the philosopher is executed, mountains and rivers all cry with tears."[41] As Socrates sacrificed himself for the good of Athens, so Cheng died for Taiwan's democratic independence. Interweaving the meaning of his self-immolation with the words of a Chinese poet and of a philosopher of the West, Cheng's Taiwanese identity was formed in the intertextual space of two worlds.

Such dramatic events accelerated the cause of democratic Taiwan. Just eleven years later in the 2000 general election, and for the first time in its history, the DPP came to power as a ruling party. It then won another general election four years later before losing to the Nationalist Party in 2008. In the general election of 2016 it came to power again, and held onto its position in 2020.

The Taiwanese intellectuals' nationalistic-democratic identity represented by the DPP, together with the Chinese identity of the mainlanders in Taiwan as represented by the Nationalist Party, was crucial in the formation of the two-party system of the island nation—markedly unlike a Western-style left/right split. Cheng's martyrdom has been formally recognized as contributing to the construction of this identity. Since 1997, the 228 Incident that Cheng sought to write into Taiwanese history has been commemorated with an annual national holiday. The site of Cheng's self-immolation was renamed "Freedom Lane" in 2012. April 7 was named Free Speech Day in 2016. As Taiwanese new concerned intellectuals, Cheng and his comrades invoked the intellectual traditions of both East and West in forging their Taiwanese identity.

Taiwan's Civil Society

In addition to state recognition of his martyrdom, on the tenth anniversary of his self-immolation, Cheng's comrades turned the site of Cheng's act into a museum and advocacy organization—the Nylon Cheng Liberty Foundation—established to promote free speech in the form of lectures, conferences, arts festivals, school visits, and essay competitions. This marks another path of institutionalization for the new concerned intellectuals' democracy movement that, along with their strong presence in the education system since the early twentieth century, charted a new path for state and society. Similarly, two retired mathematics professors from the National Taiwan University established the Humanistic Education Foundation in 1989, a body that would play a major role in the abolition of corporal punishment that had been an integral part of school life in Taiwan. The foundation challenged the authoritarian education system associated with the autocratic government, preparing the ground for a growing democratic culture.[42]

Non-governmental organizations like the Humanistic Education Foundation or Nylon Cheng Liberty Foundation blossomed in 1990s Taiwan, totaling around 100 such organizations by the start of the twenty-first century.[43] The majority were set up and run by new concerned intellectuals. The Taiwan Association for

Human Rights, to give another example, was founded on Human Rights Day in 1984, at the same time as Cheng's activism and with a similar goal of making an independent democratic Taiwan. The Association was particularly important in securing and safeguarding the right to protest and to freedom of speech that were fundamental to Taiwan's emerging democratic culture. Human rights discourse was used by the new concerned intellectuals to express their Taiwanese identity and to put pressure on the government to live up to international standards.[44]

Taiwan's Labor Party, *Laodong dang* (勞動黨), was also founded in 1989. The party had split from another left-wing organization with a similar-sounding English name, the Labor Party Taiwan, *Gong dang* (工黨), founded two years earlier. Neither have had much electoral success. In a Taiwan where the identity of being Taiwanese versus being Chinese dominated the political scene, their visibility remained low. The older labor party, however, had better publicity in 1989 thanks to its choice of candidate to stand for that year's Legislative Yuan election in the southern city Kaohsiung: representing the party was a woman called Hsu Hsiao-dan (1958–), who gained fame for her nude performance in a live experimental theater production the year before. During the 1989 election campaign, Hsu dressed in revealing thin satin while canvassing the streets, causing a sensation and drawing attention to her cause. For her use of her body to challenge the male world of politics, Hsu was nicknamed "Taiwan's Ilona Staller," after the Italian porn star politician. Hsu lost the election by a narrow margin, but her challenge to conservatism and authoritarian politics lives on as another mark of Taiwan's democratization. Like the newly widowed Yeh, Hsu challenged Taiwan's patriarchal order of authoritarian governance.

The year 1989 also saw the opening of the first Eslite Bookstore, which played a part in transforming the reading experience of Taiwanese, and that chimed well with the democratizing agenda of the concerned intellectuals. Eslite bookstores had cafes that the book-reading population frequented, and lecture series called "Eslite Forum" that were hosted by renowned public intellectuals and artists, making intellectual consumption commercially viable and forming a middle-class culture. This new urban reading culture added another layer of engagement to Taiwan's thriving civil activities.

The burgeoning political arena of 1989 was further augmented by a large-scale street protest. One consequence of a fast-growing economy of the 1980s was an exponential rise in home prices. The fruits of economic growth were not enjoyed by the majority, but rather a large portion concentrated in the hands of investors and bosses whose surplus capital went into the housing market, causing prices to soar. Stagnant, low wages meant that many people paid a high proportion of their income for housing in the capital, Taipei. On August 26, 1989, an estimated 40,000–50,000 protesters occupied the most expensive districts in Taipei's city center, sleeping on the street overnight in response to a call for protest by schoolteacher Li Xinchang (1952–). These activists named their cause "Snail without a Shell."[45]

The occupation became a movement, and the movement a permanent organization called "The United Association of the Houseless." It joined forces with a new organization of concerned intellectuals, the Taipei Society (*Chengshe*, literally, "purifying society") founded a few months earlier. The Taipei Society was formed by the most prestigious academics on the island, most with degrees from Western universities, to create a non-governmental and non-profit think tank. Their scholarly devotion to the public good was quintessential of the new concerned intellectuals. Faculty at the Graduate Institute of Building and Planning at National Taiwan University also adopted the housing campaign as their major concern, adding weight to the cause. The expanded campaign then enjoyed support from political parties, large and small, but in truth had limited success in changing Taiwan's housing policy, which remained largely a marketized system favoring the haves over the have-nots.[46]

Civil society had a limited capacity to challenge capitalist economy partly because Taiwan was on the capitalist side of the Cold War divide and partly because the economic system worked in making the island country materially prosperous. The founder of the "Snail without a Shell" movement, Li Xinchang, turned his organizational talent to entrepreneurialism, opening a chain of restaurants before joining the haves and abandoning the movement altogether.

Taiwan's civil society established in these years was, nonetheless, crucial for its democracy movement. Each civil organization addressed a specific group of issues, often joining forces in campaigning, using each other's platforms as the Taipei Society and the housing issue shows. The notorious 1997 kidnapping and murder of a young woman, Pai Shiao-yen, underlines this, bringing together as it did civil organizations to launch a joint demonstration and campaigns. Organizations like the Humanistic Education Foundation, the Taipei Society, and many women's organizations such as the Peng Wan-Ru Foundation joined to march in the streets and lobby legislators, forcing the government to tackle the issue of women's safety. These civil organizations were the "grassroots democracy" of Taiwan.[47]

Despite a rejection of Chinese identity among the most extreme independence activists, Taiwan's Chinese culture played a key role in the democratic developments, specifically, the concerned intellectuals' traditional social and political position as "book-reading people," which empowered them to speak out and act to fulfil both their own and their society's expectations. Their creative adaptation of Western democratic principles and civil society practices recast the state's role in people's lives. Rather than being fully absorbed by the state as the traditional intellectual was, the new concerned intellectuals in Taiwan served the state and society by being both outsiders to the system, as its critics, and insiders participating in the creation of a democratic government.

Being a new concerned intellectual in Taiwan in the twenty-first century, however, has become less about a lifelong commitment, or a vocation, as it was in the traditional Confucian world. The concept of the new concerned intellectual as developed in Taiwan has started to merge, in the 2010s, with the concept of "citizenship" in the Western tradition.[48] The intellectual is no longer a person but rather a persona, concerned with public affairs and bound by a duty and right to speak out and to take political action.

Conclusions: Taiwan as a Method

Much has changed in the way that the history of Taiwan is taught since I was a student in 1989. A much greater emphasis has been put on Taiwan's own past rather than on China, which is now seen as a county that shares the same Chinese culture as Taiwan, rather than as a homeland to which we would one day return. Most of today's Taiwanese students would feel no resonance with songs like "Descendants of Dragon," or the others we sang on the night of the Tiananmen massacre. The transformation of Taiwan in these years serves as an example of democracy taking root in a local environment and, given the shared Chinese culture, as a method to assess China's democratic movement. China did not lack new concerned intellectuals willing to challenge state monopoly to create a democratic culture. The protests begun by the young intellectuals of Beijing in the spring of 1989 were joined by academics, public intellectuals, journalists, and other professionals, who shared the same May Fourth spirit as their Taiwanese counterparts. Ordinary workers of Beijing also joined the movement through strikes, feeding the students, and physically blocking the People's Liberation Army entering the city. Many lost their lives in doing so. The new concerned intellectuals in communist China, just like Taiwan, played their part in demanding democratic change. China differed from Taiwan in two major ways, however: first, in its political-economic conditions and second in the concerned intellectuals' ability to check the communist party's political monopoly.

While 1980s Taiwan was ready for an opposition party and the growth of civil society to check and balance the state, China continued its hard authoritarian politics. The Communist party-state grew ever stronger in the first three decades of its existence, becoming arguably the most intrusive state China has ever seen. The deeply intertwined bureaucracies of state and party reached ever deeper into society, down to the village level, bringing individuals and families into the orbit and scrutiny of dual political control. This top-down state-led socialist revolution was not omnipotent—it had to negotiate with local forces and its own socialist discourse. But it was omnipresent, leaving little space for meaningful opposition or civil society. Under such conditions, intellectuals as a knowledge elite could do little to kick-start a democratic transformation from below in the same way the Taiwanese intellectuals could.

Even though they shared the same history prior to 1949—and even the same party-state structure until as late as the 1970s—China's political tolerance differed significantly from Taiwan's.[49] Taiwanese commitment to democratic elections might have been flawed, but opposition groups did join the system and enter the state, albeit in minuscule numbers in the early 1970s. They questioned Chiang junior and his policies as system insiders, making him aware of their Taiwanese identity at the same time. Chiang's Nationalist Party was localized in the 1970s by absorbing Taiwanese social elites into its fold for power-sharing, rather than staying aloof as a party for mainlanders.[50] The Chinese Communist Party, in contrast, tightly held its monopoly on political power as it committed to implementing the socialist revolution. China did practice village elections, but these were not an open contest as elections in Taiwan in the 1970s were fast becoming. Instead, the village elections in China were a process of confirming the local leaders who had a track record of party loyalty.[51] The same went for the central government's elections in the Politburo and National People's Congress, that was confirmation of the results of power struggles among the political elite taking place behind the scenes.

The political-economic conditions of these decades also worked against China's democratization. Following the end of the Civil War in 1949, Taiwan went through a period of political stability allowing society to develop. China instead experienced the upheavals of the Great Leap Forward (1958–62) and the Cultural Revolution (1966–76). The anti-intellectualism of these movements did not destroy the self- and social expectations of the new concerned intellectuals, but they did set China on a path of renewed authoritarianism.

As the people's trust in the government was destroyed in those years, when Deng came to power in 1978, faith in the party-state needed to be rebuilt.

Deng's economic reform compounded the tendency for authoritarian rule as his reintroduction of market economy faced opposition within the party and in society. The direction that Deng would take China became clear to the rest of the world only in hindsight. When Deng started his reforms, from the perspectives of both the street and the campus, or even within the party-state bureaucracy itself, 1980s China looked chaotic and directionless. It preached socialist revolution while at the same time privatizing many state-owned industries. Deng's developmentalism shocked the nation on both the ideological and economic fronts. The 1989 Tiananmen democracy movements, as a major outburst of young intellectuals' political activism, and the subsequent massacre, happened in these unfavorable conditions of the Deng era. The political and ideological turbulence whipped up by the demonstrations that year further intensified the party's need for political monopoly.

The two Chinas started life in the same year, 1949, with similar historical baggage, the same tradition of new concerned intellectuals, and the same political structures of Leninist party-state, despite their different political ideologies. Seven decades on, they are still each other's nemesis. Democracy became the difference that divided the two. Taiwan's route to democratic politics had its own unique trajectory and political-economic contingency, with the new concerned intellectuals playing a major role in its making. Taiwan proves that Western democratic ideas are more than compatible with Chinese culture. As the new concerned intellectuals of Taiwan set out to revolutionize themselves and their state and society, they created a democratic culture and, with it, their cultural homeland.

Notes

1 For an account from the anchor of that night's program, see UDN Globe, https://global.udn.com/global_vision/story/8662/3850579 (accessed September 16, 2021).
2 See, for example, Jeremy Brown, *June Fourth, the Tiananmen Protests and Beijing Massacre of 1989* (Cambridge: Cambridge University Press, 2021).
3 Economist Intelligence Unit, *Democracy Index 2021*.
4 Samuel P. Huntington, "The Clash of Civilizations?" *Foreign Affairs* 72, no. 3 (1993): 23–49.
5 For example, Edward Friedman and Barrett L. McCormick, eds., *What If China Doesn't Democratize: Implications for War and Peace* (Armonk, NY: ME Sharpe, 2000); Minxin Pei, *China's Trapped Transition: The Limits of Developmental*

Autocracy (Cambridge: Harvard University Press, 2006); Yun-han Chu, Larry Diamond, Andrew J. Nathan, and Doh Chull Shin, eds., *How East Asians View Democracy* (New York: Columbia University Press, 2010); Andrew J. Nathan, Larry Diamond, and Marc F. Plattner, eds., *Will China Democratize?* (Baltimore: Johns Hopkins University Press, 2013).

6   See *Modern China* (April 1993); Timothy Brook and B. Michael Frolic, eds., *Civil Society in China* (Armonk, NY: M. E. Sharpe, 1997). Traditional China's flourishing "associations of popular religion" were identified as a potential site of China's equivalent to the coffee house culture of the West. See Kenneth Dean, "Ritual and Space: Civil Society or Popular Religion," in *Civil Society in China*, ed. Timothy Brook and B. Michael Frolic (London: Routledge, 1997), 172–92; Robert P. Weller, *Alternate Civilities: Democracy and Culture in China and Taiwan* (Boulder: Westview Press, 1999); Richard Madsen, *Democracy's Dharma: Religious Renaissance and Political Development in Taiwan* (Berkeley: University of California Press, 2007).

7   Hao Chang, *Chinese Intellectuals in Crisis: Search for Order and Meaning, 1890–1911* (Berkeley: University of California Press, 1992).

8   For a study of intellectuals of this era, see Timothy Cheek, *The Intellectual in Modern Chinese History* (Cambridge: Cambridge University Press, 2016) and Rebecca Karl, *Staging the World: Chinese Nationalism at the Turn of the Twentieth Century* (Durham, NC: Duke University Press, 2002).

9   On missionary education in this period, see Paul A. Cohen, "Christian Missions and Their Impact to 1900," in *The Cambridge History of China Vol. 10, Late Ching, 1800–1911*, ed. John K. Fairbank (Cambridge: Cambridge University Press, 1978), 543–614.

10 See Wen-hsin Yeh, *The Alienated Academy: Culture and Politics in Republican China, 1919–1937* (Cambridge, MA: Harvard University Press, 1990); Rana Mitter, *A Bitter Revolution: China's Struggle with the Modern World* (Oxford: Oxford University Press, 2004); Theodore Huters, *Bringing the World Home: Appropriating the West in Late Qing and Early Republican China* (Honolulu: University of Hawaii Press, 2005).

11 Xu Xue (徐学), *Huozhong longyin: Yu Kwang-chung pingzhuan* (火中龙吟 余光中评传, *Dragons Humming in the Fire: Critical Biography of Yu Kwang-chung*) (Guangdong: Huacheng chubanshe, 2002), 36.

12 Edward Said, *Representations of the Intellectual: The 1993 Reith Lecture* (London: Vintage, 1994).

13 Confucius, *Confucian Analects, the Great Learning, and the Doctrine of the Mean by Mencius*, trans. James Legge (London: Trubner & Co., 1861), 208.

14 For Fan Zhongyan as an intellectual, see Paul Jakov Smith, "A Crisis in the Literati State: The Sino-Tangut War and the Qingli-Era Reforms of Fan Zhongyan, 1040–1045," *Journal of Song-Yuan Studies* 45 (2015): 59–137.

15 See John W. Dardess, *Blood and History in China: The Donglin Faction and Its Repression, 1620–1627* (Honolulu: University of Hawaii Press, 2002).

16 Jeffrey N. Wasserstrom, *Student Protest in Twentieth-Century China* (Palo Alto: Stanford University Press, 1991), 21–2, 281–2.

17 *New Youth* 6, no. 1 (January 1918): 10–11.

18 Lee Feigon, *Chen Duxiu, Founder of the Chinese Communist Party* (Princeton: Princeton University Press, 1983).

19 Leo T. S. Ching, *Becoming Japanese: Colonial Taiwan and the Politics of Identity Formation* (Berkeley: University of California Press, 2001).

20 Steven Phillips, *Between Assimilation and Independence: The Taiwanese Encounter Nationalist China, 1945–1950* (Palo Alto: Stanford University Press, 2003).

21 *Zhiyou Zhongguo* (自由中國, *Free China*) 18, no. 4 (1957): 111.

22 Lei Chen, *Lei Chen huiyilu zhi xindang yundong haipishu* (雷震回憶錄之新黨運動黑皮書, *Memoir of Lei Chen and the Black Book of the New Party Movement*) (Taipei: Yuanliu, 2003).

23 Ming-min Peng, *A Taste of Freedom: Memoirs of a Formosan Independence Leader* (New York: Holt, Rinehart and Winston, 1972), ch. 8.

24 See the journal's online editions: http://theintellectual.net/zh/ (accessed September 12, 2021).

25 The organization is still in existence and has an online presence, see http://www.wufi.org.tw/ (accessed September 16, 2021).

26 Edwin A. Winckler, "Institutionalization and Participation on Taiwan: From Hard to Soft Authoritarianism?" *China Quarterly* 99 (1984): 481–99.

27 On the election, see Ernest P. Young, "Politics in the Aftermath of Revolution: The Era of Yuan Shih-k'ai, 1912–1916," in *The Cambridge History of China 12, Part 1*, ed. Denis Twitchett and John K. Fairbank (Cambridge: Cambridge University Press, 1983), 208–55.

28 Shelley Rigger, *Politics in Taiwan: Voting for Democracy* (London: Routledge, 1999), 10.

29 For the history of this period, see Fupian Chen (陳佳宏), *Taiwan duli yungdong shi* (台灣獨立運動史, *A History of Taiwan's Independence Movement*) (Taipei: Yushanshe, 2006), ch. 4.

30 Ibid., ch. 5.

31 This is an ongoing controversy. See Fu-chung Li, "Weiquan tizhi xiade Guomindang dangying qiye (威權體制下的國民黨黨營企業, The Party-owned Enterprises: Under the Authoritarianism of Kuomintang)," *Guoshigugang Guangkan* (國史館館刊, *Bulletin of Academia Historica*) 18 (2008): 189–220.

32 For an introduction to this period, see Murray A. Rubinstein, *Taiwan: A New History* (Armonk, NY: M. E. Sharpe, 2007).

33 *Taiwan jianguo lieshi Cheng Nan-jun jinian ji* (台灣建國烈士鄭南榕紀念集, *Commemorative Essays of the Martyr of Taiwan Cheng Nan-jun*) (Taipei: Freedom Era Weekly, 1989), 16.

34 Ibid., 15–23, 73–5.
35 Ibid., 9, 41.
36 For the interview with Yeh, see "Yeh Chu-lan: Nylong, nihaoma, (葉菊蘭: Nylong, 你好嗎?, How Are You, Nylong?)" http://www.nylon.org.tw (accessed September 16, 2021).
37 Ibid.
38 *Taiwan Jianguo lieshi Chan I-hua jinian zhuanshu* (台灣建國烈士詹益樺紀念專書, *Commemorative Essays of the Martyr of Taiwan Chan I-hua*).
39 For the collection of news reports and public reactions, see http://www.nylon.org.tw (accessed September 16, 2021).
40 Rigger, *Politics in Taiwan*, ch. 6.
41 *Taiwan jianguo lieshi Cheng Nan-jun*, 4, 24. The words of Socrates are a creative translation. The Chinese original read: 千秋萬歲名, 寂寞身後事 … … 哲學家被處死之時, 山河都將流淚.
42 Renben jijing hui (人本教育文教基金會). See: https://hef.org.tw/ (accessed September 16, 2021).
43 Hsin-Huang Michael Hsiao (蕭新煌), "Taiwan de fei zhengfu zhuzhi, minzhu zhuanxing yu minzhu zhili (臺灣的非政府組織、民主轉型與民主治理) Non-Governmental Organizations, Democratic Transformation and Democratic Governance in Taiwan," *Taiwan Minzhu Jikan* (臺灣民主季刊) 1, no. 1 (March 2004): 65–84.
44 For the Association's work and history, see its website: https://www.tahr.org.tw/ (accessed September 16, 2021).
45 Lu, Bing-Yi (呂秉怡), "1989–2014 都市住宅運動 (Urban housing movement)."
46 For the Taipei Society, see: https://www.taipeisociety.org/ (accessed September 16, 2021).
47 Ya-Chung Chuang, "Democracy in Action: The Making of Social Movement Webs in Taiwan," *Critique of Anthropology* 24, no. 3 (2004): 235–55.
48 See Joshua A. Fogel and Peter G. Zarrow, *Imagining the People: Chinese Intellectuals and the Concept of Citizenship, 1890–1920* (Armonk, NY: M. E. Sharp, 1997).
49 For the similarities between Taiwan and China in the 1950s and 1960s, see Julia Strauss, *State Formation in China and Taiwan: Bureaucracy, Campaign, and Performance* (Cambridge: Cambridge University Press, 2019).
50 Chung-li Wu and Shih-chan Dai, "From Regime Transition to Liberal Democracy: The Case of Taiwan," in *Democracy in Eastern Asia: Issues, Problems and Challenges in a Region of Diversity*, ed. Edmund S. K. Fung and Steven Drakeley (London: Routledge, 2015), 60–79.
51 For a study on village elections, see Robert A. Pastor and Qingshan Tan, "The Meaning of China's Village Elections," *The China Quarterly* 162 (2000): 490–512.

7

The Guildford Four and *First Tuesday*: *Free to Speak*

Frances Pheasant-Kelly

This chapter examines a series of *First Tuesday* television documentaries made by Yorkshire Television for the ITV Network in the United Kingdom that aired from 1984 to 1989. The series, which focused on the wrongful conviction of the Guildford Four for the 1974 Guildford and Woolwich pub bombings in London, transformed legislative and criminal processes in the UK. Along with contemporaneous UK film productions such as the *Thin Blue Line* (1988), the *First Tuesday* series foreshadowed a broader questioning of political and legal decision-making through cinematic documentaries such as *The Panama Deception* (1991), *The Mayfair Set* (1999), *Fahrenheit 9/11* (2004), *Inside Job* (2010), and *13th* (2016). *First Tuesday* represented a visual text which helped mark 1989 as a turning point in the history of exposing judicial malpractice in the UK and led to a series of legislative amendments that transformed the British system. Aside from a judicial enquiry into the Guildford case and the release of the Guildford Four, these included a change to the laws on interrogation, amendments to the law on referring cases to the Appeal Court, and changes to the law of "disclosure." Moreover, this pivotal moment in the UK echoed a broader resistance to, and overturning of, oppressive and corrupt regimes—likewise born of earlier years—that induced seismic shifts in the global political, social, and judicial landscape.

Indeed, as the rigidities of the global Cold War order weakened, alternatives to the business-as-usual politics of an array of authorities were being dramatically put forward in East Germany and the Eastern Bloc, but also well beyond. For instance, in Venezuela, a popular insurrection against price hikes backed by the International Monetary Fund shook the established order such that political stability only returned in the form of the "Bolivarian Revolution" of Hugo

Chavez.¹ In then-Yugoslavia, the Non-Aligned Movement appealed to "the developed world to face, with maximum will and determination and without prejudice, the conflict which is older and deeper than the Cold War and bloc confrontation—the conflict between affluence and poverty."² In Finland, in a keynote address at a World Bank conference, economist and later Prime Minister of India, Manmohan Singh, called for renewed economic cooperation within the global South in an alternative to Washington-led structural adjustment.³ In the United States, a coalition of groups organized a 100,000-person Housing Now! rally in Washington, DC, to demand decent housing and jobs that had become all the more scarce after two terms of Reaganomics.⁴ Polling data indicated that most people agreed that the United States "continues to need a strong women's movement to push for changes that benefit women."⁵ The British focus on judicial malpractice exemplified by *First Tuesday*, in other words, was not a provincial one, but unfolded against a restive international backdrop where activists, intellectuals, and documentarians pushed back against an unfair status quo.

The *First Tuesday* documentaries, produced by investigative journalist Grant McKee with Ros Franey, alleged that the conviction of "the Guildford Four"—Gerry Conlon, Paddy Armstrong, Carole Richardson, and Paul Hill—was wrongful, and represented one of the greatest miscarriages of justice in British political history. The Four were accused of bombing pubs at Guildford on October 5, 1974, and Woolwich on November 7, 1974, that killed seven people. These attacks were later found to have been perpetrated by the IRA.⁶ The Four were given life sentences and subsequently spent fifteen years in prison after coerced confessions clinched convictions for unproven crimes. Despite the fact that convicted IRA members Martin O'Connell and Brendan Dowd admitted to the bombings, the Guildford Four's first appeal in 1977 was rejected.⁷ Subsequent evidence uncovered by the Four's solicitor, Gareth Peirce, contributed to the case being reopened in 1987 and their convictions being quashed by the Court of Appeal in October 1989.⁸

Crucially, the media, and notably, McKee's investigative journalism, were instrumental in initiating and sustaining the momentum of the case. Working with Ros Franey, McKee made the episodes "Auntie Annie's Bomb Factory" (1984), "The Guildford Time Bomb" (1986), and "A Case That Won't Go Away" (1987). McKee and Franey's *First Tuesday* "Free to Speak" documentary, which aired in November 1989 following the Guildford Four's release, included exclusive interviews about their time in prison. In its wake, further investigation revealed pervasive ineptitude, corruption, and discrimination in the judicial and policing systems, including in the convictions of the "Birmingham Six."[9] Analogous controversies continue to emerge, both in the UK and beyond.[10] While some commentators have recognized the contribution made by *First Tuesday*, there has been no evaluation of the program's role in the release of the Guildford Four and Maguire Seven.[11] Drawing on McKee and Franey's written account, *Time Bomb* (1988), and Gerry Conlon's 1990 autobiography, as well as archival evidence from the trial, this chapter aims to redress this gap by analyzing the content and visual style of McKee and Franey's documentaries. It also considers how the documentaries helped transform certain criminal and legal procedures, which in turn had implications for the broader legacy of television and cinema narrative content. The immediate effect, however, was for the Home Secretary Douglas Hurd to establish a judicial inquiry into the Guildford and Woolwich convictions, presided over by Sir John May.[12] As was true elsewhere in 1989, authorities had to acknowledge and bend to popular calls for accountability.

Contexts

The first three *First Tuesday* documentaries aired between 1984 and 1987, responded to increasing evidence that the Guildford Four had been wrongly convicted of the bombings at Woolwich and Guildford in 1974. These bombings had in fact been part of a campaign waged by the Provisional IRA at the height of "the Troubles," a period of political violence from 1969 to 1998 which escalated when the British government deployed troops in Northern Ireland and ended with the signing of The Good Friday Agreement. The Guildford and Woolwich attacks reflected an intensification of the republican bombing campaign on mainland Britain during the 1970s and were carried out by active service units of the provisional IRA and the Official Republican Army operating in England.[13] As well as the attacks at Guildford and Woolwich, 1974 also saw bombings in Birmingham which killed twenty-one people and injured 160 others.[14] The police therefore came under increasing pressure to arrest IRA bombers, a point repeatedly made in the four documentaries. These *First Tuesday* programs presented evidence that suggested that the Guildford Four and the Maguire Seven had been wrongfully convicted. Key to their persuasive power was their documentary style. The four programs generally assumed a documentary format, though 1989's "Free to Speak" differed substantively in its visual approach. Bill Nichols describes various types of documentary styles, including the poetic, performative, expository, observational, interactive, and reflexive modes.[15] Relevant to the four programs are the expository and observational formats with certain participatory aspects. The expository mode involves a voiceover narrator who remains unseen. While "expository texts take shape around commentary directed toward the viewer, images serve as illustration or counterpoint. The rhetoric of the commentator's argument serves as the textual dominant, moving the text forward in service of its persuasive needs."[16] The style of the first three documentaries is expositional in its use of voiceover commentary. In contrast, "Free To Speak" is entirely observational, since its aim is not to present an argument but to consider the impact that wrongful imprisonment had on its four subjects and their reactions to "freedom." As Nichols notes, the observational mode "stresses the non-intervention of the filmmaker ... to enhance the impression of lived or real time."[17] It is this format that dominates the documentary central to this chapter.

The Impact of the *First Tuesday* Documentaries

Gerry Conlon's account of his arrest, imprisonment, and exoneration, *Proved Innocent*, specifically refers to the impact of the *First Tuesday* documentaries. Conlon's solicitor, Alastair Logan, was one of the main campaigners for the Guildford Four and worked with the makers of "The Guildford Time Bomb," which was broadcast in summer 1986.[18] The first three documentaries led to other research on the Guildford Four, including Robert Kee's *Trial and Error*,[19] while Sir John May's final report for the judicial inquiry on the case credits the documentaries several times.[20] For instance, May notes how the 1986 program, "The Guildford Time Bomb," raised "doubts ... about the safety of the convictions."[21] As a result, Brian Cafferey (head of the Home Office division responsible for examining alleged miscarriages of justice) proposed to review the Guildford Four case.[22] The follow-up *First Tuesday* program, "A Case That Won't Go Away" (1987), prompted Caffarey to write to Grant McKee to request information on an alibi witness who had not previously given evidence at trial.[23] There is no doubt that the content of the *First Tuesday* programs, along with related press coverage, contributed significantly to the further investigation and ultimately to the quashing of the Guildford Four and Maguire Seven convictions.

Auntie Annie's Bomb Factory

The first of the *First Tuesday* documentaries, "Auntie Annie's Bomb Factory" (March 6, 1984), describes the arrest of the Maguire family, who were relatives of Gerry Conlon and came to be known as the Maguire Seven. They included Gerry's father, Guiseppe Conlon, who had traveled to London from Belfast. The title of the episode suggests the unlikeliness of the Maguire home serving as an IRA bomb factory, and introduces a number of prominent public figures as well as documents that challenged the likelihood that the Maguire family was part of the IRA. In so doing, the program conforms to the expository mode by emphasizing "the impression of objectivity and of well-substantiated argument."[24] In 1984, when the episode aired, Annie Maguire and her husband Patrick had been in prison for ten years. The film returns to the Maguire family home in London where the seven were arrested and subsequently convicted for handling and possession of nitroglycerine, a component of explosives. The narrator (Paul Dunstan) reports that the arrests were based on confessions by Paul Hill and Gerry Conlon during "prolonged interrogation." The two had allegedly claimed that Gerry's Aunt Annie had taught them to make bombs, illustrated in the program through a newspaper headline, a claim that was later retracted.

The voiceover constructs the timeline of the IRA campaign against a montage of scenes of destruction ranging from the M62 coach blast to the Guildford, Woolwich, and Birmingham pub bombings, the footage accompanied by sounds of ambulance and police sirens.[25] The narrator highlights the strength of public feeling as well as concerns that "the real culprits might have got away." Accounts of the arrest of the Guildford Four and the Maguire Seven follow images of the Maguire home, described as an "alleged IRA bomb factory" but portrayed as an unlikely setting for terrorist activity. McKee and Franey later commented that "Viewers ... must have felt unease at the notion of this forthright, apolitical London housewife and mother as the IRA's 'senior armourer,' 'evil Aunt Annie' who had presided over bomb-making lessons in her Harlesden kitchen."[26] The montage concludes with a framed photograph of Guiseppe Conlon, who died in prison in 1980, before cutting to an interview with Lord Fitt, a critic of republican violence, who nevertheless asserts that "Guiseppe was not involved in any way with any terrorist activity." The use of a framed photograph, with its implications of memory and family, rather than a prison mugshot contributes to an impression of Guiseppe Conlon's innocence. The program then assembles several prominent public figures to advocate its case with minimal direct intervention by the filmmaker. When the documentary moves on to footage of the two Maguire sons, Vincent and Patrick, they explain their initial reactions to finding the police in their home. Patrick comments, "I knocked on the door, I didn't have my own key, I was too young. I thought it was a party" and "they asked us silly questions like 'where's the bombs,'" leading the two youths to think they were "on 'Candid Camera.'" Both recounted how they saw their mother crying, lending further sympathy to their cause.

The Maguire Seven were convicted of handling nitroglycerine, although defense solicitor Alastair Logan identified omissions and aberrations in the police search of the Maguire home. He noted, for instance, that even though the Seven were allegedly handling explosives prior to the police search, dogs and sniffer devices failed to pick up any sign of explosives. Forensic examination was inadequate, and no evidence of bombmaking equipment surfaced, the narrator noting that the judge subsequently described the search as "without doubt, incomplete." Logan goes on to explain that "an experienced bombmaker would know instantly that nitroglycerine is absorbed through the skin of the hands and creates […] an 'NG' headache." The narrator suggests that the hand analyses that were subsequently carried out were turning points—nitroglycerine was found on the hands of six out of the seven people in the Maguire home, and that a pair of plastic gloves in a kitchen drawer also tested positive even though a sniffer device had registered nothing in the kitchen. The narrator then notes that the test on the gloves was analyzed by a seventeen-year-old trainee, while a single unconfirmed test was used for the hand analyses, with no control sample. An independent scientist, Dr. Brian Caddy at Strathclyde University, identifies a further flaw with the analyses: insufficient numbers of standard spots of nitroglycerine in the thin-layer chromatography (TLC) were used, making the tests in his opinion, "doubly unreliable." The inventor of the TLC test, former explosives chief at Woolwich, John Yallop, also testified that he was not satisfied with the testing, in terms of both the negative "sniffer" result and the lack of a confirmatory test.

The entire case against the Maguire Seven, as Logan summarizes, was based on the examination of the suspects' hands for nitroglycerine, confirmed by a "positive" test that could not be replicated because of inadequate samples and that was susceptible to interference by ordinary everyday substances. Moreover, the program highlighted the fact that the judge for the Maguire Seven, Justice Donaldson, had also heard the Guildford Four trial, where Annie Maguire was identified as a bombmaking instructor. Logan highlighted the prejudice that this brought against Annie Maguire and her family. The program then moves to the final letter Guiseppe Conlon wrote to his wife Sarah before his death in prison, the camera zooming in to the word "innocent" which is capitalized and therefore immediately captures the viewer's attention before returning to Lord Fitt, who states that "before he died, Guiseppe Conlon asked [me] to 'do everything you can to prove I didn't do this.'" The program subsequently shows footage of the funeral and close-ups of Sarah Conlon placing flowers on her husband's grave as she comments, "God knew he was innocent." But, Lord Fitt notes, "if we find them not guilty, it will open up the floodgates for others who were convicted on similar evidence." The defense solicitor, Harry Disley, concludes by saying "I think an injustice was done and I shall never think otherwise." Ultimately, "Auntie Annie's Bomb Factory" provided damning conclusions from a series of high-profile figures, together with documentary evidence and expert testimony which was consolidated by empathetic filmmaking approaches, such as the inclusion of funeral footage and the framed photograph of Guiseppe, alongside images of Annie Maguire as a young mother and unlikely explosives expert.

The Guildford Time-Bomb

The second episode of *First Tuesday*, which aired July 1, 1986, also follows the Guildford Four convictions in expository mode, and opens with a montage of the pub bombings, individual photographs of the Guildford Four, footage of their respective mothers, and a statement by defense solicitor Alastair Logan, who had defended the Maguire Seven, protesting the innocence of the Four. Presenter Jonathan Dimbleby outlines the context before the documentary opens with a reconstruction of the Guildford and Woolwich bombings. The reconstruction is overlaid with a warning from David O'Connell of the provisional IRA: "We said last week in a statement that the British Government and the British people must realize that because of the terror they wage in Ireland, they will suffer the consequences. As regards military targets, there are no warnings … there will be no warnings." The reconstruction momentarily cuts to frame O'Connell in close-up before showing, in reconstruction, a bomb being planted at the Horse and Groom pub in Guildford on October 5, 1974, followed by the sound of an explosion accompanied by a black screen, the sequence then cutting briefly to footage of a victim in hospital. The narrator thereafter recounts how the Seven Stars pub was bombed thirty minutes later, the documentary cutting to photographs and footage of the aftermath. A third reconstruction centers on the King's Arms in Woolwich, again followed by photographs of devastation. The narrator explains how the bomb used at the King's Arms was embellished with coach bolts to maximize injury—the film cutting to an extreme close-up of a coach bolt embedded in a wooden frame to illustrate its destructive capacity. The viewer then learns that, after eight weeks, the investigation had a significant breakthrough following an anonymous tip-off, resulting in the arrests of Paul Hill, Gerry Conlon, Patrick Armstrong, and Carole Richardson based solely on confessions which they later retracted. Again, defense solicitors Logan and Brian Rose-Smith, along with Lord Fitt and Northern Ireland Secretary, Merlyn Rees, expressed doubts about the convictions and the way that the confessions were obtained, leading Merlyn Rees to wonder, "Were we clouded by the emotion of the time?"

The narrator creates portraits of the Four, describing Richardson as a hippy who "wore beads, took amphetamines and LSD," and drifted from job to job, while Armstrong lived in squats and was involved with drugs and petty crime. Likewise, Conlon was a petty criminal. Hill had allegedly been involved with the IRA in the Belfast killing of a former British soldier. But, the program reports, all four lived and worked openly under their real names and were unlikely IRA candidates. Father Dennis Fall, who at that time was preparing a Vatican report on the case, reiterates this, and doubted if Hill was ever a member of the IRA. The narrator reveals that there was no evidence related to the Seven Stars bombing, so that the whole case turned on the Horse and Groom attack. A diagrammatic representation indicates all those at the pub that the police had traced and where they sat. The police claimed that they had identified everyone except a couple, later identified by the prosecution as Armstrong and Richardson. However, in eight lineups, Richardson was never picked out. Moreover, she had an alibi that was backed up by two witnesses who stated that she was in London at a rock concert that evening. It would have been difficult for Richardson to have completed the journey from the Horse and Groom to the concert; however, the jury accepted the possibility despite its unlikelihood. The program also revealed another alibi for Richardson provided by Frank Johnson.[27] Johnson informed police of his alibi for Richardson but was himself arrested under the Prevention of Terrorism Act and interrogated for three days. He retracted his alibi, but in court reverted to his original account of meeting with Richardson. This was corroborated in detail in John May's 1989 judicial inquiry, which clearly demonstrates Richardson's innocence.[28]

"The Guildford Time-Bomb" establishes that the Four's convictions relied on confessions, with no forensic evidence and no positive identification of the four suspects. The lack of coherence between the statements was noted, as was the fact that Richardson was hysterical and undergoing amphetamine withdrawal during her interrogation. (Gareth Pierce, Conlon's solicitor, later discovered that

Richardson had also been injected with pethidine—which intensifies withdrawal symptoms—whilst in police custody.)[29] Armstrong was on drugs too. These ongoing revelations resulted, in 1984, in an overhaul of the law on confessions, and instigated the Royal Commission on Criminal Procedure during Police Interrogation.[30] Barrie Irving, director of the Police Foundation, was following the Guildford Four convictions, and particularly Armstrong's case. His research for the Royal Commission on Criminal Procedure (1981) led to the Police and Criminal Evidence Act (PACE). As Irving explains during the documentary, the change in law considered the effects of drugs, adequacy of rest, and access to a solicitor on suspects under interrogation. Each of these issues was relevant to the Guildford Four interrogations, the final point especially because all statements made by the Guildford Four were taken before they had access to a solicitor. Professor Lionel Hayward, lead forensic psychologist for the defense, had hypnotized Armstrong and claimed that his confession was false and was made to alleviate an intolerable situation. The weakness of the case was further highlighted by the Four's solicitor, Logan, who identified more than 100 discrepancies between their statements, later confirmed in May's judicial inquiry.[31] Indeed, the police records of interrogation had not been written during the interviews but "had been typed in draft and then transcribed later in handwriting."[32] As May notes, "the discovery of rough typed notes with handwritten amendments, from … which the handwritten notes appeared to have been copied," lent considerable weight to the case for reviewing the convictions.[33]

The most significant fact in the documentary, though, is that in December 1975, the IRA claimed responsibility for the Guildford and Woolwich bombings. This led to an appeal in 1977, which was rejected despite the fact that IRA members—the Balcombe Street Gang—gave precise details about the bombings and about the bombs themselves, whereas the Guildford Four's statements were vague, brief, and technically inaccurate. Despite the Balcombe Street Gang's coherent, logical explanations and claims of responsibility, they were never charged with the Guildford bombing. Furthermore, evidence was suppressed that indicated the Gang's involvement: "A government forensic scientist had placed Woolwich first in a series of bombings done by the [Balcombe Street] gang, but had later deleted it from his report at the request of a Sergeant [from] the Bomb Squad."[34] Despite the specific details given by the IRA, the errors in the Guildford Four statements were overlooked, even while there was no evidence to link the Guildford Four to the Balcombe Street Gang.

The end of the documentary features two of the Four's mothers, one of the alibi witnesses for Richardson, along with key political figures, Merlyn Rees and Lord Fitt, who reiterated their doubts about the validity of the convictions. As Michael Naughton notes, "governmental changes to the way in which post-appeal allegations of miscarriages of justice" were dealt with, would not have happened without efforts, including the *First Tuesday* series, that kept faith with the Guildford Four.[35]

A Case That Won't Go Away

The third *First Tuesday* documentary—"A Case That Won't Go Away" (March 3, 1987)—continues in the same expository style. Within twenty-four hours of the previous program, the Home Office had ordered a review of the Guildford Four and Maguire Seven cases, as well as that of the Birmingham Six—Hugh Callaghan, Patrick Hill, Gerard Hunter, Richard McIlkenny, William Power, and John Walker—who were sentenced to life in prison in 1975, following false convictions for bombing two pubs in Birmingham. Despite the flaws that *First Tuesday* had uncovered, by 1987 only the Birmingham Six case had been appealed. Because there was no new evidence regarding the Guildford Four or the Maguire Seven cases, no action was taken. But the Four's solicitor, Gareth Peirce, had in fact uncovered further new evidence: an alibi witness for Conlon whose statement had allegedly been taken before the trial and labeled "not to be disclosed to the defense,"[36] and that Richardson had been injected with pethidine in police custody.[37] The documentary extends the case for appeal even further by reconstructing the Woolwich bombing (using stylized imagery and red-toned night-time camerawork as the supposed route of the getaway driver is followed). The voiceover notes that the time of the bombing was 10:17 p.m. and that it was reported in a newsflash at 10:26 p.m. Twelve miles away, as an alibi witness claims, Paul Hill—the alleged getaway driver—was watching the newsflash.

"A Case That Won't Go Away" features interviews with Cardinal Hume and Lord Devlin, and their responses to Home Secretary Douglas Hurd's refusal to reassess the case. Cardinal Hume remarks that "common sense dictates that this case should be looked at again." Indeed, Hume led a delegation to see Hurd in July 1987, and was later singled out in parliamentary debate regarding the Guildford Four appeal in January 1989, with Lord Ferrers commenting that Hurd was "grateful to all those whose genuine concern for justice had led them to take an interest in this case."[38] Conlon notes in his biography that Hume had visited his father in prison: "when Cardinal Hume left he said to the screws, 'Make sure you treat these men well, because there may have been a miscarriage of justice.'"[39]

"A Case That Won't Go Away" blends new evidence and testimony—following an interview with Richardson on April 30, 1986, forensic psychiatrist, Dr. James MacKeith, and forensic psychologist, Professor Gisli Gudjonsson, stated that "the validity of the confessions must be seriously questioned"—with previous footage of the Guildford Four arrests and previous interviews, including one with Barry Irving who states, "Today the Guildford Four confessions would be inadmissible." Lord Devlin indicates that it was a "thin case" and highlighted a number of procedural errors, later acknowledged by the judicial inquiry final report.[40] In conclusion, when asked to summarize the justice afforded to the Four, Lord Devlin replies "none."

Guildford Four: Free to Speak

The final *First Tuesday* documentary revolves solely around the Guildford Four immediately after their release and aired on the fifteenth anniversary of the Woolwich bombing. It differs from the previous three programs, primarily in its observational style and lack of intervention but also in certain stylistic features, and captures the absolute rawness of their experiences, both through their verbal accounts and through facial expressions, emotional disposition, and vocal intonation. The immediacy is captured through static camerawork that unflinchingly frames their emotions. "Free to Speak" moves away from a purely factual and narrativized account of the bombings and subsequent convictions to the Four's experiences. The presenter briefly summarizes the Guildford Four case that culminated in their release in October 1989, recapping with photographs and footage from the previous documentaries, but with each of the Four framed in their respective domestic settings, the viewer therefore afforded a more personalized impression. For example, Conlon's home—which features a piano, a violin, and several stacks of papers—suggests a cultured background and an industrious nature, while good luck cards are visible in both Hill and Armstrong's homes, details that generate further empathy as does the strategy of moving back and forth between photographs of the Four before their imprisonment and the interview in the present. The use of before and after imagery shows how prison has traumatized them.

An early segment also features exterior shots of Richardson riding a horse. In voiceover, she states, "I went through prison wanting to do it. It's a dream and carried me through fifteen years," highlighting the freedom she yearned for. This contrasts with the language she uses to describe prison life but correlates with later commentary when she talks about "coming alive" after the sentence was quashed. The documentary here breaks even further with the visual style of the previous episodes, through rapid panning camera movements and long shots to frame Richardson riding through woods—conveying a sense of her freedom. The rural setting also departs distinctly from the urban footage featured in previous programs. There is no other commentary and no interviewer is audible, although the Four seem to be responding to prompts. The attention to experiences and emotions prevails throughout, with each of the Four struggling to come to terms with freedom. A pale-looking Armstrong, smiling and viewed in close-up, describes his first morning out of prison as being "very strange—I sat there for about half an hour waiting for the door to open." Hill talks about the hardships of prison and comments that "I'm trying to keep it in, but the dam will burst." Conlon says, "I'm scarred—I don't know if we're ever going to recover."

All four describe what they were like before the convictions, with frank accounts of their behavior—for instance, Conlon readily admits to petty theft and describes himself as a "drunken idiot." In talking about their arrests, all four express their naivety, and comment on the subsequent abuse that they suffered. Conlon tells how he was made to strip, was humiliated, and left in a cold cell with no clothes. Richardson describes the process as threatening: whilst in custody, she was informed that she could not have a solicitor and could be held for seven days. She states that she signed the confession to get away from the abuse. She also remarks that she did not expect to be convicted and appears repeatedly distraught at memories of the photographs of the bomb victims that she was shown. Throughout the film, she cries intermittently and at times is unable to speak. At other times, her dialogue is labored, and her eyes stare blankly, or she looks downward. The static camera does not cut away from these discomforting moments, so that the film fully reveals the trauma she suffered. Likewise, Armstrong refers to the arrest as a "very frightening experience" and subsequently comments that he "hates the police, courts and judge," and "can never forgive them." Conlon is perhaps the most animated, saying that "it actually went through my head that I'd done it." In police custody, he was threatened with his mother's safety: "They were capable of murdering my mother. I really believed that." Similarly, Paul Hill explains that he "was absolutely terrified."

"Free to Speak" then details the significance of the Guildford Four's release in relation to the Maguire Seven, whose case would now be reviewed by a new judicial enquiry. This section of the program reveals how prison life affected the Four, with Hill stating that he was moved fifty-one times and spent years in solitary confinement. In Manchester prison, his clothing was removed at 3:30 p.m. so that the rest of the day he was undressed. He also described the beatings he received: to survive these "you just go down and cover yourself." A common feature in their commentaries is the way that time passed, with nothing significant to mark it. For Hill, the passage of time was made apparent by the dramatic changes in his daughter; for Richardson, through the fact that she was unable to recognize her own mother. Time for Armstrong was marked by the fact that his mother could only afford to see him once a year. Richardson, in contrast to the vocabulary used to describe her release, describes prison time in fractured dialogue as "hell ... electronic doors, talking into boxes ... everyone seemed so severe, camera ... control room ... worse than a nightmare." She reveals that she was "permanently on medication—dulls it, makes you forget what else there is in life," and often refers to an inability to exercise any control. Sam Poyser explains that for victims of miscarriages of justice, such a sense of powerlessness is typical.[41] Armstrong too says that he "had a couple of breakdowns," while Conlon comments that "there were dark and despairing moments." At this point, the documentary cuts to a close-up of the photograph of Guiseppe Conlon that featured in the initial *First Tuesday* film: the overall effect is to convey Guiseppe's death in prison as one of his son Gerry's bleakest moments.

The release of the Guildford Four is an emotional moment, with Conlon recalling how he stipulated that he was "going out the front door," where he made his now famous declaration: "I've spent fifteen years in prison for something I haven't done, for something I knew nothing about. I watched my father die in prison for something he didn't do. He's innocent, the Maguires are innocent, the Birmingham Six are innocent. Let's hope they're next."[42] The strength of public feeling is clear in the footage of crowds cheering. The moment is mitigated, however, by the way that the Four find it difficult to adapt to life outside prison. Exterior shots that are filmed in slow motion frame Armstrong and Richardson together as they talk about "getting to know each other again." Hill remarks that "I just want to live. I've clung on by my fingertips and I'm on the brink of insanity, knowing if I let go, that's it, I'll fall into the abyss and be totally lost." Richardson asks "Where does it end? Who do you blame? But they knew before we left the police station that they were wrong and that I can never forgive them for. I've had to wait for fifteen years cos they just wouldn't say 'we were wrong.'" Conlon picks up this melancholic thread: "I feel very, very lonely at times ... I don't know what to do with myself," a point which becomes evident in his memoir *Proved Innocent*. He recounts how the television network had arranged a reception for them, but during the night Conlon suddenly felt "utterly lonely. I wanted to go to the window and call out to the next room for some contact. But this wasn't D wing at the Scrubs. It was the Holiday Inn, and I didn't even know the people in the next rooms. It had been my greatest fear ever since I knew I would be coming out. After fifteen years inside, would I be able to communicate with the outside?"[43]

The traumatizing effects of wrongful imprisonment on the Four that emerge in the documentary are substantiated by a 2004 study by Adrian Grounds who examined the psychological consequences of wrongful conviction and imprisonment. The study included one of the Guildford Four and four of the Birmingham Six. Grounds likens the difficulties encountered as similar to those experienced by war veterans and other groups of people who have suffered chronic psychological trauma.[44] Such difficulties include enduring personality change, post-traumatic stress and other psychiatric disorders, physical and psychological suffering, problems of adjustment, relationship difficulties, and a sense of lost time. Many of these difficulties were expressed by the Four in "Free to Speak," though Conlon was able to give his trauma a purpose: "If this stops capital punishment ever coming back, the time I've spent in prison will be well worth it, if this gets the Birmingham Six out, it'll be well worth it."

Since 1989, Conlon and Richardson have died, Conlon at the age of sixty and Richardson at the age of fifty-five. Hill married, but was later divorced. His daughter died of an accidental overdose. Armstrong has since married and lives in Dublin. For him, "what happened, happened, and it was awful, but I don't want to let it take over my life—and I won't let it."

Transformations

The documentaries leading to the release of the Guildford Four in 1989 were transformative for several reasons. Aside from the immediate result of the judicial inquiry, one of the most significant repercussions was a change to the laws on interrogation.[45] Forensic psychologist Barrie Irving, who featured in the documentaries, was instrumental in shaping the 1984 Police and Criminal Evidence Act, which involved the implementation of several Codes of Conduct relating to stop and search, arrest, detention, investigation, identification, and interviewing of detainees.[46] In particular, the Act required that suspects' interviews be tape-recorded and that suspects be informed of their right to free legal advice before interrogation. It also "introduced the role of 'appropriate adult': a person, independent of the police, to act as an additional safeguard in interviews with vulnerable suspects."[47]

Furthermore, the law on referring cases to the Appeal Court was changed with the establishment of the Runciman Royal Commission that led to the Criminal Appeal Act of 1995, and the creation of the Criminal Cases Review Commission. Members of the Royal Commission read the judicial inquiry on the Maguire case, and "a number of points of concern arising from the Guildford and Woolwich cases" were considered before the Commission completed its report in June 1993.[48] As Michael Naughton notes:

> In resolving the public crisis in confidence in the cases of the Guildford Four, Birmingham Six, and so on, one of the most significant amendments spawned by the Royal Commission on Criminal Justice was the Criminal Appeal Act (1995), which took away the power of referral from the Home Secretary, and established the Criminal Cases Review Commission, an independent public body with the task of investigating alleged or suspected miscarriages of justice that have already been through the appeals system and have not succeeded.[49]

Likewise, changes to the law on "disclosure" of documents resulted from the Guildford Four, Maguire Seven, and Birmingham Six cases.[50] Indeed, when it was revealed that detectives in the Surrey police force had fabricated statements and suppressed significant evidence, the quashing of the Guildford Four case directly led to a review of the Maguire Seven case, which was similarly overturned. Details of the Birmingham Six case unveiled concerns about the West Midlands Serious Crime Squad and "an investigation into the conduct of the police resulted in the disbandment of the Squad in 1989."[51] Gerry Conlon's release in 1989, a highly emotional scene that was captured in the "Free to Speak" documentary, was revisited in Jim Sheridan's film *In the Name of the Father* (1993). Conlon himself wrote a book about the experiences of the Guildford Four and their attempts at appeal, as did Robert Kee in *Trial and Error: The Maguires, The Guildford Pub Bombings and British Justice* (1989). These publications, the *First Tuesday* documentaries and the evidence that they provided, and Sheridan's semi-fictionalized film, featured prominently in the judicial inquiry and its final report.[52] As Abraham Miller makes clear, "the Guildford episode is about coerced and drug-induced confessions, suppressed and fabricated evidence, and of a society under siege rushing to judgement. But it is also a story about the media—of responsible electronic media that refused to let the case die and exposed judicial inconsistencies to public scrutiny."[53] In 1989, popular calls for justice were heard around the world. These calls resonated in the UK, where the creativity and political commitment of *First Tuesday*'s producers shook the foundations of trust in an unjust judicial system.

Notes

1. Margarita López Maya, "The Venezuelan 'Caracazo' of 1989: Popular Protest and Institutional Weakness," *Journal of Latin American Studies* 35, no. 1 (February 2003): 117–37; George Ciccariello-Maher, *We Created Chávez: A People's History of the Venezuelan Revolution* (Durham: Duke University Press, 2013), especially 13–15.
2. *Final Document: 9th Summit Conference of Heads of State or Government of the Non-Aligned Movement—Belgrade* (New York: UN Security Council, 1989), 11; Kripa Sridharan, "G-15 and South: South Cooperation: Promise and Performance," *Third World Quarterly* 19, no. 3 (September 1998): 357–73.
3. Vijay Prashad, *The Poorer Nations: A Possible History of the Global South* (New York: Verso, 2012), 143–5.
4. Allan R. Gold, "Thousands March on Washington in Protest against Homelessness," *New York Times*, October 8, 1989. Available online: http://www.nytimes.com/1989/10/08/us/thousands-march-on-washington-in-protest-against-homelessness.html. Emily McNeill, *The National Union of the Homeless: A Brief History* (Washington: Poverty Initiative, 2011), 10.
5. Linda Greenhouse, "Battle Over; Now, a War," *New York Times*, July 5, 1989. Available online: http://www.nytimes.com/1989/07/05/us/battle-over-now-a-war.html; Ruth Rosen, *The World Split Open: How the Modern Women's Movement Changed America* (New York: Penguin, 2000), 337–8.
6. John May, *Final Report of the Inquiry into the Convictions Arising from the Bomb Attacks in Guildford and Woolwich in 1974* (London: HMSO, 1994), 15.
7. Ibid., 173.
8. Ibid., 2.
9. McKee, the key investigative journalist and co-producer for these *First Tuesday* programs, collaborated with Chris Mullin on Channel Four's *World in Action*, which included an account of the Birmingham Six convictions.
10. For example, in relation to the BBC, the Catholic Church, and a number of British and US police forces. The most recent illustrations include the murders of George Floyd in the United States and Sarah Everard in the UK by serving police officers.
11. Abraham Miller, "Preserving Liberty in a Society under Siege: The Media and the 'Guildford Four,'" *Terrorism and Political Violence* 2, no. 3 (1990): 305–23.
12. "Public House Bombings (Guildford and Woolwich)," *UK Parliament Hansard*, October 19, 1989. Available online: https://hansard.parliament.uk/Commons/1989-10-19/debates/45293b1a-ab80-425d-b967-ccd1bf98cd52/PublicHouseBombings (GuildfordAndWoolwich)?highlight=guildford%20four#main-content (accessed October 18, 2021).
13. Miller, "Preserving Liberty in a Society under Siege," 308.

14 Paul Dixon and Eamonn McKane, *Northern Ireland since 1969* (London and New York: Routledge, 2011), 45.
15 Bill Nichols, *Representing Reality* (Bloomington: Indiana University Press, 1991).
16 Ibid., 35.
17 Ibid., 38.
18 Gerry Conlon, *Proved Innocent: The Story of Gerry Conlon of the Guildford Four* (London: Penguin, 1990), 206.
19 Robert Kee, *Trial and Error: The Maguires, the Guildford Pub Bombings and British Justice* (London: Hamish Hamilton, 1987).
20 May, *Final Report*, 8.
21 Ibid., 254.
22 Ibid., 254.
23 Ibid., 258.
24 Nichols, *Representing Reality*, 35.
25 On February 4, 1974, a bomb allegedly planted by the IRA detonated on a coach carrying off-duty British soldiers, killing twelve people.
26 Grant McKee and Ros Franey, *Time Bomb: Irish Bombers, English Justice and the Guildford Four* (London: Bloomsbury, 1988), 440.
27 "The 'Guildford Four' Appeal," *UK Parliament Hansard,* January 16, 1989. May, *Final Report*, 113–24.
28 May, *Final Report*, 96–112.
29 May, *Final Report*, 282.
30 Barrie Irving, *Royal Commission on Criminal Procedure: Police Interrogation* (London: HMSO, 1980).
31 May, *Final Report*, 37.
32 Ibid., 228.
33 Ibid., 4.
34 Conlon, *Proved Innocent*, 166.
35 Michael Naughton, *Rethinking Miscarriages of Justice: Beyond the Tip of the Iceberg* (London and New York: Palgrave, 2007), 33.
36 Conlon, *Proved Innocent*, 215.
37 Ibid., 213.
38 "The 'Guildford Four' Appeal."
39 Conlon, *Proved Innocent*, 186.
40 May, *Final Report*, 282.
41 Sam Poyser, Angus Nurse, and Rebecca Milne, *Miscarriages of Justice: Causes, Consequences and Remedies* (Bristol: Polity Press, 2018), 71.
42 Conlon, *Proved Innocent*, 4.
43 Ibid., 231.

44 Adrian Grounds, "Psychological Consequences of Wrongful Conviction and Imprisonment," *Canadian Journal of Criminology and Criminal Justice* 46, no. 2 (2004): 165, 178.
45 Andrea Shawyer, Becky Milne, and Ray Bull, "Investigative Interviewing in the UK," in *International Developments in Investigative Interviewing*, ed. Tom Williamson, Becky Milne, and Stephen Savage (London and New York: Routledge, 2012), 24.
46 See https://www.gov.uk/guidance/police-and-criminal-evidence-act-1984-pace-codes-of-practice#pace-codes-of-p (accessed October 18, 2021).
47 Poyser et al., *Miscarriages of Justice*, 22.
48 May, *Final Report*, 8.
49 Naughton, *Rethinking Miscarriages of Justice*, 2.
50 "The Guildford Four: May Report," *UK Parliament Hansard*, June 30, 1994. Available online: https://hansard.parliament.uk/Lords/1994-06-30/debates/b96f8eff-e126-4308-be17-56fd566631b5/TheGuildfordFourMayReport?highlight=guildford%20four#contribution-60bdc6a0-aaba-4264-a028-301a735f4619 (accessed October 18, 2021).
51 Clive Walker, "Miscarriages of Justice in Principle and Practice," in *Miscarriages of Justice: A Review of Justice in Error*, ed. Clive Walker and Keir Starmer (Oxford: Oxford University Press, 1999), 50.
52 May, *Final Report*, 12.
53 Miller, "Preserving Liberty in a Society under Siege," 307.

8

George H. W. Bush's Panama War Speech: Realist Policy as "Just Cause"

Wassim Daghrir

In December 1989, the United States, under the presidency of George H. W. Bush, invaded Panama. Codenamed "Operation Just Cause," the invasion was a pivotal event in the United States inter-American relationship. Indeed, it marked the start of a new chapter in the US approach to foreign affairs in what would soon be called the post-Cold War era. Accordingly, it is important to look into the rhetorical justifications used by the Bush administration to gain public support for the first military intervention abroad unrelated to the "immanent" threat of Communism and the USSR. In this regard, this chapter sets out to explore Bush's use of propaganda devices and persuasion in his speech justifying the invasion of Panama to the American public. After providing some background for Just Cause, this chapter will use critical discourse analysis (CDA) to offer a close reading of the text of Bush's speech and reveal its propagandist qualities.

The strategic use of language in foreign policy discourse can be highly productive in creating political myths that are mainly meant to manipulate the public and rally them around a particular understanding of social reality. In this regard, political leaders often turn to certain linguistic tropes that help them persuade audiences and harness support for certain foreign policy agendas. Propaganda represents one of the most efficient linguistic strategies to exert considerable political effects. In an attempt to define propaganda and emphasize its efficiency in shaping people's perceptions of political issues, Jowett and O'Donnell maintain that "propaganda ... attempts to achieve a response that furthers the desired intent of the propagandist" as well as changes public opinion.[1] In the American context, Chuck Hagel asserts that propaganda represents one of the pillars of American foreign policy discourse, given its intricate and flexible nature. He argues that America's foreign policy requires "a strategic agility that, whenever possible, gets ahead of problems, strengthens US security and alliances, and promotes American interests and credibility."[2] While perhaps more readily recognizable in examples from the Communist world of 1989—not least in attempts by the People's Republic of China and German Democratic Republic to depict dissent as entirely in the service of Western imperialism—propaganda is a useful and appropriate way to make sense of US foreign policy pronouncements and the ideological work they perform.

To analyze examples of propaganda such as Bush's Panama speech, it is necessary to look at the rhetoric and language through which foreign policy agendas are expressed. Politics, after all, is largely the use of language, and presidential speech is the government speaking.

In fact, the power of the presidency depends on its ability to persuade. The application of power is often legitimized through rhetorical persuasion; and, in the case of American presidents, such power, and its associated rhetoric, becomes the fulcrum upon which many global issues turn. Bush's 1989 speech sought to legitimize the American intervention in Panama to topple the Noriega government. The US 1989 invasion of Panama was a symbolic event: it was the first American use of force since 1945 not directly related to the Cold War. The invasion occurred at a time when the world's geopolitical structure was changing and when the ideological and strategic grounds behind previous US interventions were evaporating. In this way, the US invasion of Panama opened a new post-Cold War era of inter-American relations. Why, then, in the absence of Cold War considerations did the United States deem it necessary to rely on a large-scale military intervention? To address this question, I will deal in detail with the official explanations issued by the Bush administration to justify its December 1989 invasion of Panama.

Panama's leader, Manuel Noriega, enjoyed a close relationship with the US government while he assisted the Reagan administration's anti-Sandinista campaign in Nicaragua.[3] Relations between the United States and Panama began to deteriorate, however, after Noriega refused to allow Panama to be used as a staging ground for a US attack on Nicaragua.[4] Consequently, the Reagan government shifted to an anti-Noriega agenda, and President Bush inherited the Reagan administration's hostility toward Panama. Bush, who as a CIA director had valued, employed, and strengthened Noriega, was faced with a dictator operating in open defiance of the United States. The Bush White House tried various overt as well as covert tactics to force Noriega out of power. Before Panama's May 1989 elections, Bush authorized the CIA to spend about $10 million to influence the results.⁵ When Noriega voided those results, Bush publicly encouraged members of the Panamanian Defense Forces (PDF) to rebel against their leader: "We share the Panamanian people's hope that the PDF will stand with them and fulfill their constitutional obligation to defend democracy," Bush declared.⁶ Bush sought to reassure the PDF that the US objection was to Noriega, not to the military, saying: "A professional PDF can have an important role to play in Panama's democratic future."⁷ Encouraged by the Bush administration, elements of the PDF attempted a military coup on October 3, 1989. They expected US military support, which never arrived, and the coup failed. The Bush administration's failure to support to the plotters brought severe criticism of the president for his inaction. Bush, whose "manhood" had been questioned in the past, was particularly anxious to overcome the "wimp factor" that weakened his image in clearly gendered terms. In a long tradition of presidential policy in relation to Latin America that ran back through John Kennedy to Theodore Roosevelt, Bush wanted to appear suitably manly in his response to Noriega.⁸ Geopolitical calculations influenced Bush's thinking and rhetoric. So did gender politics.

The growing hostilities between Panama and the United States led to a series of provocative acts between the PDF and American troops stationed in Panama. Following rumors of a pending US intervention, the Panamanian National Assembly passed a resolution naming Noriega "chief of the government." The resolution also stated that "the Republic of Panama is declared to be in a state of war while the [US] aggression lasts."⁹ A number of incidents followed, resulting in the death of one US Marine, the beating of a US serviceman, and the sexual assault of the serviceman's wife. Using these incidents as pretext, Bush decided to intervene militarily in Panama. After Reagan and Bush's policies of economic sanctions, political pressure, blackmail, and covert interference had failed to drive out Noriega, Bush launched "Operation Just Cause." On December 20, 1989, just weeks after the opening of the Berlin Wall, 24,000 US troops landed in Panama, battled the PDF, and, within three days, controlled the country. About 1,000 Panamanians and 21 US soldiers were killed in the invasion. Guillermo Endara, who had reportedly won the May 1989 elections, was sworn in as president in a US base on the day of the invasion. Noriega was arrested, sent to the United States, and put on trial for drug trafficking.

Noriega had been a close ally of the US government. He was trained as an army intelligence officer by the CIA and remained close to the agency for many years. Despite his involvement with drug trafficking, money laundering, and various other misdeeds, Noriega was long regarded by the US government as a precious asset: "When he committed crimes and abused his power, Washington looked the other way."¹⁰ In 1979, for instance, senior officials in the Carter administration blocked federal prosecutors from bringing drug trafficking and arms smuggling indictments against Noriega because they preferred to continue receiving the intelligence he provided.¹¹ In mid-1986, when the press in the United States uncovered Noriega's involvement in the narcotics trade as well as his CIA connections, the Reagan administration made no change in its Panamanian policy, considering Noriega's utility.¹² Most probably, the United States needed his involvement in narcotics to fund various Central American covert ventures of the 1980s. After Noriega met Vice-President Bush in December 1983, he told his top aides that he had picked up the following message from the meeting: the US government wanted help for the Contras so badly that it would turn a blind eye to money laundering and setbacks to democracy in Panama.¹³ Noriega had been a close US ally for more than three decades. What happened?

Relations between the United States and Panama began to deteriorate after Noriega reportedly refused to cooperate further in Washington's anti-Sandinista plans or to allow Panama to be used as a staging ground for a possible US attack on Nicaragua.¹⁴ Support for Noriega in Washington was also undermined by developments within Panama. The Reagan administration began, in fact, to move away from its close relationship with Noriega in mid-1987, in response to Panama's political troubles and chaotic social situation. After pro-Noriega demonstrators in Panama stoned the US embassy, the US government began to criticize Noriega openly and suspended economic and military aid.¹⁵ The debate intensified within the administration over the most appropriate policy to adopt. On the one hand, the State Department argued that Noriega was a danger to Panama and a liability to the United States and that Washington must pressure him to step down. The CIA and the Defense Department, on the other hand, were reluctant to abandon an ally who had been useful for so long.¹⁶ The Reagan administration was compelled to confront the problem that Noriega had become after Panamanians rejected him in the elections, after the Iran-Contra revelations, and especially after US courts indicted him on drug trafficking charges, the February 1988 indictments making front-page news in the United States. Consequently, the Reagan administration shifted to a vigorous anti-Noriega policy. In an election year, in which the drug problem had become a significant campaign issue, "the US government could not afford to be seen coddling a drug lord after its own courts called for his prosecution."¹⁷ Actually, the new US position toward Noriega used narcotics as a pretext, and its deeper causes were both large scale, in terms of reorienting the US posture after the Cold War, and very specific, in terms of overcoming the Iran-Contra debacle.

The administration launched an aggressive public campaign against Noriega, the White House pressured Noriega to resign, and the government used economic sanctions and military intimidation tactics to force him out. In March 1988, the US government offered to drop the drug indictments if Noriega retired. Noriega rejected the deal and denounced the Reagan administration.[18] This played a critical role in the path toward "Operation Just Cause."

The Panama invasion signaled a new US posture toward the world in the aftermath of the Cold War. With the Cold War order in crisis and a new global order emergent, the US government found new arguments in favor of its December 1989 invasion of Panama. Like any other military action, "Operation Just Cause" was backed by a well-orchestrated public relations campaign meant to gain the support of the US Congress, press, and public and, therefore, to generate a national consensus over the administration's most crucial decisions. The Bush administration advanced four main grounds to justify the US military action as just and legal: (1) to protect American citizens; (2) to restore democracy in Panama; (3) to stop drug trafficking and to arrest Noriega, who had been indicted in the United States for drug trafficking; and (4) to protect the integrity of US rights under the Panama Canal Treaty. All these arguments deserve a close analysis.

Obviously, Bush's December 20, 1989, speech was used to "sell" the invasion of Panama to the American public. Based on a CDA analysis, this article highlights the propagandist nature of George H. W. Bush's "Operation Just Cause" speech.[19] It is salient to note that discourse is neither a neutral nor an innocent practice of language. To define discourse, one would undoubtedly get lost in the concept's various interdisciplinary uses and interpretations. The renowned scholar of text linguistics and discourse analysis, Teun Adrianus Van Dijk, perceives discourse as a "text in context."[20] This definition of discourse is relevant to this chapter's particular scope of focus: discourse transcends mere textual structures to reveal a "whole process of social interaction."[21]

Critical discourse analysis aims to study discourse as a social practice. CDA considers social context in its examination of a text. It studies the connections between textual and social structures, and interprets the interactions between the two. In political science, CDA is employed to explore power relations, for example, those exercised by the political leadership in order to govern the public through speeches or gatherings. Espousing a CDA approach to discourse perceives power as an instrument of control. In this regard, propagandists gain control over their audiences by means of communication, as we can see by identifying the discursive strategies Bush used to legitimize American intervention in Panama. Building on Norman Fairclough's *Analyzing Discourse: Textual Analysis for Social Research*, this chapter considers genre, conjunctions and clauses, knowledge representation, polarization, euphemism, and myth in Bush's speech.[22]

Genre

On the morning of the invasion, President Bush issued the following words:

> My fellow citizens, last night I ordered US military forces to Panama. No president takes such action lightly. This morning I want to tell you what I did and why I did it.
>
> For nearly two years, the United States, nations of Latin America and the Caribbean have worked together to resolve the crisis in Panama. The goals of the United States have been to safeguard the lives of Americans, to defend democracy in Panama, to combat drug trafficking, and to protect the integrity of the Panama Canal treaty. Many attempts have been made to resolve this crisis through diplomacy and negotiations. All were rejected by the dictator of Panama, General Manuel Noriega, an indicted drug trafficker.
>
> Last Friday, Noriega declared his military dictatorship to be in a state of war with the United States and publicly threatened the lives of Americans in Panama. The very next day, forces under his command shot and killed an unarmed American serviceman; wounded another; arrested and brutally beat a third American serviceman; and then brutally interrogated his wife, threatening her with sexual abuse. That was enough.
>
> General Noriega's reckless threats and attacks upon Americans in Panama created an imminent danger to the 35,000 American citizens in Panama. As president, I have no higher obligation than to safeguard the lives of American citizens. And that is why I directed our Armed Forces to protect the lives of American citizens in Panama and to bring General Noriega to justice in the United States. I contacted the bipartisan leadership of Congress last night and informed them of this decision, and after taking this action, I also talked with leaders in Latin America, the Caribbean, and those of other US allies.
>
> At this moment, US forces, including forces deployed from the United States last night, are engaged in action in Panama. The United States intends to withdraw the forces newly deployed to Panama as quickly as possible. Our forces have conducted themselves courageously and selflessly. And as Commander in Chief, I salute every one of them and thank them on behalf of our country.

Tragically, some Americans have lost their lives in defense of their fellow citizens, in defense of democracy. And my heart goes out to their families. We also regret and mourn the loss of innocent Panamanians.

The brave Panamanians elected by the people of Panama in the elections last May, President Guillermo Endara and Vice Presidents Calderon and Ford, have assumed the rightful leadership of their country. You remember those horrible pictures of newly elected Vice President Ford, covered head to toe with blood, beaten mercilessly by so-called 'dignity battalions.' Well, the United States today recognizes the democratically elected government of President Endara. I will send our ambassador back to Panama immediately.

Key military objectives have been achieved. Most organized resistance has been eliminated, but the operation is not over yet: General Noriega is in hiding. And nevertheless, yesterday a dictator ruled Panama, and today constitutionally elected leaders govern.

I have today directed the Secretary of the Treasury and the Secretary of State to lift the economic sanctions with respect to the democratically elected government of Panama and, in cooperation with that government, to take steps to effect an orderly unblocking of Panamanian government assets in the United States. I'm fully committed to implement the Panama Canal treaties and turn over the Canal to Panama in the year 2000. The actions we have taken and the cooperation of a new, democratic government in Panama will permit us to honor these commitments. As soon as the new government recommends a qualified candidate—Panamanian—to be administrator of the Canal, as called for in the treaties, I will submit this nominee to the Senate for expedited consideration.

I am committed to strengthening our relationship with the democratic nations in this hemisphere. I will continue to seek solutions to the problems of this region through dialog and multilateral diplomacy. I took this action only after reaching the conclusion that every other avenue was closed and the lives of American citizens were in grave danger. I hope that the people of Panama will put this dark chapter of dictatorship behind them and move forward together as citizens of a democratic Panama with this government that they themselves have elected.

The United States is eager to work with the Panamanian people in partnership and friendship to rebuild their economy. The Panamanian people want democracy, peace, and the chance for a better life in dignity and freedom. The people of the United States seek only to support them in pursuit of these noble goals. Thank you very much.[23]

Bush's speech offers a case study of highly ritualized political discourse that strategically legitimizes American intervention in Panama. This discourse is a two-way non-mediated speech in which President Bush is assigned an almost patronizing authority over the American people. This form of communication is emphasized by Fairclough, who underscores that communication between organizations and the public is acutely hierarchical given its influence and power over individuals.[24] Accordingly, Bush's authoritative position can be detected through his use of authority-connotative titles like "President" and "Commander in Chief" and his constant repetition of the first personal pronoun, which is used seventeen times in the speech. This strategy not only confirms the President's higher status but also shows his personal involvement and readiness to take action whenever US national security is allegedly threatened.[25]

Such discursive features exemplify Aristotle's three methods of persuasion, particularly his use of ethos which allows the speaker to position himself as an expert, a leader compelled to act on behalf of his people. Aristotle's persuasion model is reinforced by CDA-oriented legitimating strategies that demonstrate the importance of certain discursive practices and their role in rendering policy proposals understandable, ethical, and even cherished. The most frequent legitimating strategies that Bush adopts are position-based authorization and knowledge-based authorization which unveil the hidden ideological motifs behind the use of expressions like "Commander in Chief" and "President." Bush's speech carries the implication that his recommended course of action is best. No further reasons need to be provided because the president recommends this action to preserve American national security.[26] Consequently, such tropes can be highly effective in rationalizing Bush's policies and most importantly in anchoring in his audience's cognitive process a desire for protection against foreign foes.

What this implies is that, through his speech, President Bush creates a sense of emergency that necessitates immediate action in order to protect American national interest and save American people from foreign aggression. In so doing, Bush establishes national security as a leitmotif in legitimizing foreign policy decisions and harnessing public support. These legitimating strategies are enhanced by the elaborative sentences that Bush opts for throughout his speech.

Conjunctions and Clauses

Language relations often provide discursive information about social actors and their actions such as their distance and proximity. As such, clauses and conjunctions play an important role in Bush's discourse. In this analysis I have chosen three examples of conjunctions that highlight the propagandist aspect of Bush's speech:

Elaborative Clauses

In discourse analysis, elaborative clauses are considered for their role in adding to or explaining previous information. In the text presently under analysis, there are two cases in which elaborative clauses are deployed to serve as a justification of the US government's actions. Through his assertion that "no president takes action lightly," Bush seeks mainly to align himself with all world leaders and therefore to spark the impression that his decision is the only choice to be pursued. This is evidence of Van Leeuwen's legitimating forms, particularly the authority of conformity which creates the impression that decision-makers opt for certain actions "because that's what everybody else does, or because that's what most people do." The implied message is that "everybody else is doing it, and so should you, or most people are doing it, and so should you."[27] In the context of Bush's speech, this reasoning renders US military intervention a socially accepted convention that all world leaders would readily follow had they been in a similar situation.

The second elaborative clause used in the speech is "that's enough." Indeed, the use of the adjective "enough" alludes to the gravity of General Noriega's crimes, which necessitate an immediate military action. Additionally, the highly subjective tone of the clause underscores the impression that President Bush is both compassionate and willing to defend the American nation from any threat. This discursive practice draws heavily on Aristotle's emphasis of the use of pathos as a tool to appeal to the listeners' emotions and galvanize them.

The Conjunction "and"

The prominence of the additive conjunction "and" serves a strategic political purpose. Throughout the text, Bush uses the conjunction "and" or "also" whenever he mentions US allies. In this vein, he underscores that "the United States, nations of Latin America and the Caribbean have worked together to resolve the crisis in Panama." In fact, the use of such coordinating conjunctions emphasizes the equivalence of the two subjects and most importantly unveils their shared traits and objectives. It reveals that Bush's perception of American foreign policy is bent on global cooperation and collective action. Echoes of such arguments are found in Fairclough's assertion that the use of subject positions can be highly productive in fixing meaning and therefore in homogenizing social actors.[28] The effects of such conjunctions are even more reinforced with the use of elaborative clauses which play a paramount role in leveraging the audience and prompting them to adopt Bush's political stance. Causal clauses operate in a similar vein, as they are often used to justify foreign policy agendas and make foreign policy decisions as rational as possible.

Causal Clause

To justify US operations in Panama, Bush provides multiple causes. The declared causes are the following: safeguarding the lives of Americans, defending democracy, combating drug trafficking, and protecting the integrity of the Panama Canal Treaty. The use of such justifications invokes the enduring legacy of the missionary strand of American exceptionalism, which assigns to the United States the role of the moral crusader. The belief in American exceptionalism provides an essential element of the cultural and intellectual framework for the making and conduct of US foreign policy. It has always had a powerful presence in American discourse. Every president has invoked the theme of a unique America in some way or another. Consequently, a recurring theme is that foreign policy choices are made for moral reasons. At a minimum, exceptionalism assumes that the United States is morally and culturally equipped to offer an example to the world. More proactive interpretations of exceptionalism support the promotion of American values abroad through the use of various aspects of US power and influence.

Van Leeuwen refers to this legitimating discursive practice as moral evaluation.[29] In this vein, he cites Berger and Luckmann's assertion that "legitimation provides the 'explanations' and justifications of the salient elements of the institutional tradition. It 'explains' the institutional order by ascribing cognitive validity to its objectivated meanings and justifies the institutional order by giving a normative dignity to its practical imperatives."[30] Legitimating practices, particularly moral evaluation, cannot be held in isolation from the moral values that characterize different nations. Such values do not need justification, as they can be easily anchored in the popular imagination. As Leeuwen notes, such values are often presented in very simple and subtle ways by using adjectives like "good" and "bad," or "moral" and "immoral." When combined with legitimating authority, these discourses of moral values become even more credible and powerful, as they help naturalize the power of political leaders and therefore generate mass loyalty.

Bush's endeavor to anchor such moral values within the national popular imagination, and to vindicate America's full commitment to promoting freedom and democracy, is illustrated in his assertion that "the Panamanian people want democracy, peace, and the chance for a better life in dignity and freedom" and that "the people of the United States seek only to support them in pursuit of these noble goals." This moral zeal that characterized post-Cold War American foreign policy sought to create a suitable international environment in which the United States could flourish and bolster its interests with little or no resistance. In an attempt to critically analyze post-Cold War foreign policymaking, Christopher Layne maintains that nearly all post-Cold War administrations subscribed to the Wilsonian school of thought, which entails that "democracies are stable, pacific, and never fight each other." Therefore, "seen from this perspective, spreading democracy is not a policy based on woolly-headed idealism but rather is a hard-headed strategy that aims at enhancing US security."[31] This idea is in harmony with the third reason that propelled the US intervention in Panama, which was the protection of the Panama Canal Treaty. Indeed, under Article IV of the Canal Treaties, the United States is given the right and the power to safeguard the canal. This justification remains highly controversial, however, since Noriega did not violate nor openly threaten the security of the canal or the treaties.

Drug-trafficking is another important argument deployed in the "Operation Just Cause" speech. In fact, this argument draws heavily on Reagan's War on Drugs agenda in the late 1980s, which set the stage for a "zero-tolerance" policy. The reference to Noriega's drug trafficking targeted and heightened anxieties in relation to drugs. Manufacturing hysteria has been considered one of American propaganda's indispensable strategies: it is a common practice for US politicians to endeavor to "scare the hell" out of the American people to advance their goals.[32] The Noriega drug scandal was classified under the effects doctrine, which legitimizes taking legal measures beyond the US borders in case the crime has a negative impact on American citizens.[33] Subsequently, drug trafficking became another argument that served to legitimate American intervention in Panama, given that Noriega's government was depicted as directly threatening the US population.

Knowledge Representation

Representation plays an important role in political discourse since it deals with the way knowledge is communicated. Halliday describes language as the "interlocking options or network of systems for creating meaning."[34] Indeed, when analyzing Bush's discourse in the "Operation Just Cause" speech, we notice that knowledge is presented in the form of declarative sentences. The grammatical structure of theses sentences is basic: they all follow a subject-verb-object format. Declarative sentences usually state facts and let the audience know something specific. In this case, President Bush is the knowledge-initiating actor who reports US achievements in Panama to American listeners. The prevalence of declarative statements in Bush's discourse suggests, however, a knowledge deficiency on the part of his audience. This gap gives Bush the upper hand since he claims the sole source of information, a power device he uses to sell the invasion of Panama to a reluctant and tired post-Cold War public opinion.

Time and space representation also play an important role in shaping political propaganda discourses. According to Fairclough, "space, time, and 'space-times' are routinely constructed in texts," greatly affecting how social events are constructed.[35] Bush's discourse oscillates between the past and future tenses. The past tense is used when referring to the American operation in Panama or to the Noriega dictatorship. Since the action was already executed by one actor—the US forces—the American people are dismissed from the social action and are therefore subjected to and influenced by the propaganda discourse of the state given its ideological power privilege. On the other hand, although he does not give clear ideas or strategies that the United States would pursue after toppling the Noriega administration, the use of the future tense can be a highly effective way of carving out the image of a peaceful and democratic nation. As such, the use of "prediction" in this context may serve as a legitimizing strategy to justify the US authorities' intervention. In both contexts, temporality reinforces the power of the American agenda to frame the discourse according to its interests.

Additionally, the importance of space representation cannot be ignored, as it contributes to the division of the international arena into distinct places. In fact, this division is mainly meant to create two major contrasting spaces: an authoritarian external space and a democratic internal one. However, it is important to note that Bush does not bluntly create this distinction. Rather, it is subtly maintained throughout the whole speech. Moreover, this distinction is primarily imagined: state borders appear fluid and therefore the realm of secure spaces can be easily widened through the creation of like-minded governments that subscribe to the American worldview. External spaces are only those that do not conform to the American model. Hence, the overall implication of this division is that alternatives to the American way would not lead to the establishment of a harmonious and secure international system, but they would rather create a chaotic and threatening system that would endanger the safety of

Americans and the world. This Manichean understanding of the international landscape is evident in the discourse of polarization, which carves out set boundaries that differentiate in-groups and out-groups.

Polarization

At the heart of American presidential discourse exists a coherent worldview, one that presidents have applied with remarkable consistency and uncompromising conviction. This view holds that the global arena can be understood as a conflict between the forces of Good and Evil, and that America is called upon to defend the former from the latter. This premise requires the identification of Evil—an enemy that, by its nature, cannot be engaged, negotiated with, understood, managed, contained, or ignored. It can only be hated, attacked, and destroyed. One way of achieving this is by using legitimizing language that will positively represent the favored worldview or the approved approach to global phenomena, as well as those who support this view or approach. Legitimizing language is usually accompanied by its counterpart, delegitimizing language, which negatively depicts the opposing worldview as well as those who hold these different opinions and values. Such binary conceptualizations frequently take on the form of a polarization between a legitimized insider group ("us") and a delegitimized outsider group ("them").[36]

In discourse analysis, polarization implies a group's opposition and sense of superiority to another group. According to Brewer, individuals are usually connected by certain common features, principles, or set of goals.[37] Rejection is triggered when one group's interest is threatened by other groups or individuals. In this regard, Bush's speech illustrates this in-group, out-group division, which is deliberately used to delineate certain social actors in the popular national imagination. This Manichean discourse is further reinforced with the use of a legitimizing language that extols American values and way of life, and a delegitimizing language that denigrates the opposing worldview and those who share it. Indeed, all negative attributes, such as violence, or sexual and physical abuse, are associated with and ascribed to the Noriega regime. On the other hand, Americans are portrayed as innocent victims of the Panamanian dictator's brutality. This ideologically motivated representation of the "other" is a major source of bias and division, and therefore makes an effective political tool in propaganda speeches. The use of such strategies can be perceived as part of a framing war, implying an "us versus them" dichotomy that portrays the global arena as a battle between the forces of good and evil, giving such dualism a moral function: to offer a sense of moral certitude, which leaves no room for doubt or regret. In fact, discourses rooted in "good" and "evil" legitimate any action undertaken in the name of good, no matter how destructive, on the grounds that it is attacking evil, leaving no room for different interpretations. This positions the United States as the bastion of goodness and defender of righteousness in the world. Such dramatic binary opposition seems likely to facilitate the assuaging of guilt associated with war.

Bush's speech not only seeks to legitimize US military intervention in Panama, however, but to create a sense of solidarity by citing violence against individual Americans, including the suggestion of sexual violence against a civilian woman. Bush's allusion to American victims of Noriega's regime aims to deepen his audience's hostility toward the Noriega administration and therefore prompt Americans to endorse their government's decision.

What makes this type of communication so important is its capacity to create a false dilemma. In fact, binary constructions present a limited view of the world and, often, force a decision between two options that, in actuality, are not the only outcomes available. A "good versus evil" battle is much more likely to gain the attention and approval of the American public, since it reduces a potentially complex scenario to an easily accessible question of morality and identity. When Americans expect their interventions to be grand heroic crusades on a worldwide scale, the fate of the world in a struggle between Light and Darkness hangs on the outcome. President Bush's Panama speech was strategically framed to meet such a worldview.

Euphemism

Euphemism, in the words of Eliecer Crespo-Fernández, is "a discursive strategy that politicians use to approach unsettling, embarrassing, distasteful, [or] taboo topics without appearing inconsiderate to people's concerns."[38] Given that political language is "purpose-oriented," politicians are often careful when addressing issues that can be sensitive, unpleasant, or discomfiting. Although the reception of the US military operation was generally positive in both America and Panama, certain voices expressed concern about the consequence of the war. To alleviate these anxieties, Bush opts for discursive tactics which aimed to mitigate the human cost of the war. He emphasizes the achievements of American soldiers during the operation by offering a review of the US forces' accomplishments in Panama, and their role in securing democracy and peace in the country. This is achieved through the use of adverbs such as "selflessly" and "courageously," which depict the US forces as defenders of liberty and democracy and as bulwarks against corruption and dictatorship. The glorification of the American soldiers' achievements creates a sense of pride and patriotism which emotionally prepares the audience for the negative news. Indeed, Bush only briefly mentions American and Panamanian causalities to avoid negative or violent reaction: he refers to death only once. To justify the loss of life, Bush magnifies the sacrifices of the victims by linking them to greater purposes such as America's moral principles and patriotic duty.

Myth

Narratives and moral tales are of paramount importance in generating social and cognitive obedience and therefore in legitimizing certain decisions. In this regard, Van Leeuwen asserts that "in moral tales, protagonists are rewarded for engaging in legitimate social practices or restoring the legitimate order."[39] The efficiency of these discursive practices lies in their emphasis on a ready-made repertoire of images which is often used to create a particular understanding of reality. Moral tales—along with the collective symbolism they draw upon—can lead to the normalization and even the institutionalization of certain actions that are sometimes illegitimate.

A case in point is the speech under consideration here, which relies heavily on a moral, legitimating discourse based on American values. Religion represents an important tenet of US foreign policy: major presidential speeches have constantly exhibited high religious-moral content. President Truman's March 1947 "Truman Doctrine" speech, for example, clearly had religious-moral connotations.[40] It grew out of a conviction that international politics were dominated by a clash between two totally antithetical value systems. Nations of the world, Truman maintained, were being compelled to choose between "two alternative ways of life" represented by the United States and the Soviet Union. Truman believed that the Communist menace was as dangerous for American society as the earlier fascist threat. In this way, Truman's Manichean rhetoric proclaimed a new diplomatic crusade.

In this same vein, President Reagan told the people of West Berlin in June 1982 that "theirs was a meeting place of light and shadow, tyranny and freedom. To be here is truly to stand on freedom's edge and in the shadow of a wall that has come to symbolize all that is darkest in the world today."[41] In Reagan's words, "the forces of good" must ultimately rally if they are to "triumph over evil." The "great civilized ideas" of "individual liberty, representative government, and the rule of law under God" are "menaced by an evil neighbor." Communism, like fascism, glorified "the arbitrary power of the state" while denying "the existence of God" and those "God-given liberties that are the inalienable right of each person on this planet."

Similarly, many of President George W. Bush's speeches were filled with references to the United States being "called" or given a "mission" by the "Maker of Heaven" and "Author of Liberty."[42] Bush junior's speeches exceeded those of his predecessors in the sheer number of references to God, but there was nothing unusual in a US president describing the nation's role in the world in religious terms. Many US presidents have invoked the same mission—that the United States, as the "city upon a hill" and the "indispensable nation," has been called by God to achieve "the expansion of freedom in the entire world."[43] That religious conceptions have dictated goals and color understandings of the world in which these goals have to be met is seen in John Adams' inaugural address, in which he thanked an "overruling Providence which had so signally protected this country."[44] In 1919, Woodrow Wilson promised that by supporting the League of Nations, the United States would lead in the "redemption of the world."[45] During the Second World War, Franklin D. Roosevelt declared in his 1942 message to Congress: "We on our side are striving to be true to [our] divine heritage."[46]

Such American values are rarely questioned, as they are deeply rooted in American national identity. As religion and democracy intertwine, American political discourse serves as a collective cultural symbol that can be highly effective in rallying people around certain foreign policy proposals. This can be noticed throughout the speech as President Bush employs a linguistic register with democratic, moralistic connotations. His assertion that "Panamanians will put this dark chapter of dictatorship behind them" elicits feelings of fulfillment among the American people given that their values are well protected by the government. What this implies is that democracy becomes a propaganda asset and a legitimatizing argument given its high status as a sacred convention that is rarely questioned by the American people.

Conclusion

American foreign policy discourse is often characterized by the use of propaganda as a major tool of legitimization and agenda setting. Indeed, in order to influence American public opinion, President Bush's speech relies on a variety of discursive strategies that aim to appeal to the American people's values and emotions and reinforce the portrayal of the United States as a moral crusader. This vision of American leadership is enshrined in various speeches and strategy documents that put considerable emphasis on the importance of security commitments and their role in sustaining American grand strategy objectives.

What then are the lessons of the Panama episode? The invasion was attractive to the Bush administration for diverse reasons: to counter the impression that Bush was insufficiently strong and masculine, the need to be seen as acting decisively against drugs, the desire to terminate the "Vietnam Syndrome," and, especially, the desire to prove to the world Washington's determination to defend US credibility in the international arena. In a changing international environment, the US government believed that it had to act as the sole remaining superpower. In fact, if the United States could not cope with low-level defiance in its own hemisphere, how would it deal with far more serious international challenges?

The unexpected disintegration of the Soviet Union led to dramatic changes in world politics and compelled the United States to contemplate the features of the post-Cold War world. The years 1989 through 1991 witnessed some of the most dramatic changes in global politics since 1945. In 1989, the wall separating East Berlin from West Berlin, long a symbol of the Cold War, was dismantled. The speed and depth of this political revolution (the sudden end of the Cold War) caught American leaders by surprise and left them faced with the urgent need for a total reorganization of the country's foreign policy objectives and the adoption of new strategies and new master plans. Were there any major threats left? How should the United States reinstate its policies in various parts of the world? How and to what extent should the CIA and the Defense Department be reorganized? What strategy should the United States now pursue in Europe, Asia, Russia, and the Third World? What would the most important interests be, as the twenty-first century approached? Under what conditions should the United States be willing to use force on behalf of its foreign policy goals? These were some of the major questions that needed answering by the US political and intellectual elite.

The "Communist threat" had been the glue that held the US system together. It justified upholding more than 375 US military bases abroad, and the deployment of more than half a million US troops on foreign soil. It led to enormous wealth and power for the military-industrial complex and for the managers of the US National Security establishment. It also diffused tensions in a divided society by focusing attention on a "common enemy." For all of these reasons, the end of the Cold War left the United States without a sense of foreign policy purpose to replace that of containing Communist expansion. The United States searched instead for a global policy that could be translated into clear guidelines, a new roadmap to the country's role as sole superpower. At the same time, US projections of power, especially in Latin America, preceded the Cold War, and so in some ways the invasion of Panama was in keeping with longer histories of US interference in what its elites thought of as their backyard. As was often the case, and as the people of Iraq would soon find out, US empire in Latin America, with or without accompanying Cold War propaganda, provided the template for imperialism elsewhere.[47]

The Panama invasion occurred at a time when the Soviet and American blocs were reconciling, and the Cold War disappearing. So, international affairs observers did not necessarily expect the United States to revert to its interventionist policy in Latin America. Yet, Washington perceived new threats and advanced "new" arguments in favor of its military action. The ideological "combating Communism" was replaced by "combating drugs." There were hence still threats to be afraid of and enemies to deal with. In a way, the variety of reasons used and the shift in threat discourse could be perceived as a testing out of potential new foreign policy discourse going forward into the post-Cold War era. The Panama invasion was indeed "sold" to the American public and it paved the way for a new interventionist future for the United States.

President Bush and his advisers talked about a "New World Order" but neither he nor his advisers ever put much flesh on the bare bones of a policy. The Bush administration, famous for missing "the vision thing," was a "process administration" (gradual, cautious, and transitory).[48] In fact, the Bush team never articulated a new foreign policy for America, never set forth clear goals and a doctrine to replace the Containment Doctrine of the Cold War, and never designed a clear strategy to implement the New World Order concept. Indeed, the Bush White House lacked vision to put its ambiguous concept into a policy. Consequently, the one-term Bush administration left no clear future guidelines for the country's approach to international affairs.

Notes

1. Gareth S. Jowett and Victoria O'Donnell, *Propaganda & Persuasion* (Los Angeles: Sage, 2006).
2. "The Nomination of Dr. Condoleezza Rice to Be Secretary of State," *Hearings before the Committee on Foreign Relations, United States Senate* (Washington: US Government Printing Office, 2005).
3. Max Hilare, *International Law and the United States Military Intervention in the Western Hemisphere* (The Hague: Kluwer Law International, 1997), 96.
4. Ibid.
5. John Stockwell, *The Praetorian Guard: The US Role in the New World Order* (Boston: South End Press, 1991).
6. Linda S. Robinson, "Dwindling Options in Panama," *Foreign Affairs* 6, no. 5 (Winter 1989/90): 192.
7. Ibid.
8. Fay S. Joyce, "Bush Challenges Mondale on Demand for Apology," *New York Times*, October 18, 1984, D26; Margaret Garrard Warner, "Bush Battles the 'Wimp Factor,'" *Newsweek*, October 19, 1987. Available online: https://www.newsweek.com/bush-battles-wimp-factor-207008 (accessed November 14, 2021); Matt Taibbi, "A Brief History of Everything That Happened because of George H.W. Bush's Insecurity," *Rolling Stone*, December 7, 2018. Available online: https://www.rollingstone.com/politics/politics-features/george-h-w-bush-wimp-766076/ (accessed November 14, 2021); Kirstin L. Hoganson, *Fighting for American Manhood: How Gender Politics Provoked the Spanish-American and Philippine-American Wars* (New Haven: Yale University Press, 2000); Robert D. Dean, *Imperial Brotherhood: Gender and the Making of Cold War Foreign Policy* (Amherst: University of Massachusetts Press, 2003).
9. Hilare, *International Law and the United States Military*.
10. Eytan Gilboa, "The Panama Invasion Revisited: Lessons for the Use of Force in the Post Cold War Era," *Political Science Quarterly* 110, no. 4 (1995): 539–62.
11. Ibid.
12. Thomas Carothers, *In the Name of Democracy* (Berkeley: University of California Press, 1991).
13. Mark Cook and Jeff Cohen, "The Media Go to War: How Television Sold the Panama Invasion," *Extra!* (January/February 1990), 5.
14. Hilare, *International Law and the United States Military*.
15. Carothers, *In the Name of Democracy*.
16. Ibid.
17. Robinson, "Dwindling Options."
18. Carothers, *In the Name of Democracy*.

19 Available online: https://www.americanrhetoric.com/speeches/ghwbushpanamainvasion.htm (accessed October 23, 2021).
20 Teun Adrianus Van Dijk, "Discourse, Power and Access," in *Texts and Practices: Readings in Critical Discourse Analysis*, ed. Carmen Rosa Caldas-Coulthard and Malcolm Coulthard (London: Routledge, 1995), 84–104.
21 Norman Fairclough, *Critical Discourse Analysis: The Critical Study of Language* (London: Longman, 1995).
22 Norman Fairclough, *Analysing Discourse: Textual Analysis for Social Research* (New York: Routledge, 2003).
23 Ronald H. Cole, *Operation Just Cause: The Planning and Execution of Joint Operations in Panama February 1988–January 1990* (Washington, DC: Joint History Office, Office of the Chairman of the Joint Chiefs of Staff, 1995).
24 Fairclough, *Analysing Discourse*.
25 Nicolette Bramley, "Pronouns of Politics: The Use of Pronouns in the Construction of 'self' and 'other' in Political Interviews" (PhD Thesis, Australian National University, 2001).
26 Theo van Leeuwen, *Discourse and Practice: New Tools for Critical Analysis* (New York: Oxford University Press, 2008).
27 Theo van Leeuwen cited in Mohd Muzhafar Idrus and Nor Fariza Mohd Nor, "Legitimation Analysis: Exploring Decision-Making and Power in *Hot Bench*." *Gema Online Journal of Language Studies* 16, no. 2 (June 2016): 33–45.
28 Fairclough, *Analysing Discourse*, chapter 8.
29 Van Leeuwen, *Discourse and Practice*, 117.
30 Peter L. Berger and Thomas Luckmann, *The Social Construction of Reality: A Treatise in the Sociology of Knowledge* (New York: Doubleday, 1966), 111.
31 Christopher Layne, "The Waning of US Hegemony: Myth or Reality? A Review Essay," *International Security* 34, no. 1 (Summer 2009): 147–72.
32 Denise M. Bostdorff, *Proclaiming the Truman Doctrine: The Cold War Call to Arms* (College Station: Texas A&M University Press, 2008), 72.
33 Charles Maechling, "Washington's Illegal Invasion," *Foreign Policy* 79 (Summer 1990): 113–31.
34 Michael Halliday, *An Introduction to Functional Grammar* (London: Edward Arnold, 1985).
35 Fairclough, *Analysing Discourse*, 151.
36 Tanja Collet and Tom Najem, "Word Choices in Post-9/11 Speeches and Identity Construction of the Other," *The Canadian Political Science Association*. Available online: https://www.cpsa-acsp.ca/papers-2005/Najem.pdf (accessed October 22, 2021).
37 Marilynn B. Brewer, "The Psychology of Prejudice: Ingroup Love and Outgroup Hate?" *Journal of Social Issues* 55, no. 3 (1999): 429–44.

38 Eliecer Crespo-Fernández, "Euphemism as a Discursive Strategy in US Local and State Politics," *Journal of Language and Politics* 17, no. 6 (December 2018): 789–811.
39 Van Leeuwen, *Discourse and Practice*, 117.
40 Andrew Preston, *Sword of the Spirit, Shield of Faith: Religion in American War and Diplomacy* (New York: Knopf, 2012), 429–30.
41 Available online: https://commons.wikimedia.org/wiki/File:President_Reagan%27s_Speech_at_Charlottenburg_Palace_in_West_Berlin_on_June_11,_1982.webm (accessed November 16, 2021).
42 See, for example, "Inaugural Address by George W. Bush," *New York Times*, January 20, 2005. Available online: https://www.nytimes.com/2005/01/20/politics/inaugural-address-by-george-w-bush.html (accessed November 16, 2021).
43 Ibid.
44 "Inaugural Address of John Adams," March 4, 1797. Available online: https://avalon.law.yale.edu/18th_century/adams.asp (accessed November 16, 2021).
45 Woodrow Wilson, "Final Address in Support of the League of Nations," in *Woodrow Wilson: Essential Writings and Speeches of the Scholar-President*, ed. Mario R. DiNunzio (New York: NYU Press, 2006).
46 Franklin D. Roosevelt, "State of the Union Address," January 6, 1942. Available online: https://www.presidency.ucsb.edu/documents/state-the-union-address-1 (accessed November 16, 2021).
47 Greg Grandin, *Empire's Workshop: Latin America, the United States, and the Making of an Imperial Republic* (New York: Macmillan, 2006).
48 Robert Ajemian, "Where Is the Real George Bush?: The Vice President Must Now Step Out from Reagan's shadow," *Time*, January 26, 1987. Available online: http://content.time.com/time/subscriber/article/0,33009,963342-2,00.html (accessed November 16, 2021).

9

Poptivism on the Cold War's Edge: *Breakthrough/Rainbow Warriors* and the "1989" Sound

Roxanne Panchasi

Prelude

There is a crackling static between 1989's personal affective residue and what that year now signifies in my historian's mind. For most of those twelve months, I was seventeen years old. I became a university undergraduate in September, and celebrated my eighteenth birthday in late December, just two days before the end of the decade. It was a pretty big year.

I think I first learned about the protests and violence of Tiananmen watching TV with my high school boyfriend. And the bicentennial of the French Revolution, that major set of late-eighteenth- and early-nineteenth-century events that would become so important to me as an eventual historian of France and empire? I cannot remember whether or not I took note of the occasion that summer. If so, it was with a very limited sense of what that anniversary could possibly mean. I remember discussing the fall of the Berlin Wall with friends before a class months later, during my first semester as a History major.

My recollections of the scenes, moments, and feelings of the year suggest that I was never not listening to music in 1989. But while I remember just about all—and even know the words to many—of the songs included, I do not remember either *Breakthrough* or *Rainbow Warriors*, the fundraising albums that Greenpeace released in 1989, first in the Soviet Union, and then worldwide. History and memory are never the same.

Side One: How to Read a Record

Five years after the Band Aid anti-famine charity single "Do They Know It's Christmas?" and the year before the release of *Red, Hot + Blue*, the first in a series of AIDS fundraising albums, *Breakthrough* and *Rainbow Warriors*, assembled a crew of the music industry's conscientious citizens to raise money and awareness, this time in support of Greenpeace, the largest environmental organization on the planet.[1] A sonic clearinghouse for some of the most popular music of the 1980s, *Breakthrough*, was the first fundraising compilation of "Western" music to reach a Soviet audience, and the first album of its kind released behind the "Iron Curtain" before its distribution elsewhere. Launched in the Soviet Union on March 6, 1989, by the state company Melodiya Records, the double album brought together over two dozen big-ticket acts, including Peter Gabriel, Talking Heads, U2, Eurythmics, Aswad, Sting, Sade, REM, Dire Straits, and more. Several of the artists had participated in similar projects previously, and some had even donated in support of Greenpeace before.[2] A few months later, the album appeared in repackaged form under a new name: *Rainbow Warriors*.[3] Produced and promoted by several record companies and Greenpeace offices in locations across the globe, *Rainbow Warriors* became "the most distributed album in recording history" by June 1989.[4] In a promotional video, Greenpeace International (GPI) spokesperson and executive director Steve Sawyer confirmed: "It's being released in virtually every country ... where they sell records around the world, and we're doing new deals all the time."[5]

What kind of "texts" were *Breakthrough* and *Rainbow Warriors*? At a basic level, the records consisted of music and lyrics by multiple artists. Hanging together fairly loosely, these were not original compositions, but songs recorded and released from the early through the mid-1980s, then donated for use by the fundraising project. The artists waived any compensation or royalties, and all profits went to support Greenpeace's work in the USSR (from *Breakthrough*) and elsewhere throughout the world (from *Rainbow Warriors*). Performed by musicians from both sides of the Atlantic and from Australia, the songs represented the 1980s in their own ways. Missing were the sounds of key popular genres like heavy metal, post-punk, hip-hop, or rap, however. The artists featured on the albums were also overwhelmingly white and male.[6]

Some of the tracks explicitly took up issues Greenpeace had been working on for almost two decades: the dangers of nuclear power and weapons, the vulnerabilities of nature, and a humanity capable of, but not always moved to take, sufficient care or action with respect to peace and the environment.

A diagnosis and warning, the collection issued its call for change to a global "Ship of Fools" (World Party), "Throwing Stones" (The Grateful Dead), and careening toward "The End of the World" (REM). U2's "Pride (In the Name of Love)" opened the album with the 1968 assassination of Dr. Martin Luther King Jr. The British reggae group Aswad's "Set Them Free" asked people and governments around the world to take a stand against South African Apartheid. The Pretenders' "Middle of the Road" called out the complacency of the comfortable in the face of poverty and suffering. Songs like INXS's "This Time," Terrence Trent D'arby's "Let's Go Forward," and "When Tomorrow Comes" by the Eurythmics expressed anxieties and hopes for the future. Others tapped into a shared humanity, reminding listeners to "Look Out Any Window" (Bruce Hornsby), to see a "City of Dreams" (Talking Heads), and a "Small World" (Huey Lewis), to consider that "Heaven Is a Place on Earth" (Belinda Carlisle) and that "We Are the People" (John Cougar Mellencamp). Artists like Sade, Thompson Twins, Sting, and Bryan Adams sang about friendship and love.

Titles, lyrics, musical and emotional registers are not the only way to read these albums, however. They also belong to what poet and critic Joshua Clover has designated "1989, the category" and "1989, the concept," two ways of approaching that year that are also ways of thinking about pop music in/as history.[7] Released in 1989, both *Breakthrough* and *Rainbow Warriors* were expressions of a poptivism (pop music + activism) on the Cold War's edge. Enacting a "world" including buyers/listeners, potential Greenpeace supporters, and members, the two albums released on either side of an ideological divide in flux hold imbricated narratives of geopolitics and consumption. Together, they sold copies into the millions and generated approximately $8 million for Greenpeace.[8] In the late 1980s, compilations like *Breakthrough* and *Rainbow Warriors* were also necessarily physical cultural artifacts. Appearing in the form of vinyl LPs, CDs, and cassette tapes, they were commodity-objects of a specific moment in the material history of music production and distribution. Carrying different meanings for fans and collectors, these media relied on technologies essential to their production and enjoyment, provoking diverse visual and tactile experiences, from their packaging (protective covers and sleeves, liner notes, etc.) to the sound media itself, and the haptic, visual, and auditory chains of experience involved each time they were then, and can still now be, played.

Breakthrough and *Rainbow Warriors* happened, then, on the brink of a heterogeneous obsolescence, and at the busy intersection of major historical forces: imperialist and Cold War conflict, later capitalism with its attendant forms of cultural and political marketing, and growing concerns about the destructiveness of what many now refer to as the "Anthropocene."⁹ The biographies of these two albums reveal multiple symptoms and contradictions of a historical moment when the meanings of politics, culture, the environment, and the world itself were up for grabs in myriad ways. Beyond the content and form of the albums themselves, there is a rich and detailed documentation of the before, during, and afterlives of *Breakthrough* and *Rainbow Warriors* as organizational, musical, and marketing projects. That repository resides primarily with Greenpeace International (GPI), the group's worldwide umbrella. Record companies, management agencies, promoters, and media outlets based in multiple countries also participated in the making, distribution, and reception of these albums. Situating *Breakthrough* and *Rainbow Warriors* as cultural and political texts means reading this meta-compilation of historical footprints, stories, and points of view.

Interlude

I ordered my copy of the double LP *Breakthrough* from a used record seller in Germany in 2019 and it took several weeks to arrive. The hazy imagery of its cover art intrigues me. As I slid record one (of two) out of its sleeve to play it for the first time, I wondered about the album's original owner. It was a bit of a thrill to touch this artifact, to feel its textures and edges, to hear it and think on what this might have been like for that first listener. I was delighted as a music lover, a collector, and a historian.

Side Two: A World Music Story

Doug Faulkner, Greenpeace's chief fundraiser of many years, claimed he was the "person who, at the beginning of 1987, suggested … that Greenpeace do a fundraising album in the USSR."¹⁰ According to Faulkner, he and Greenpeace chairman and cofounder David McTaggart "had been inspired by Peter Gabriel whilst visiting him at his farmhouse in Bath."¹¹ Faulkner shared this story in a July 1989 letter to Ian Flooks, head of the London-based Wasted Talent Agency that was so instrumental in securing the musical acts featured on both albums. Faulkner did not end up coordinating the planning and promotion, however.¹² Working with Flooks, Wasted Talent, and the Greenpeace national office in the UK, chaired by Cornelia Durrant, GPI oversaw the venture, setting up an eventual "record project base" in Los Angeles, headed up by Kate Karam. That office sorted out details and liaised with music industry representatives, particularly as things moved forward worldwide. Communication, coordination, and regular tensions between the different parties involved in the project were a persistent concern. Expressing fissures within the organization, they indicated a real struggle between Greenpeace's global aspirations and initiatives, and the grassroots efforts and philosophy at the heart of the group's founding mission.

In his 1992 survey of recent "mass media music projects," musicologist Neal Ullestad included *Breakthrough* and *Rainbow Warriors* among his "seven challenges to the status quo" in 1980s pop.[13] Live Aid (a major concert event following on the success of the Band Aid single) "jump-started" a series of music/activist efforts such as Farm Aid, the Artists United against Apartheid hit song "Sun City," Amnesty International's "Conspiracy of Hope" and "Human Rights Now!" concert tours, as well as the Greenpeace albums of 1989.[14] Resisting the bipolar belligerence of a Cold War apparently in its final stages, *Breakthrough* and *Rainbow Warriors* launched at a peak moment of "Western"/"Northern" anxious and benevolent fascination with the Communist East and Global South that was a turning point in the history of music philanthropy and activism.[15] It was also a critical juncture in the history of environmental crises, and of Greenpeace's activist and educational work. In a December 1988 update for Greenpeace's national offices shortly before the Soviet record came out, GPI referenced a "whole series of environmental disasters and scares over the past seven or eight months [that] ... helped move the environment closer to people's hearts and way up the political agenda."[16] Indeed, Greenpeace itself had been a big part of this process, drawing attention to and spreading information about these issues around the world. In addition to various regional and international campaigns since the group's founding, Greenpeace was, in 1989, getting ready to launch the *Rainbow Warrior II*, a new vessel to take up the work of the ship French secret service agents had bombed in Auckland Harbor, New Zealand, in July 1985. Crucial to Greenpeace's protests against French nuclear imperialism in the Pacific, the *Rainbow Warrior* had been making international headlines for years before the bombing. The attack killed one person, photographer Fernando Pereira. It also irreparably damaged the boat that had become such an icon of the group's work, and of environmentalist direct action more broadly. In addition to the scandal and diplomatic crises that followed, an international arbitration process resulted in an $8.2 million settlement in Greenpeace's favor.[17]

Alternately referred to as the "East/West album," the "Soviet record," the first phase of the "Greenpeace record project," or "compilation album," and its eventual proper name, *Breakthrough* also came together at a major turning point in Soviet history. The transformations of the Gorbachev era that began in 1984 included emergent policies of *glasnost* (openness) and *perestroika* (restructuring), reforms propelled forward in part by the impact of the disaster at the Chernobyl nuclear power plant in Ukraine after a failed electrical test on April 26, 1986. The effects of the resulting environmental and health catastrophe continued to reverberate decades later. Apart from the multiple deaths caused by the explosions and ensuing fire at the reactor site, the disaster spread high levels of extremely harmful radiation throughout the area surrounding the plant, the broader region, and internationally. Chernobyl's far-reaching impact made it clear in unprecedented ways that national and ideological borders did not hold when it came to large-scale environmental threats like those Greenpeace had been protesting for years.[18]

The Greenpeace personnel responsible for the "Soviet record" expressed excitement about the project's "great potential not just for raising money ... but for raising awareness of environmental problems and the importance of everyone, whether in Minsk or Des Moines, taking active responsibility for the solutions."[19] It was Greenpeace's hope that this initiative might "provide a platform to talk about the environment at a time when people are perhaps more than ever ready to listen."[20] The record project could be a way to reach a broader Soviet population unfamiliar with the range of Greenpeace's efforts around the world. The organization's previous interactions with the Soviet Union had been focused on opposing the whaling industry. While Greenpeace refused participation in politics in a traditional sense, those clashes between the environmentalist group and Soviet whalers cannot be isolated completely from the era's Cold War context.[21] The record project had potential as a departure from this confrontational past.

Greenpeace regarded *Breakthrough* as exactly what the album's title suggested, an opening echoing *glasnost*, one that might lead to "a wide range of projects with the Soviets from public education to a cleanup of the Danube."[22] Ian Flooks of Wasted Talent described the album as "a real example of perestroika in action."[23] *Breakthrough* also seemed to meet a Soviet state need at the time. According to a British journalist who previewed the album before its release, the Soviet authorities were "keen to be seen to be responding to citizens' protest against pollution" in the wake of Chernobyl and "other local pollution scandals."[24] Soviet state support for the project corroborated this view from outside. Greenpeace had the endorsement of Dr. Yevgeny Velikhov, vice-president of the Soviet Academy of Sciences, a physicist who had served as an adviser to Gorbachev following the Chernobyl disaster. Clearing a path in various ways, the Soviet government supported the collaboration with Melodiya Records, permitted Greenpeace to set up a bank account in Moscow, and approved plans for the album's promotion and release in early March 1989, including a widely publicized launch that brought several of the artists to the Soviet Union.[25] Beyond the establishment of a local office, Greenpeace hoped to gather and share information about Soviet air and sea pollution, and to develop East-West programs and exchanges aimed at educating Soviet children about environmental issues.[26]

While some of the acts featured on *Breakthrough* may have been familiar to Soviet music fans in 1989, access to music from "the West" had been subject to different forms of denunciation and censorship historically. "Western" sounds had certainly gotten through in previous decades, however. The World Youth Festival held in Moscow in 1957 introduced thousands of young people to fashion, dance, and music (especially jazz) from outside the Soviet Union.[27] The Beatles had made their mark since the 1960s. Radio broadcasts the authorities had not managed to jam successfully, as well as smuggled and bootlegged versions of albums, also contributed to what Soviet fans were able to take in over the years. Sanctioned tours by artists such as Cliff Richards and Elton John in the 1970s, and the legal releases of albums by groups like Jethro Tull and the Moody Blues also happened along the way. Things relaxed considerably into the 1980s, as the Gorbachev regime's cultural and other reforms opened space for Soviet artists as well as foreign music and musicians.[28] Still, much of the contemporary "Western" music that circulated in the Soviet Union continued to do so via an "underground home-taping network" involving "cassettes traded on the street by tourists for hats, flags, or other military collectibles."[29]

"'Greenpeace' Album Is The World" read the title of a September 1988 *Billboard* magazine article anticipating *Breakthrough*.[30] The record project performed and insisted on border-crossing, the removal of political and state barriers to a better, more sustainable future. And young people would be essential to this future. According to David McTaggart, Greenpeace "ha[d] been looking for a way to make a breakthrough in the Soviet Union, to get [their] message to Soviet youth particularly" and the Soviet record promised as much. Featuring contemporary songs and acts, this unprecedented release would (it was hoped) appeal to a fresh generation open to change on a number of fronts, including the environment. Music could be a particularly effective strategy for reaching out. As McTaggart noted in an interview prior to the album's release, "music is an international language that has great credibility with youth. They know that the content of these songs is not controlled by any government. And there is definitely a message for Soviet youth and for the youth of the world—pollution doesn't respect international borders."[31] Always good for a soundbite, Flooks described *Breakthrough* as "a record of unity, of concern, of commitment."[32]

Designed by Neville Brody, *Breakthrough*'s front and back covers featured "greenpeace" in lower case letters (without the organization's logo), and the album title, as well as images of a cheetah, a mountain range, and a swath of tropical rainforest partially destroyed. The album leaned into these visuals of a planet at risk, a world of interdependent species and landscapes rather than competing militarized states, economies, or ideologies. Hoping to make their own motives for participating as explicit as possible, the artists involved with *Breakthrough* had requested the production of a detailed set of liner notes outlining areas of global environmental concern alongside song descriptions and background information about each performer or group. The result was a sixteen-page booklet, produced by Greenpeace, that went into every double album. It featured dramatic photographs, text in Russian, and a cut-away form that purchasers could fill out and mail in to find out more information, become members, or donate.[33]

The booklet opened with "Blue Marble," an arresting photographic view of Earth from the 1972 Apollo 17 space mission. This was the indivisible whole *Breakthrough* was meant to evoke. From the album's very first lines and lyrics, the reader/listener would be reminded of this planet situated within a vast universe, a world of more consequence than any single individual, group, or state. The message throughout was that "everything on Earth is interconnected" and that "human activity can impact planetary systems." A "common language," music was a force belonging to all of humanity. The album was "a first step," calling on listeners to "do something" to preserve the world they shared.[34] The pages that followed pursued themes of destructive technology and ways of living: nuclear weapons and power; the exploitation of the Earth's natural resources—its oceans, air, lands, and non-human inhabitants—a "global life-support system" to be safeguarded against "national prerogatives and parochial interests."[35]

The Soviet launch of *Breakthrough* expressed Greenpeace's intention to forge a global community and work toward a future transcendent of political and ideological division. Several of the artists traveled to Moscow for the occasion with a group that also included Flooks, Greenpeace and record company representatives, and a group of international journalists. Documenting the three-day launch, Greenpeace's archival footage tracks the stages of the trip from the arrival of artists Brinsley Forde, John Farnham, Chrissie Hynde, The Edge,

Alannah Currie, Tom Bailey, Peter Gabriel, David Byrne, Jerry Harrison, Annie Lennox, Karl Wallinger, Guy Chambers, and their entourage at the Moscow airport through the series of promotional events that followed. The group toured the city, held a major press conference and gave smaller interviews to the Soviet media, attended a children's concert, and paused here and there for autographs and photos. Annie Lennox and The Edge also shot an unprecedented promotional TV ad for the album. The popular Soviet program *Before and after Midnight* (produced by Vladimir Davydenko and hosted by Vladimir Molchanov), a show with a viewership of 200,000,000 people throughout the Soviet Union, featured the project as well.[36]

On March 6, hundreds of people turned up at the Moscow Melodiya Records store for the double album's release, to see the musicians, and to get their records signed.[37] Aleksey Kiselev, who later became an activist with the organization, remembers this as "the beginning of [his] story with Greenpeace." "I stood outside in freezing weather for six hours hoping to buy a very expensive LP," Kiselev recalls.[38] Indeed, each album sold for nine rubles, the equivalent of one-tenth of the average Soviet monthly salary.[39] Another Soviet observer remembers that *Breakthrough* was "a valuable album" because it "was the first introduction to many of the performers":

> The day the record was released, the record shop on Kalininskiy Prospekt (now Novy Arbat) was taken by storm. It looked like the line-up stretched all the way to the Kremlin. It was entered into the Guinness Book of Records as the world's longest line! By May 1989, the number of copies sold exceeded one million.[40]

From Greenpeace's perspective, the launch was a resounding success. Cornelia Durrant of Greenpeace UK described "[t]he organization of the event" (the coordination of visas, travel arrangements, the itinerary, media appearances, etc.) as a "nightmare."[41] In her July 1989 report to Steve Sawyer, Durrant nevertheless claimed that "Greenpeace *Breakthrough* had one of the most successful and visible launches of any album anywhere."[42] The musicians' Moscow trip had generated extraordinary enthusiasm for the record that carried over after their departure. *Breakthrough* remained at the top of the Soviet music charts long after the release, and Greenpeace received thousands of requests for more information from purchasers who used the liner booklet cutaway. One of the organizers on the Soviet side had joked: "Every time you plug in an electric appliance in the Soviet Union, you hear the Greenpeace album."[43] More than a year after the launch, Flooks reported that 80,000 people had written in for more information, and he hoped that many of them would become Greenpeace supporters and members.[44]

On his return from the Moscow trip in March 1989, John Preston, the Chairman of BMG Records, the company that planned to distribute *Breakthrough* throughout Eastern Europe and elsewhere under the name *Rainbow Warriors*, concluded that "there could hardly have been a better promo trip for the record company."[45] The buzz around *Breakthrough* would generate excitement about the upcoming release of *Rainbow Warriors* outside the Soviet Union. Preston did, however, note a glitch: "The little ripple from Mr. Sukhardo [of Melodiya Records] in respect of the vast numbers he obviously wishes to export to my part of the world ... an interesting interpretation of the old phrase 'free world.'"[46] His comments made clear the persistence of boundaries that rhetoric about the planet, nature, a shared humanity, and the whole Earth could not transcend. There were cracks in the foundation of *Breakthrough*'s mission to bring people together with song in the interests of global environmental change. The entire enterprise was caught up with state and corporate interests from the start. The Soviet record project was exactly that in some ways, a project sanctioned by the state, bounded by the borders of the Soviet Union, and segregated from *Rainbow Warriors* in name, presentation, production, distribution, contracts, and more. Soviet Communism and the divisions of the Cold War may have been on the wane in 1989, but the financial and other territorialities of capitalism were non-negotiable. New barriers would emerge in the years to come.

Interlude

Apart from some differences in the track list, *Rainbow Warriors* sounds a lot like *Breakthrough*. As objects, the vinyl versions of these records also share dimensions, the regular fold characteristic of the double album, the pockets, sleeves, etc. The textures of their paper jackets differ, however, and so do the style and tone of their visual designs overall. *Breakthrough* and *Rainbow Warriors* feel like they are not only from different places, but also from different times. I can almost hear a world between them, even when the songs I am listening to are the same.

Side Three: What Is a Rainbow Warrior?

An official music video to promote the worldwide release of *Rainbow Warriors* beginning in June 1989 featured clips from several songs played over footage of spectacular natural landscapes and bright, smiling human faces, many of them belonging to children. At the end of this collage of image and sound, two paragraphs of text scrolled up on screen over footage of the *Rainbow Warrior II* (also launched that summer), sailing proudly in the background. As Steve Sawyer explained in another promotional clip, the album was "called *Rainbow Warriors* after the ship, which was the heart and soul of our organization for so many years."[47] He also referred to the naming of that original vessel after a "North American Indian legend which foretells a time when the Earth is being spoiled by mankind, and a group of people of all colors and all races around the world get together to try to bring about change." This explanation for the album name, and the names Greenpeace gave to its first and second flagships, appeared in the liner notes to both *Breakthrough* and *Rainbow Warriors*, and elsewhere in the planning and promotional materials for both records.[48]

Months earlier, in January 1989, Kate Karam of the LA-based record project office had confirmed that *Rainbow Warriors* would be the title of the worldwide album. In a report including a section called "The Name Game," Karam explained, "The record companies and product managers [had] advised that the cover art and the name 'Breakthrough' were too 'soft' for the West." Karam acknowledged that there might be some hesitation over the new name:

> I know what you're going to say, 'cause Cornelia [Durrant, of Greenpeace UK] and I had the same reaction. 'Rainbow Warriors?' 'It's too hippy.' 'It's too reminiscent of the bombing and doesn't reflect how we've grown.' 'Indigenous groups are going to flip out.' But if you're outside the organization and you're not a granola-head, you're just an average Joe (Jose, Giuseppe, etc.) who knows a little about what Greenpeace is, you know that it has something to do with the environment, and most importantly you've seen pictures of its actions in newspapers around the globe. And most likely, the *Rainbow Warrior*.[49]

The name of the vessel was recognizable, an important element of the Greenpeace "brand" that had continued to resonate strongly in the years after the 1985 bombing. Indeed, it had more than one new lease on life in 1989. Apart from the new Greenpeace ship and the album, it was also the name of a video game launched (aboard the *Rainbow Warrior II*) that year.[50]

Taking up the origin story Greenpeace has repeatedly represented as an Indigenous "legend," the *Rainbow Warriors* album provoked questions about the true meaning and mission of the organization.[51] Intended to raise money and awareness, and to attract new Greenpeace members and supporters around the world, the record project had noble aspects. At the same time, multiple record company deals and contracts, planning and promotional strategies for the album, and the marketing and sales hoopla that ensued came into repeated conflict with some of Greenpeace's basic principles and practices. Greenpeace had always insisted it was a non-governmental organization, unaligned with any particular politics, and completely free of ties to corporate interests. Peace, environmental protection, and sustainability were its goals. Already, in January 1989, there was trouble between the record project team and other members of the organization over the *Rainbow Warriors* album. For example, Cornelia Durrant and Kate Karam were both keen on tying the release of the album with the launch of Greenpeace's new vessel.[52] Insistent that the *Rainbow Warrior II*'s inauguration had a distinct significance that demanded an occasion of its own, Steve Sawyer and David McTaggart ultimately rejected the idea.[53] While both men supported the record project, they expressed concerns along the way that this initiative not overshadow the other work of the organization.

The album design and plans for the *Rainbow Warriors* marketing campaign provoked pushback from a number of Greenpeace national offices, whose help GPI and the record project staff expected with promotion in various countries around the world. The liner notes and inserts for *Rainbow Warriors* posed a different set of problems than those for *Breakthrough* because the former would be released in multiple places with different official languages. This was one of the reasons the team adopted a "comic book" design developed by Andy Gammon and John May, the author of the original English liner text for *Breakthrough*. Underlining once again an "undivided world" focus, Kate Karam noted in her January 1989 report that "[a]lmost every culture in the world has its own favourite comics." "It is an almost ancient way of communicating," she continued. "It's so deceptively simple that it takes people in without them even really knowing it … It needs no explanations."[54] Illustrator Dave Gibbons's vibrant artwork featured images of environmental hazards (nuclear weapons, waste, etc.), a Doomsday Clock-style wristwatch, and a set of Greenpeace activists powering forward in a Zodiac inflatable boat.

Running with these themes and this aesthetic, the marketing strategy Kate Karam and Cornelia Durrant outlined for the album included promotional merchandise that would, ideally, "make everyone want to be a Rainbow Warrior in 1989."[55] Pushing the myth, the strategy hailed the musicians involved with the album as "Rainbow Warriors." Potential buyers/listeners would be encouraged to emulate these artists, beginning with their purchase of the album and promotional merchandise, including shirts, jackets, baseball caps, sunglasses, decals, and more. Finally, they'd be given suggestions for ways they might adjust their own behavior in service of the environment: refraining from using Styrofoam, aerosols, or diesel fuel; making recycling a priority; supporting and perhaps becoming members of Greenpeace. Karam and Durrant suggested distributing inflatable Zodiacs to record stores for use in *Rainbow Warriors* displays, offering free merchandise to world leaders and celebrities to help promote the album, and an ad campaign in the form of "fake 'I'm a Rainbow Warrior' testimonials from people like the Ayatollah Khomeini, Lenin, Thatcher, Flipper, Skippy, Karl Marx, etc." that would superimpose *Rainbow Warriors* merchandise onto images of these famous figures.[56]

Reactions to these ideas on the part of representatives from Greenpeace's national offices ranged from hesitation to outright refusal. Greenpeace Sweden expressed concern, given their "policy ... to avoid producing and selling products that contributes [*sic.*] to pollution."[57] Another representative, from the Hamburg office of Greenpeace Germany, was also opposed to certain products and materials including "highly white paper." "In our merchandise ..., " he explained, "we try to sell only products that are very solid and not harmful for the environment ... And we don't sell baseball caps."[58] In the end, Greenpeace had the liner booklet for *Breakthrough* printed on "non-toxic chlorine-free Scanmatt paper." Kate Karam's June 1989 press release for Greenpeace offices announced that *Rainbow Warriors*' "record jacket and insert materials" had been "printed on specially milled non-chlorine bleached recycled paper," making it the first "environmentally friendly record."[59]

The environmental footprint of the project was important, but so too was the proposed messaging regarding different understandings of what Greenpeace did and should mean. Wladimir Zalozieckyj of Greenpeace Austria had some of the strongest words for Karam and Durrant on the subject of the marketing campaign:

> I am extremely concerned by the approach you want to take when marketing this album. What does Greenpeace want to achieve? ... I was very irritated when I read your ten-point plan ... This name is a symbol for us, for our way to work, to fight. It contains the spirit of our organization! ... Please realize that 'Rainbow Warrior' is different from Lacoste, Benetton etc. You can't buy 'Rainbow Warrior.' And you do not become a Rainbow Warrior simply by buying the album.[60]

Some national offices also objected to what they perceived as the "militarism" of the *Rainbow Warriors* cover and liner art and its incompatibility with the promotion of peace essential to the organization. A spokesperson from Greenpeace Germany, for example, noted, "We have here a strong peace and environmental movement which is very sensitive to any military things."[61] Steve

Sawyer also worried about the "image of Greenpeace." Wondering whether the artwork for *Rainbow Warriors* could "run the risk of being accused of 'Ramboism'" in certain places, he echoed suggestions that an alternative to the *Rainbow Warriors* cover art be used in some national contexts.[62]

Other matters pitted the national offices against GPI and *Rainbow Warriors*' promotion. As with *Breakthrough*, the matter of record companies and licensing came up, but it was even more complicated given that this second album involved a worldwide release. In the case of the Soviet Record, there had been concerns about Melodiya selling albums in Germany and perhaps other areas outside the territory covered by their contract. When it came to *Rainbow Warriors*, issues arose because individual national offices had their own promotional materials and deals with suppliers. Some of those arrangements included proprietary names and images that could not be used legally by other companies for merchandise sales within the same territory, for example. This raised the more fundamental problem of the autonomy of Greenpeace's offices throughout the world in relationship to GPI and its efforts on behalf of the organization "as a whole." Ward Dossche of Greenpeace Belgium underlined the significance of this autonomy when he broached the question of "competitive merchandising," perhaps unintentionally alluding to his country's own painful history of struggle against oppressive outsiders. "The invasion of countries by the record is acceptable," he admitted, "but you should not start additional fundraising-efforts in other countries, that's violating national territory ...."[63] While music might be a shared language of humanity, the legal and financial realities of licenses, contracts, and jurisdictions emphasized "the crescents" rather than "the whole of the moon."[64]

Interlude

Preparing this essay, I collected almost all of the versions and physical formats of both *Breakthrough* and *Rainbow Warriors*.[65] I needed to see the different covers and sleeves, the art, the texts that made these two pieces of a larger project distinct. I also wanted to return to the forms of music-as-object in 1989. The cardboard and vinyl. Those hard plastic CD and cassette cases that click open and shut, sometimes getting stuck or breaking. Removing the media, listening, putting it back, reading the notes that line these shells. I regularly think historically without props from the era, but this time, I had a craving.

Side 4: Did the End of the Cold War Make a Sound?

On the first page of his 1989 essay "The End of History?" Francis Fukuyama pointed to "the ineluctable spread of Western consumerist culture" in various parts of the world as evidence of the "triumph of the West, the Western *idea*." Examples of this spread included the "color television sets now omnipresent in China, the cooperative restaurants and clothing stores opened in the past year in Moscow ... and the rock music enjoyed alike in Prague, Rangoon, and Tehran."[66] It made sense that Fukuyama would cite the ubiquity of "rock music" as a marker of change with respect to historical global conflict. In the Soviet Union, as elsewhere in the "East," rock music had been the target of suspicion and repression as a decadent cultural form, the expression of a bourgeois capitalist and consumerist faux rebellion that could only corrupt Communist workers and citizens.

Fukuyama also characterized "the end of history" as "a very sad time":

> The struggle for recognition, the willingness to risk one's life for a purely abstract goal, the worldwide ideological struggle that called forth daring, courage, imagination, and idealism, will be replaced by economic calculation, the endless solving of technical problems, environmental concerns, and the satisfaction of sophisticated consumer demands.[67]

The interdependent biographies of *Breakthrough* and *Rainbow Warriors* were not likely on Fukuyama's radar when he wrote those words. There is also much more to say about the range of issues raised by Fukuyama's piece that other contributors to this volume have addressed in different ways. What strikes me most here, however, reading these 1989 words about which so much has been written, is that they refer to ideas and ideals that these two Greenpeace albums released that same year were also entangled with in their own ways. From the planning stages through their worldwide promotion and distribution, *Breakthrough* and *Rainbow Warriors* negotiated and attempted to respond to, even bring about, a new "world," a world as a planet in need of human protection, a world not riven with borders, ideologies, or exploitative, unsustainable corporate exploitation and interest. At the same time, these Greenpeace projects turned with unprecedented intensity toward those very same forces for support, attempting to nourish a mission of change within existing political, financial, and cultural structures. In among the other sounds these landmark albums offered, hummed polyphonic preverberations and echoes, impending extinctions and persistent, if shifting, divides.

Notes

1. Founded in Vancouver, Canada in the early 1970s, the international NGO now has a membership of over 3 million people and offices in 55 countries. I would like to thank the International Institute of Social History (IISH), Greenpeace International (Amsterdam) Archives (GPI Archives), and its archival and reproductions staff. Many thanks also to Brian Connolly, as well as the editors and other contributors to this volume, for their invaluable suggestions.
2. Peter Gabriel, Eurythmics, and Pretenders had all appeared on *Greenpeace-The Album* in 1985, a Greenpeace UK effort. See "British Acts Team up for Greenpeace Album," *Billboard*, August 17, 1985, 78.
3. *Breakthrough* on vinyl included twenty-five songs on two LPs. The cassette added an additional song, "Small World" by Huey Lewis and the News. *Rainbow Warriors* on vinyl featured twenty-seven songs, the same as the Soviet cassette version, with Lou Reed's "Last Great American Whale" added. The cassette included Blue Rodeo's "Rebel," but the CD added "Balance" by Little Steven, The Silencers' "Scottish Rain," Hothouse Flowers' "Hard Rain," and "Somewhere Down the Crazy River" by Robbie Robertson instead. Format capacity and licensing arrangements seem to have determined these differences, and I found no evidence of other considerations in GPI's documentation regarding the project.
4. Dan Collins, "Putting Peace in the Groove," *Cork Examiner*, June 22, 1989.
5. "Steve Sawyer on Rainbow Warriors Album-Interview," Greenpeace Media, 1989. Available online: https://media.greenpeace.org/archive/Steve-Sawyer-on-Rainbow-Warriors-Album---Interview-27MZIFJ89JUMI.html (accessed October 15, 2021).
6. Journalist Robert Hilburn pointed out that the album was "not a total survey of what's happening today in rock," citing these genres as notably absent while acknowledging the success of the record. Robert Hilburn, "'Rainbow Warriors' Smashes Sales Records in Soviet Union," *Los Angeles Times*, June 24, 1989.
7. Joshua Clover, *1989: Bob Dylan Didn't Have This to Sing About* (Berkeley: University of California Press, 2009), 5.
8. Hilburn, "'Rainbow Warriors' Smashes Sales Records."
9. On the origins and use of the term, see Will Steffen, Jacques Grinevald, Paul Crutzen, and John McNeill, "The Anthropocene: Conceptual and Historical Perspectives," *Philosophical Transactions of the Royal Society A* 369 (2011): 842–67.
10. Doug Faulkner (Greenpeace International) to Ian Flooks (Wasted Talent Agency) et al., July 10, 1989. International Institute of Social History (hereafter IISH), Greenpeace International Archives (hereafter GPI Archives), Amsterdam, ARCH02587/1500.
11. Ibid.

12. The original idea was to hold a benefit concert in Moscow, but the album project proved more practical ultimately. Faulkner to Flooks et al., July 10, 1989. IISH, GPI Archives, ARCH02587/1500.
13. Neal Ullestad, "Diverse Rock Rebellions Subvert Mass Hegemony," in *Rockin' the Boat: Mass Music and Mass Movements*, ed. Reebee Garofalo (Boston: South End Press, 1992), 37–53, 39.
14. See Ullestad, "Diverse Rock Rebellions Subvert Mass Hegemony"; Lucy Robinson, "Putting the Charity Back into Charity Singles: Charity Singles in Britain, 1985–1995," *Contemporary British History* 26, no. 3 (2012): 405–25; and Andrew Jones, "Band Aid Revisited: Humanitarianism, Consumption, and Philanthropy in the 1980s," *Contemporary British History* 31, no. 2 (2017): 189–209.
15. See Robinson, "Putting the Charity Back into Charity Singles"; Cheryl Lousley, "'With Love from Band Aid': Sentimental Exchange, Affective Economies, and Popular Globalism," *Emotion Space and Society* 10, no. 1 (February 2014): 7–17 is useful for thinking about how projects such as Band Aid attempted to forge a "global community" through benevolent consumption. For an analysis of the shift to individual and "market-driven" activisms in this period, see Jones, "Band Aid Revisited."
16. "Greenpeace Compilation Album: Update for Offices," December 1, 1988, IISH, GPI Archives, ARCHO2597/1501.
17. On the first ship and the 1985 bombing, see Michael King, *Death of the Rainbow Warrior* (New York: Penguin Books, 1986) and David Robie, *Eyes of Fire: The Last Voyage of the Rainbow Warrior* (Philadelphia: New Society Press, 1987).
18. See Zhores Medvedev, "Chernobyl: A Catalyst for Change," in *Milestones in Glasnost and Perestroika*, ed. A. Hewett and Victor H. Winston (Washington, DC: The Brookings Institution, 1991), 19–30. Kate Brown, *Manual for Survival: A Chernobyl Guide to the Future* (New York: W. W. Norton & Co., 2019) is a recent history that explores new archives and questions. See also Svetlana Alexeivitch, *Voice of Chernobyl: The Oral History of a Nuclear Disaster*, trans. Keith Gessen (London: Dalkey Archive Press, 2005).
19. "Greenpeace Compilation Album: Update for Offices," December 1, 1988, IISH, GPI Archives. ARCHO2597/1501.
20. Ibid.
21. See Jason M. Colby, "Conscripting Leviathan: Science, Cetaceans, and the Cold War," *Diplomatic History* 44, no. 3 (June 2020): 466–78.
22. "Greenpeace Compilation Album: Update for Offices," December 1, 1988, IISH, GPI Archives. ARCHO2597/1501.
23. Terry Trucco, "A Rock Album Aimed at Soviet Youth," *New York Times*, September 14, 1988.

24 Richard Palmer, "Greenpeace Goes Pop in Soviet Campaign," *Sunday Times*, September 11, 1988. See Laurent Coumel and Marc Elie, "A Belated and Tragic Ecological Revolution: Nature, Disasters, and Green Activists in the Soviet Union and the Post-Soviet States, 1960s–2010s," *The Soviet and Post-Soviet Review* 40, no. 2 (January 2013): 157–65.
25 "Greenpeace Compilation Album: Update for Offices," December 1, 1988, IISH, GPI Archives. ARCHO2597/1501. Melodiya Records guaranteed a fixed revenue per album produced (not sold) to be split equally between Greenpeace and the International Foundation for the Survival and Development of Humanity, a new, independent, non-governmental organization based in the Soviet Union.
26 Jennie Walsh, "Breakthrough for the Environment," *Pravda International* 3, no. 5 (1989): 22.
27 Pia Koivunen, "The 1957 Moscow Youth Festival: Propagating a New, Peaceful Image of the Soviet Union" in *Soviet State and Soviet Society Under Nikita Krushchev*, ed. Melanie Ilic and Jeremy Smith (London: Routledge, 2009), 46–65.
28 Sabrina Petra Ramet, Sergei Zamascikov, and Robert Bird, "The Soviet Rock Scene" in *Rocking the State: Rock Music and Politics in Eastern Music and Russia*, ed. Sabrina Ramet (Boulder, CO: Westview Press, 1994), 179–216.
29 Glenn Baker "Rock around the Bloc," *The Australian Magazine*, 1989. IISH, GPI Archives. ARCHO2597/1501 (Press clippings). See also Robert Rauth, "Back in the USSR: Rock and Roll in the Soviet Union," *Popular Music and Society* 8, no. 3–4 (1982): 3–12; and *Youth and Rock in the Soviet Bloc: Youth Cultures, Music, and the State in Russia and Eastern Europe*, ed. William J. Risch (Lanham, MD: Lexington Books, 2015).
30 Edwin Riddell, "'Greenpeace' Album Is the World," *Billboard* 100, no. 36, September 3, 1988.
31 David McTaggart (GPI), Letter to Ian Flooks, re: Greenpeace Breakthrough-Rainbow Warriors, March 10, 1989, IISH, GPI Archives. ARCHO2597/1501.
32 Ian Flooks quoted in Michael Parks, "Rock to Carry Greenpeace Message to Soviet Union," *Los Angeles Times*, October 28, 1988.
33 See David McTaggart to Greenpeace Board, "Greenpeace Pamphlet in Melodia [sic] Record," October 10, 1988, IISH, GPI Archives. ARCHO2597/1500. The text of the booklet was prepared by John May and Michael Howard Brown, author of *The Greenpeace Story*, a history of the organization since its founding published the same year (Toronto: Prentice Hall, 1989). The text was then translated into Russian for the Soviet record. While I did not find the original English text in the Greenpeace archives, I did find discussion of the booklet's content and overall look. Translations from Russian to English are by Marina Khonina.
34 John May, *Breakthrough* album liner booklet, 9.
35 Ibid.

36 For footage from the Moscow launch, including the press conferences, interviews, clips from Soviet television, and the Melodiya record signing event, see the *Breakthrough* Album Release in the Soviet Union (Photo & Video) Collection (GP0STSF4H). Available online: https://media.greenpeace.org/collection/27MZIFJWQJS24 (accessed October 15, 2021).

37 The crowd apparently became so agitated that the artists had to leave suddenly. On that first day alone, *Breakthrough* sold 500,000 copies in the Soviet Union.

38 Aleksey Kiselev, "Stroili velikuju Rossiju, a vyshel torgovyi tsentr" [We were building Great Russia and ended up with a shopping mall] *Lenta.Ru* (2016). Available online: https://m.lenta.ru/articles/2016/01/28/greenpeace/ (accessed October 15, 2021).

39 Lionel Rotcage, "Chez les Soviets," *Rolling Stone* (April 1989).

40 S. Sychev, "Grinpis sobiraet zvezd [Greenpeace Brings Stars Together]," *Radiola* (2018). Available in Russian online: http://tabloid.net.ru/radiola-god-1989/ (accessed October 15, 2021).

41 Cornelia Durrant (Greenpeace UK) to Steve Sawyer (GPI), March 10, 1989. IISH, GPI Archives: ARCHO2597/1502.

42 Cornelia Durrant, "Greenpeace Album-Report" to Steve Sawyer, July 31, 1989, 4. IISH, GPI Archives: ARCHO2597/1502.

43 Ibid. See also Kate Karam to Steve Sawyer et al., "tass says gp no 1," June 3, 1989. IISH, GPI Archives: ARCHO2597/1500.

44 Ian Flooks to David McTaggart, June 11, 1990. IISH, GPI Archives: ARCHO2597/1502.

45 John Preston (BMG Records) to Ian Flooks (Wasted Talent) and Cornelia Durrant (Greenpeace UK), March 15, 1989. IISH, GPI Archives. ARCHO2597/1501.

46 Ibid. A subplot of the Soviet record story included allegations that Melodiya was responsible for "black-market" copies of the Soviet LPs being sold in Germany. While Sukhardo denied vehemently any involvement on Melodiya's part, Greenpeace representatives expressed concern on a number of occasions about the company violating the territorial limits of its contract.

47 "Steve Sawyer on Rainbow Warriors album-Interview," Greenpeace Media, 1989.

48 Ibid.

49 Kate Karam to Steve Sawyer et al., re: album update, January 31, 1989. IISH, GPI Archives: ARCHO2597/1501.

50 See the information and description at the website for Moby Games: https://www.mobygames.com/game/rainbow-warrior (accessed October 15, 2021).

51 See Frank Zelco, "Warriors of the Rainbow: The Birth of an Environmental Mythology," *Arcadia* 16 (2013). Available online: https://doi.org/10.5282/rcc/5625 (accessed October 15, 2021). Zelco explains that the myth came from William Willoya and Vinson Brown's *Warriors of the Rainbow: Strange and Prophetic*

Dreams of the Indians (Healdsburg, CA: Naturegraph, 1962), an evangelical tract supporting Indigenous conversion to Christianity. Greenpeace co-founder Bob Hunter found the book compelling, and this is how the story became an integral part of the organization's mythos.

52 Durrant began encouraging this idea in the fall of 1988. In a November 10 note to Sawyer, she suggested that timing the album and ship launch together "would help the promotion campaign immeasurably." IISH, GPI Archives: ARCHO2597/1500. See also Durrant's communication to Sawyer on December 29, 1988, underlining this point, IISH, GPI Archives: ARCHO2597/1501.

53 Steve Sawyer to Martin Leeburn, "re: books and boats," January 3, 1989. IISH, GPI Archives: ARCHO2597/1501.

54 Kate Karam to Steve Sawyer et al., re: album update, January 31, 1989. IISH, GPI Archives: ARCHO2597/1501.

55 Kate Karam and Cornelia Durrant to David McTaggart, Steve Sawyer et al., re: Rainbow Warriors-Draft Promotion Ideas, April 3, 1989. IISH, GPI Archives: ARCHO2597/1501.

56 Ibid.

57 Lena Davidsson (Greenpeace-Sweden) to Kate Karam, March 17, 1989. IISH, GPI Archives: ARCHO2597/1501.

58 Reply from Hamburg office to Greenpeace Stichting Council et al., March 9, 1989. IISH, GPI Archives: ARCHO2597/1500 ("merchandise" folder).

59 Kate Karam to Greenpeace Offices re: press release for Rainbow Warriors pt. one, June 7, 1989. IISH, GPI Archives: ARCHO2597/1500 ("media/press" folder).

60 Wladimir Zalozieckyj (Greenpeace Austria) to Kate Karam et al., April 5, 1989. IISH, GPI Archives: ARCHO2597/1501.

61 "Wally" (Greenpeace Germany) to Steve Sawyer, March 16, 1989. IISH, GPI Archives: ARCHO2597/1501.

62 Steve Sawyer to Cornelia Durrant, March 13, 1989. IISH, GPI Archives: ARCHO2597/1501. One alternative was to return to the artwork for *Breakthrough* in sites where the other design posed a problem. See also Kate Karam to Elke Martin (Greenpeace Germany), "re: album cover," April 11, 1989; and Elke Martin to Cornelia Durrant, April 12, 1989. IISH, GPI Archives: ARCHO2597/1501.

63 Ward Dossche (Greenpeace Belgium) to Kate Karam, re: Merchandising-effort with "Rainbow Warriors," March 10, 1989, ARCHO2597-1500.

64 The reference is to a line from "The Whole of the Moon" by The Waterboys, a song featured on both albums: "I saw the crescent/You saw the whole of the moon."

65 I did not acquire the rare and relatively expensive Soviet cassette version, but have consulted a number of photographs online.

66 Francis Fukuyama, "The End of History?" *The National Interest* 16 (Summer 1989): 3.

67 Fukuyama, "The End of History?" 17.

10

A Tale of Two Periodicities: Indigenous and Settler Continuities amid Neoliberal Transformation at the St. Alice Hotel

John Munro

It's a strange sensation, writing about a time in history that sits within my living memory, a time for which one of my sources (primary or secondary? I'm not sure) is my own mind. Like so many others back in 1989, my attention was drawn to the momentous events of the day. Watching the world from Vancouver, I was awed by the bravery of a man who stood down the tanks of Tiananmen, unsure just what to make of the events in Berlin, and aghast at the massacre in Montreal and the pundits whose main concern seemed to be that this horror not be "politicized" by mentioning the misogyny that motivated the murder of fourteen women at the École Polytechnique and permeated the society in which I lived. History might not have ended the year I turned eighteen, but perhaps it crashed, cracked, or, in Daniel Rodgers' apt phrase for the late-twentieth-century era, fractured.[1]

One of the many things I didn't understand in 1989 was that all around me, capacious categories into which people organized their ideas and themselves seemed to be breaking down. An influential collection of essays diagnosed the end of the "New Deal Order" that once seemed such a stable political formation, and the United Nations said of the collective generational category of children that "the child should be fully prepared to live an individual life in society."[2] In terms of race, Stuart Hall argued that "the language of binary oppositions and substitutions will no longer suffice," and Kimberlé Crenshaw made the case that gender and race were not solid, homogeneous categories but rather cut across one another, while David Harvey turned to the indeterminacy of such apparent fundamentals as time and space.[3] These landmark publications can easily be read as retrospective signposts of fragmentation, as can the introduction in 1989 of

Microsoft Office, Nintendo's Gameboy, and the first pocket-sized mobile phone, all milestone individualizations in the experience of technology.[4] Swedish pop-rockers Roxette added to the atomization of the moment with "Listen to Your Heart," the first number one music single not released on vinyl, denoting the ascendancy of the solitary song over the long-playing record and the dissolution of the aural landscape.[5]

At the very moment that "Listen to Your Heart" outpaced the tunes taken up by Roxanne Panchasi elsewhere in this book to find itself atop the music charts, the Berlin Wall opened, and economic and political individualism rushed in to challenge and ultimately overwhelm the collective visions of society and human rights that had prevailed under Communism in the German Democratic Republic and beyond.[6] This triumph for capitalism gave neoliberalism two green lights. One was to expand spatially into those parts of the globe in Moscow's camp.[7] The other, of which Wal-Mart's 1989 toppling of Sears as top US retailer marked but one indicator, was to accelerate within "the West."[8] That quickening could take place much more smoothly with the elimination of Communist alternatives that had given impetus to the creation and maintenance of Keynes-inspired conceptions of the state in the first place.[9] These developments, and the neoliberal ascendancy they represented, were certainly subject to resistance.[10] They nonetheless wrought diverse transformations around the world. But it is those within the "First World," particularly at the urban level, that I want to think about here. To do so, the "text" I want to read, not unlike some of the others in this collection, is an unconventional one.

And that text—a Vancouver-area single-room occupancy hotel I want to use this essay to think with, as we'll soon see—can help us make sense of the multiple takes on 1989. Before the wall came down, as Molly Geidel's chapter reminds us, a congratulatory interpretation had already been given voice in Francis Fukuyama's celebration of the "unabashed victory of economic and political liberalism" that announced history's individualist terminus.[11] A less sanguine view registered a deterritorialized globalization characterized by intensified forms of exploitation, exemplified by sociologist Saskia Sassen's claim that "1989 marks the rise of histories other than those of democracy and freedom."[12] Other writing on the end of the Cold War and the rise of neoliberalism has emphasized the ways in which phenomena predating the late 1980s, such as the alterations in cultural politics, the escalation of terrorism and counterinsurgency, or crises in state socialism, modernization theory, and the Keynesian welfare state were at least as important in the creation of our times as were the spectacular events that saw three worlds dissolve into one.[13] Each of these ways of understanding the post-Cold War world has compelling qualities. All see the 1989 era, if not that specific year itself, as a moment of great transformation.

I see it differently. The year 1989 matters for the history of the Cold War and neoliberalism, yes, but what I want to do here is to ask how histories of the Cold War's decline and neoliberalism's ascent look when considered in light of settler colonialism and what Kanaka Maoli scholar Kēhaulani Kauanui calls "enduring Indigeneity."[14] Themes of imperialism are not absent from the scholarship that informs many Cold War periodizations, and there has been excellent work that recasts the entire 1945–89 era as continuous with imperial histories that become visible once cold war lenses are traded for decolonial ones.[15] But putting settler colonialism and ongoing Indigenous resurgence, rather than empire more generally, in the foreground of any account of 1989 does more than contextualize. It shows "1989" to be something closer to what anthropologist Raymond Fogelson calls a "nonevent," it demonstrates how some histories are very much ongoing, and it calls attention to certain forms of resistance and structures of dominance that turn out to be not that fractured after all.[16]

My argument—that neoliberalism, at least in North American cities, can only be properly understood in light of enduring Indigeneity and the long-duration structure of settler colonialism—departs, then, from both celebratory and critical interpretations of 1989 as transformative turning point. To make this case, I turn not to the tearing down of one of the world's most famous walls, but to the demolition of the obscure St. Alice Hotel in North Vancouver, Canada. Unlike the wall in Berlin, which divided First from Second Worlds and fell to great ado, the walls of the St. Alice housed a meeting place of First and Fourth Worlds and were demolished in 1989 without public fanfare. I know this because I've researched this topic, but also because I lived in the neighborhood. I don't think I ever went into the St. Alice, but I walked or rode my skateboard past it countless times, and older members of my family liked to go there for drinks after work or on a weekend evening. When it was torn down, the five-story building had been a single-room-occupancy hotel with an unruly beer parlor, and its residents and patrons—many of them Indigenous, most of them poor— were in the way of neoliberal redevelopment plans for this area of the city. The displacement of these people made way for a new building: a twenty-eight-story, high-end condominium tower, which as the tallest structure in its neighborhood is aptly named The Observatory.

But these details are foreshadowing. In order to establish how this forgotten moment in urban history might tell us something about what stayed the same amid all that changed in 1989, I want to proceed in three parts. In the

Figure 10.1 St. Alice Hotel, 1980s. Courtesy North Vancouver Museum and Archives.

Figure 10.2 The Observatory, 2013. Courtesy Rebecca Cook and JP Fulford.

first two sections to follow, my goal will be to draw lessons from scholarship on neoliberalism and settler colonialism, in general and at the city level. These lessons will guide my reading of the St. Alice and its destruction in my third section, before I conclude by coming back to what all of this might mean for how we think about a momentous year in transnational intellectual and political history.

Explaining Neoliberalism

A lot has been said about neoliberalism, from Michel Foucault's 1979 definition— "a state under the supervision of the market rather than a market supervised by the state"—to Quinn Slobodian's definitive account of markets encased from democratic challenge.[17] From a vast literature, I draw four main lessons that are worth keeping in mind when considering neoliberalism in relation to the city and to 1989. The first is that place matters, in that to see neoliberalism across the globe is not to negate regional specificity. Neoliberalism, in other words, is not a place-neutral phenomenon.[18] Secondly, neoliberalism is not merely an ideological extension of a particular form of economics. Rather, ideas in their own right have been crucial to the preponderant role of market individualism.[19] Third, just as it might be tempting to give ideas a second-string role in the history of neoliberalism in favor of the supposed primacy of the economy, it is also quite possible to think of neoliberalism as somehow only secondarily concerned with cultural difference or racial and gender hierarchies in comparison to the goal of universalizing capitalist market relations. Race, gender, and culture are, however, not superstructural.[20] Lastly, pronouncements of shrinking governments notwithstanding, the state is not in retreat.[21]

At the city level, urban renewal and gentrification, two broad subjects with their own respective literatures, are the most relevant contexts for what came before and what has accompanied the neoliberal turn in municipal governance. In terms of urban renewal, recent work has begun to locate the phenomenon as an aspect of intellectual and cultural history, while also confirming an earlier wave of scholarship from the 1970s and 1980s which saw links between white racism and private property that deepened inequality.[22] Modernist urban renewal and more recent entrepreneurial urbanism are not interchangeable, but the latter has often mapped itself, sometimes quite literally, on to the former.[23] "Gentrification," meanwhile, was coined by sociologist Ruth Glass in her analysis of late 1950s London, where she observed a middle-class "invasion," which once begun, "goes on rapidly until all or most of the original working class occupiers are displaced, and the whole social character of the district has changed."[24] Popular interest in gentrification—not least as themes in two landmark films of 1989: Spike Lee's *Do the Right Thing* and Michael Moore's *Roger and Me*—has, alongside scholarly literature, only increased with the phenomenon's acceleration and expansion over the past three decades. In the new cityscape, gentrification is only one aspect of a revived entrepreneurialism in which municipal possibilities have been considerably narrowed by the threat of capital flight and the power of financial institutions, especially the International Monetary Fund, World Bank, and bond rating agencies.[25] Even the specific literature on the neoliberal city is large, but it substantiates that the four general claims about neoliberalism referred to above all hold true at the urban level.[26] In the neoliberal city, entertainment projects and spectacles of consumption are key components of urban management. Though often legitimated through appeals to nationalism or civic pride, the construction of entertainment complexes and convention centers or the staging of expositions and corporate sporting events have tended to link transnational class interests between the local elites of a given city and visiting consumers with sufficient wealth to make use of such facilities and occasions.[27] Vancouver's Expo 86 typified this phenomenon.

At the same time, in the North American setting, there are distinctions as well as enmeshments between Canadian and US urban neoliberalisms, which in themselves have become a matter of some contention. In fact, two discussions have become entangled around the question of the salience of national specificity in the development of cities in Canada and the United States: over whether a "continentalist" view of the North American city illuminates similarities or muddles distinctiveness, and over whether gentrification is a component of emancipatory cultural potential or heavy-handed economic revanchism.[28] In looking at the history of the St. Alice hotel, my contribution here to the first disagreement will be to take the continentalist view that neoliberalism's individualism (and colonial underpinnings) does make Canadian cities more like than unlike those of the United States.[29] 1989 matters once again here, as the year when the Free Trade Agreement between Canada and the US first went into effect and drew the economies of the two countries closer together. In terms of the second debate, rather than take a staunch position over whether neoliberal gentrification has been primarily emancipatory or revanchist (though I tend decidedly toward the latter), I want to underscore the inattention, on both sides, to the history of settler colonialism and Indigeneity.

The Settler-Colonial Complex

Historian Patrick Wolfe, whose work has become the de rigueur citation on settler colonialism, also provides one of its most useful definitions: "an inclusive, land-centered project that coordinates a comprehensive range of agencies, from the metropolitan center to the frontier encampment, with a view to eliminating indigenous societies."[30] Like neoliberalism, settler colonialism has given rise to a large and growing literature, from which I wish to note four points pertinent to my analysis of the St. Alice Hotel. First, as will come as no surprise this far into the transnational turn, settler colonialism has not been contained within hermetic national borders.[31] Second, while a broadly binaristic logic sets Indigenous peoples apart from settlers, the history of settler colonialism is also one of relational differentiations structured in dominance.[32] Lines around whiteness and settlement, for instance, have been created through varied processes of gender formation.[33] Third, the process of formal decolonization has made nations of colonies, but not postcoloniality of colonialism. Never total, always contested, and often genocidal, forms of settler control posit permanent invasion in shaping state structures, emotions of belonging, ways of remembering and forgetting, and modes of intellectual argumentation.[34] Aspirations notwithstanding, the settler structure has also been unstable and incomplete, and thus rightfully characterized by Mohawk anthropologist Audra Simpson as a project of "ongoing existence and simultaneous failure."[35] Fourth, colonial dispossession enables capital accumulation. There is now a growing body of work on the ways in which settler colonialism has shaped North American capitalism.[36] There is also an emerging literature—one this chapter aims to contribute to—that looks at the entanglement of settler colonialism and neoliberalism more specifically.[37]

Alongside these broad insights into settler colonialism and enduring Indigeneity, themselves the interdisciplinary product of the work of scholars and activists, historians have also linked empire and the city for some time. In 1940, Arthur Schlesinger Sr. characterized the contest for resources and transportation routes between nineteenth-century New York, Baltimore, and Philadelphia as one of "urban imperialisms."[38] More recently, William Cronon and Eugene Moehring have shown how the connection between metropolis and hinterland, and between networks of cities and towns, was instrumental to the colonial conquest of the US West.[39] With James Belich's 2009 *Replenishing the Earth*, the role of the city in settler colonial history has been rendered in impressive depth and breadth at a transnational level. Belich's book, which opens by comparing Chicago and Melbourne with London and New York, puts capitalism and technology at the center of its argument about the rise of a trans-continental Anglo-world during the nineteenth century. Over and over in *Replenishing the Earth*, we see how cycles of boom, bust, and "export rescue" (in which the original colonizing power would renew trade links with settler colonies after an economic crash in the latter) were anchored by cities.[40] The urban locale remains as important as ever to how power operates under settler colonial conditions. Enter the St. Alice.

Reading the St. Alice

Of course we can't enter the now-demolished St. Alice, even if the hotel can enter my argument about 1989 representing more of the same alongside true transformation. Nonetheless, the building remains legible if not visible. If, as historian Tom Wilkinson has it, a "textual analysis of buildings can be a fruitful one," what, then, did the St. Alice say?[41] Although a space and not a literal text, it can still say something about the place in which it stands. And it can say different things at different times.

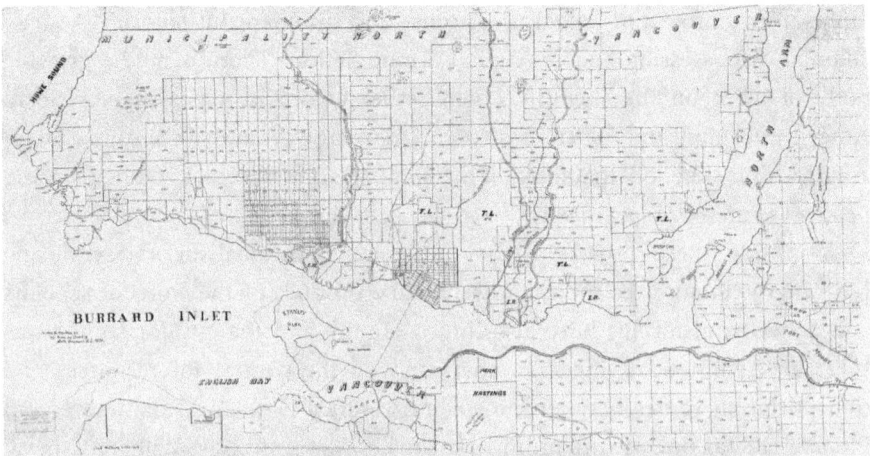

Figure 10.3 Municipality of North Vancouver. This 1899 map indicates land subdivision in North Vancouver and provides a sense of the spatial relationship between North Vancouver and Vancouver, which are separated by Burrard Inlet. The St. Alice was located within the densely plotted area of North Vancouver close to the straight line that spans Burrard Inlet on this map. Courtesy City of Vancouver Archives.

A potent symbol of settler colonialism at the city level, the St. Alice emblematized different phases of colonial and capitalist development upon its construction in 1912 and demolition seventy-seven years later. Built near the waterfront in North Vancouver, which lies just across the Burrard Inlet from Vancouver's downtown, the hotel was, in its early years, the brickwork pride of wealthy colonial moderns on land that was part of sovereign Squamish Nation territory. If this building is a text, then brick was its font. "Brick meant progress" and a racialized claim on the future, as William Deverell has written of early-twentieth-century Los Angeles.[42] Indeed the St. Alice's original owner, Antonio Gallia, called for 200,000 bricks in his original building application.[43] "Texts," literary critic Gesa Mackenthun writes in words that work well for what the St. Alice represented upon its construction, "did play an important role in the history of conquest."[44] With seventy rooms, a dining hall, banquet room, lounge, and other facilities, the St. Alice in its early days was the most impressive and imposing building on Vancouver's north shore.[45] It was also not exceptional. In cities across North America during the early twentieth century, "hotels represented their cities as progressive and sophisticated and often marked their place in the world."[46] Places like the St. Alice boosted claims to space, but also to time. The time of the future, marching on from a fading Indigenous past toward a permanent place of the white, propertied settler. Like the photography of Edward Curtis, statues from Luigi Perisco's *Discovery of America* (1844) to James Earle Fraser's *End of the Trail* (1915), or paintings from John Gast's

Figure 10.4 St. Alice Hotel, ca. 1913. Courtesy North Vancouver Museum and Archives.

American Progress (1872) to Emily Carr's *Skedans* (1912, the year the St. Alice opened), the hotel can and should be read as pronouncing settler futurity and Indigeneity as past.

In the spatial setting I'm considering here, the process of settler colonialism formally began in 1792, when Captain George Vancouver arrived in what is for now called Burrard Inlet. As the reach of European maritime capitalism became established through the Pacific Northwest, the relationship between Natives and newcomers was based on trade. Throughout the course of the nineteenth century, this equation changed as Indigenous communities found access to their land and resources severely curtailed, since the beneficiaries of the settler society that became the province of British Columbia dispossessed as they accumulated.[47] The tools and technologies which made this dispossession possible were varied and numerous: including direct violence, an imperial state, a colonial culture, epidemics, European technologies of transport and terror, maps which managed space in Eurocentric terms, numbers which quantified in order to control populations, a legal apparatus which protected settler property, and residential schools designed to extinguish Indigenous epistemologies, systems of language, standards of learning, and ways of life.[48]

National and provincial empire building also had a specifically municipal manifestation during and after the nineteenth century. Once Vancouver was officially founded in 1886, officials began working to annex even the slivers of land allocated as Native territory within the city. Part of this process involved the forced removal of Squamish residents from the village of Senákw, which became in part property of the Canadian Pacific Railway, across Burrard Inlet to reserves in North Vancouver in 1913, just a year after the St. Alice opened its doors.[49] Designated by the 1876 Indian Act as land set aside for First Nations communities, reserve space was controlled by the Canadian state and subject to unilateral expropriation through a civilizational discourse that posited settlers as uniquely productive occupants of the land. As one newspaper editorial complained in 1933, "the city is suffering, as it has suffered these forty years or more, from a useless, undeveloped, untaxable piece of waste land impinging on the populous area."[50] Meanwhile, expropriated Indigenous terrain and resources generated incomes for business owners in North Vancouver, as did Indigenous labor along the shoreline's lumber mills and docks.[51]

For Indigenous people in North Vancouver, dispossession was not accompanied by rights. The Indian Act not only designated reserve territory but also controlled every aspect of Native life, including leisure time. Indigenous people in Canada were legally prohibited from purchasing alcohol until 1951, although even after that in British Columbia, as activists like Squamish leader Andy Paull pointed out, racial restrictions remained.[52] Furthermore, many private clubs and government-controlled liquor stores excluded Indigenous patrons by regulation, and many more offered an unwelcoming atmosphere by custom for all but white clientele.[53] During and after the 1950s, beer parlors such as that of the St. Alice, then, were among the few places where Indigenous people could socialize in a licensed environment.[54]

The evolution of the St. Alice was also the result of transformed economic relations in North Vancouver. By the mid-twentieth century, the first wave of capital accumulation through primary resource extraction had for the most part run its course, the waterfront was lined with large industrial ship-building yards, and North Vancouver's well-to-do had moved outward and upward from the city center. And with this economic and cultural shift comes a plot twist in how we might read the St. Alice. No longer the preserve of local elites, it became a place of habitation and congregation for working-class and poor locals, both Indigenous and non-Indigenous. Purpose-built as a statement of settler permanence and futurity, it became a symbol of settler colonial failure. Indigenous contestation, in other words, prompts us to read the postwar St. Alice against the grain of its original authorial intent. From this perspective, 1989 appears as the tail end of what Yellowknives Dene political theorist Glen Coulthard calls the "culmination of a near decade-long escalation of Native

Figure 10.5 View from the St. Alice Hotel of North Vancouver Shipyards, Burrard Inlet, and Vancouver (across the inlet) during the Second World War. Courtesy North Vancouver Museum and Archives.

frustration."⁵⁵ As Phanuel Antwi points out in conversation with Amira Ismail in this volume, if the "Oka Crisis" appeared to flash up before many Canadians as an unexpected standoff between Mohawk warriors and Canadian police and military forces, for Indigenous participants and observers it was the product of long-simmering colonial tensions. Enduring Indigeneity, yet again, as ongoing accompaniment to the settler structure.

As the postwar decades wore on, a major shift took place throughout both Canada and the United States: an economic, political, cultural, and imaginative shift in continental orientation from Atlantic world to Pacific Rim. 1989 was a pivotal moment in this reorientation, it being the year when the massacre at Tiananmen Square in Beijing ensured that there would be no democratic

Figure 10.6 St. Alice Hotel, 1960s. Courtesy North Vancouver Museum and Archives.

challenge to the authoritarian capitalist project begun under Deng Xiaoping in the People's Republic of China, and when other capitalist Pacific powers got together in Canberra, Australia to form Asia-Pacific Economic Cooperation, or APEC. Even by the time my own family of Scottish shipbuilders, ironworkers, and retail employees arrived in North Vancouver in the 1970s, the industrial economy was in notable decline. By the 1980s, British Columbia was caught in the grips of a recession. As crises often do, this one contained profitable opportunities for those in a position to take them. Just across Burrard Inlet, the organizers and allies of Vancouver's 1986 World Exposition, or Expo '86 (itself a celebration of Vancouver's Pacific Rim location), found themselves in just such a spot. Claiming that people living in single occupancy hotels were "guests" rather than residents, Vancouver's city council and provincial government sided with developers who swept single-room occupancy hotels of their tenants in mass evictions that made room for well-heeled tourists. Expo was at once human displacement in the most predictable of colonial traditions and an advertisement to property speculators that Vancouver was not only scenic but also for sale. During and after Expo, Vancouver embodied traits of "the neoliberal city," but in this instance, colonial history and Pacific Rim spatial location also had important roles to play.[56]

The residents of the St. Alice were just far enough away from the Expo site to be spared eviction during the World's Fair, but by the mid-1980s, the hotel's days were nonetheless numbered. Not because the building had become unable to provide housing, albeit modest, for those who might otherwise be homeless. Not because it ceased to be an important community-gathering place. And not because this structure was in danger of collapse. The St. Alice's days were numbered because of the land it sat on, which overlooked Burrard Inlet and was increasing in value; because its residents, many surviving on social assistance, generated little wealth for local elites; and because the neighborhood in which the St. Alice stood had been subject to an ongoing campaign of representation by local media that emphasized dereliction, delinquency, and decline.[57] Such thematic staples of neoliberal gentrification discourse appeared in the local press alongside a steady stream of coverage exemplifying settler anxiety about North Vancouver's ongoing settler structure, including various anti-Indigenous pronouncements from a Member of British Columbia's Legislative Assembly, Jack Davis.[58] Most notoriously, this anxiety played out through the open racism of local columnist and Holocaust-denier Doug Collins toward Squamish and Tsleil-Waututh communities.[59] I remember how, under the cover of "free speech," the *North Shore News* celebrated having this noxious figure on its staff.

With a prominent platform for the likes of Collins and a general anti-Indigenous tenor pervading the area's main news source, *North Shore News* readers were left to make connections between a dilapidated neighborhood and discreditable Indigenous claims on settler society. In 1989, as had been the case before and would continue to be after, Indigenous people impeded settler progress. No great transformation to see here. The St. Alice's days were also numbered because it had become so known for its beer parlor, whose clientele consisted of the last of the shipyard workers from an industry closing up shop on the North Shore, residents of the local public housing project, where I lived, on the adjacent bloc, and local Indigenous patrons.[60]

When the owner of the St. Alice received an offer for the property from Cressey Development, a corporation that had previously gained attention for poor upkeep and gouging tenants, the hotel's owner explained to city councilors that he "did not believe there would be a serious dislocation of long-term tenants in the hotel, in the event the building is demolished."[61] The council agreed to let the sale and demolition proceed, and once the St. Alice tenants were issued eviction notices, a motion to consider emergency housing for those thrown out failed to pass.[62] By the late 1980s, with Vancouver's glass-tower and leaky condo boom on the horizon, brickwork no longer bespoke the settler future. Now, as Cressey's own "Heritage Potential" report said disparagingly with reference

Figure 10.7 St. Alice Hotel interior, 1980s. Courtesy North Vancouver Museum and Archives.

Figure 10.8 St. Alice Hotel demolition, 1989. Courtesy North Vancouver Museum and Archives.

to the 1910s, the St. Alice "represents architectural and building methods and materials typical of that era."[63] The Observatory would require new material and lend itself to a new neoliberal reading, but both buildings would tell an ultimately continuous story of settler ambition. In any case, many of those evicted from the St. Alice likely headed for Vancouver's downtown eastside, itself by then in the grips of an affordable housing shortage in the aftermath of Expo. In great contrast to the global attention that was to be trained on the fall of the Berlin Wall just a few months later, when the wrecking ball took aim at the St. Alice in the spring of 1989, and The Observatory was put up in its place, few people seemed to notice.

Conclusion

What conclusions can we draw from this story? For one, the history of the St. Alice Hotel makes clear that we need an analysis of settler colonialism in order to begin to understand neoliberal gentrification in the North American city. Coming to terms with the economic dimensions of neoliberal gentrification is certainly necessary, but hardly sufficient for understanding the displacement of residents from a space imagined as inhabited by poor and especially by

Indigenous people. In addition, the history of the St. Alice gets us further away from US or Canadian exceptionalisms when we consider cross-border comparisons at the end of the era we call the Cold War. Seattle, for example, lost hundreds of low-income housing units as the 1980s came to an end, while in the San Francisco Bay area, the Loma Pietra earthquake of October 1989 ushered in a round of disaster capitalism in which thousands of single occupancy rooms were removed from the housing market. Canadian and US national histories of neoliberalism and settler colonialism are not identical, but their resemblances are readily apparent.

Finally, the history of the St. Alice Hotel confronts us with a tale of two periodicities. On the one hand, 1989 marks a break with the Cold War, the geopolitical form of organization which supposedly determined global life from the late 1940s until that point, and which gave way to a globalized neoliberalism thereafter. On the other hand, we have the possibility of alternate timelines. Periodization is political, and Cold War periodizations, for all they reveal, also obscure through reduction to a two-camps logic. The history of the St. Alice encourages us to reckon with other histories rendered inconspicuous by the 1945–89 timeline, to wit settler colonialism for which neither the Cold War's beginning nor its end constitutes watershed events. The St. Alice was the site of many meetings over the decades, and when neoliberalism and settler colonialism met there in 1989, the results were not happy ones for its residents and patrons. But if it was the worst of times for the displaced, for elites across the capitalist world—as the period of Communist challenge ended and the era of neoliberalism got fully underway—the times were about the best they could be. All the while and still, the contested settler structure remained.

I no longer live in Vancouver, but whenever I visit, conversations inevitably and repeatedly turn to the cost-of-housing issue. The neighborhood where the St. Alice once stood is now unrecognizably transformed from what it looked like in the 1980s, and with hindsight everyone can see that The Observatory's rise marked an initial surge in a wave of condo building that would price many people out of a rapidly rising rental market. But seem as it might that this tale can only conclude in neoliberal entrenchment of the settler order, the real coda to this story—the construction to come of Senákw—offers one last plot twist to how we might read the St. Alice, this time in its aftermath. Also in 1989, as it turns out, the Canadian Pacific Railway put some of the land it had acquired decades earlier at the site of Senákw up for sale. Legal proceedings ensued, resulting in 2002 in the return of a portion of what had been taken.[64] The Squamish Nation is now building a new housing development on the site, scheduled for completion in 2030, described as the "Largest First Nations economic development project in Canadian history."⁶⁵ If the St. Alice was a settler space that became indigenized over time, Senáḵw looks to be a recovered Indigenous site that will offer relatively affordable housing for residents, challenging both neoliberal regimes of property and settler principles of sovereignty. Enduring Indigeneity indeed.

Notes

1. Daniel T. Rodgers, *Age of Fracture* (Cambridge, MA: Harvard University Press, 2011).
2. "United Nations Convention on the Rights of the Child," *United Nations Human Rights Office of the High Commissioner* (November 20, 1989), https://www.ohchr.org/EN/ProfessionalInterest/Pages/CRC.aspx (accessed March 3, 2022).
3. Steve Fraser and Gary Gerstle, eds., *The Rise and Fall of the New Deal Order, 1930–1980* (Princeton: Princeton University Press, 1989); Stuart Hall, "New Ethnicities," in *Stuart Hall: Critical Dialogues in Cultural Studies*, ed. David Morley and Kuan-Hsing Chen (1989; New York: Routledge, 1996), 442; Kimberlé Crenshaw, "Demarginalizing the Intersection of Race and Sex: A Black Feminist Critique of Antidiscrimination Doctrine, Feminist Theory and Antiracist Politics," *University of Chicago Legal Forum* 139 (1989): 139–67; David Harvey, *The Condition of Postmodernity* (New York: Blackwell, 1989).
4. "Microsoft Offering Apple Office CD," *New York Times*, August 3, 1989; "It's Serious Business as Nintendo's Gameboy Goes Head-to-Head with Atari's Lynx," *Los Angeles Times*, November 20, 1989; "Motorola Has a Pocket-Size Cellular Phone," *Los Angeles Times*, April 26, 1989.
5. Joshua Clover, *1989: Bob Dylan Didn't Have This to Sing about* (Berkeley: University of California Press, 2009), 92, 105–6.
6. Ned Richardson-Little, *The Human Rights Dictatorship: Socialism, Global Solidarity, and Revolution in East Germany* (Cambridge: Cambridge University Press, 2020), 180–254.
7. See Ambalavaner Sivanandan, "New Circuits of Imperialism," *Race & Class* 30, no. 4 (April 1989): 1–19.
8. "1990 Sales Lift Wal-Mart into Top Spot," *Fort Lauderdale Sun Sentinel*, February 15, 1991. The definitive history of Wal-Mart is Nelson Lichtenstein's *The Retail Revolution: How Wal-Mart Created a Brave New World of Business* (New York: Metropolitan Books, 2009).
9. Eric Hobsbawm, "Goodbye to All That," in *After the Fall: The Failure of Communism and the Future of Socialism*, ed. Robin Blackburn (New York: Verso, 1991), 115–25. As David Harvey has put the matter more recently, "The collapse of

communism in 1989 removed the external pressure on states to either look to the wellbeing of their populations or face strong political opposition." David Harvey, *Seventeen Contradictions and the End of Capitalism* (New York: Oxford University Press, 2014), 165.

10 One notable example is the Black radical protests against racial neoliberalism at Howard University in the spring of 1989, as charted in Joshua M. Myers, *We Are Worth Fighting For: A History of the Howard Student Protest of 1989* (New York: New York University Press, 2020).

11 Francis Fukuyama, "The End of History?" *The National Interest*, no. 16 (Summer 1989): 3–18.

12 Michael Hardt and Antonio Negri, *Empire* (Cambridge, MA: Harvard University Press, 2000); Saskia Sassen, "The Return of Primitive Accumulation," in *The Global 1989: Continuity and Change in World Politics*, ed. George Lawson, Chris Armbruster, and Michael Cox (New York: Cambridge University Press, 2010), 51.

13 Michael Denning, *Culture in the Age of Three Worlds* (New York: Verso, 2004); Mahmood Mamdani, *Good Muslim, Bad Muslim: America, the Cold War, and the Roots of Terror* (New York: Three Leaves Press, 2004); Michael E. Latham, *The Right Kind of Revolution: Modernization, Development, and US Foreign Policy from the Cold War to the Present* (Ithaca: Cornell University Press, 2011); Odd Arne Westad, "Beginnings of the End: How the Cold War Crumbled," in *Reinterpreting the End of the Cold War: Issues, Interpretations, Periodizations*, ed. Silvio Pons and Federico Romero (New York: Routledge, 2005), 68–81.

14 Kēhaulani Kauanui, "A Structure, Not an Event: Settler Colonialism and Enduring Indigeneity," *Lateral* 5, no. 1 (Spring 2016). Available online: https://csalateral.org/issue/5-1/forum-alt-humanities-settler-colonialism-enduring-indigeneity-kauanui/ (accessed October 21, 2021).

15 William Pietz, "The 'Post-Colonialism' of Cold War Discourse," *Social Text* nos. 19/20 (Autumn 1988): 55–75; Matthew Connelly, "Taking Off the Cold War Lens: Visions of North-South Conflict during the Algerian War for Independence," *American Historical Review* 105, no. 3 (June 2000): 739–69; Wen-Qing Ngoei, *Arc of Containment: Britain, the United States, and Anticommunism in Southeast Asia* (Ithaca: Cornell University Press, 2019); Monica Popescu, *At Penpoint: African Literature, Postcolonial Studies, and the Cold War* (Durham: Duke University Press, 2020).

16 Raymond D. Fogelson, "The History of Events and Nonevents," *Ethnohistory* 36, no. 2 (Spring 1989): 133–47.

17 Michel Foucault, *The Birth of Biopolitics: Lectures at the Collège de France, 1978–1979* (New York: Picador, 2004), 116; Quinn Slobodian, *Globalists: The End of Empire and the Birth of Neoliberalism* (Cambridge, MA: Harvard University Press, 2018).

18 For example, Gillian Hart, *Disabling Globalization: Places of Power in Post-Apartheid South Africa* (Berkeley: University of California Press, 2002); Nancy MacLean, "Southern Dominance in Borrowed Language: The Regional Origins of American Neoliberalism," in *New Landscapes of Inequality: Neoliberalism and the Erosion of Democracy in America*, ed. Jane L. Collins, Micaela di Leonardo, and Brett Williams (Santa Fe: School for Advanced Research Press, 2008), 21–37.

19 Kim Phillips-Fein, *Invisible Hands: The Businessmen's Crusade against the New Deal* (New York: W. W. Norton, 2009); Johanna Bockman, "The Long Road to 1989: Neoclassic Economics, Alternative Socialisms, and the Advent of Neoliberalism," *Radical History Review* 112 (Winter 2012): 9–42; Radhika Desai, "Second-Hand Dealers in Ideas: Think-Tanks and Thatcherite Hegemony," *New Left Review* 203 (January/February 1994): 27–64; Leigh Claire La Berge, "The Rules of Abstraction: Methods and Discourses of Finance," *Radical History Review* 118 (Winter 2014): 93–112.

20 Bethany Moreton, "Why Is There So Much Sex in Christian Conservatism and Why Do so Few Historians Care Anything about It?" *Journal of Southern History* 75, no. 3 (August 2009): 717–38; Deborah Cowen and Amy Siciliano, "Surplus Masculinities and Security," *Antipode* 43, no. 5 (November 2011): 1516–41.

21 Stuart Hall, Chas Critcher, Tony Jefferson, John Clarke, and Brian Roberts, *Policing the Crisis: Mugging, the State, and Law and Order* (New York: Palgrave Macmillan, 1978); Ruth Wilson Gilmore, *Golden Gulag: Prisons, Surplus, Crisis, and Opposition in Globalizing California* (Berkeley: University of California Press, 2007); Paula Chakravartty and Denise Ferreira da Silva, "Accumulation, Dispossession, and Debt: The Racial Logic of Global Capitalism," *American Quarterly* 64, no. 3 (September 2012): 361–85; Jordan T. Camp, *Incarcerating the Crisis: Freedom Struggles and the Rise of the Neoliberal State* (Oakland: University of California Press, 2016).

22 Christopher Klemek, *The Transatlantic Collapse of Urban Renewal: Postwar Urbanism from New York to Berlin* (Chicago: University of Chicago Press, 2011); Samuel Zipp and Michael Carriere, "Thinking through Urban Renewal," *Journal of Urban History* 39, no. 3 (May 2013): 359–65, Katherine G. Bristol, "The Pruitt-Igoe Myth," *Journal of Architectural Education* 44, no. 3 (May 1991): 163–71.

23 Annemarie Sammartino, "Mass Housing, Late Modernism, and the Forging of Community in New York City and East Berlin, 1965–1989," *American Historical Review* 121, no. 2 (April 2016): 492–521; Jesus Hernandez, "Redlining Revisited: Mortgage Lending Patterns in Sacramento, 1930–2004," *International Journal of Urban and Regional Research* 33, no. 2 (June 2009): 291–313.

24 Ruth Glass, "Aspects of Change," in *London: Aspects of Change*, ed. Ruth Glass et al. (London: MacGibbon and Kee, 1964), xviii–xix.

25 David Harvey, "From Managerialism to Entrepreneurialism: The Transformation in Urban Governance in Late Capitalism," *Geografiska Annaler* 71, no. 1 (1989): 3–17; Jason Hackworth, *The Neoliberal City: Governance, Ideology, and Development in American Urbanism* (Ithaca: Cornell University Press, 2007), 17–38, 123–49; Ted Rutland, "The Financialization of Urban Redevelopment," *Geography Compass* 4, no. 8 (August 2010): 1167–78.

26 Loretta Lees, "A Reappraisal of Gentrification: Towards a 'Geography of Gentrification,'" *Progress in Human Geography* 24, no. 3 (September 2000): 389–408; Don Mitchell, *The Right to the City: Social Justice and the Fight for Public Space* (New York: Guilford Press, 2003).

27 Peter Eisinger, "The Politics of Bread and Circuses: Building the City for the Visitor Class," *Urban Affairs Review* 35, no. 3 (January 2000): 316–33; George Lipsitz, *How Racism Takes Place* (Philadelphia: Temple University Press, 2011), 73–94; Kirsteen Paton, Gerry Mooney, and Kim McKee, "Class, Citizenship, and Regeneration: Glasgow and the Commonwealth Games 2014," *Antipode* 44, no. 4 (September 2012): 1470–89.

28 On continentalism, see Maurice H. Yeates and Barry J. Garner, *The North American City* (New York: Harper & Row, 1971); Michael A. Goldberg and John Mercer, *The Myth of the North American City: Continentalism Challenged* (Vancouver: University of British Columbia Press, 1986); and Richard Harris, "More American than the United States: Housing in Urban Canada in the Twentieth Century," *Journal of Urban History* 26, no. 4 (May 2000): 456–78. On the emancipatory versus the revanchist city, see Jon Caulfield, "'Gentrification' and Desire," *Canadian Review of Sociology and Anthropology* 26, no. 4 (August 1989): 617–32; David Ley, *The New Middle Class and the Remaking of the Central City* (New York: Oxford University Press, 1996); Neil Smith, *The New Urban Frontier: Gentrification and the Revanchist City* (New York: Routledge, 1996). Tom Slater's work provides a good starting place for these discussions. See Tom Slater, "Looking at the 'North American City' through the Lens of Gentrification Discourse," *Urban Geography* 23, no. 2 (February/March 2002): 131–53.

29 Roger Keil, "'Common-Sense' Neoliberalism: Progressive Conservative Urbanism in Toronto, Canada," *Antipode* 34, no. 3 (July 2002): 578–601.

30 Patrick Wolfe, "Structure and Event: Settler Colonialism, Time, and the Question of Genocide," in *Empire, Colony, Genocide: Conquest, Occupation, and Subaltern Resistance in World History*, ed. A. Dirk Moses (New York: Berghahn Books, 2008), 108.

31 Ian Tyrell, "Beyond the View from Euro-America: Environment, Settler Societies, and the Internationalization of American History," in *Rethinking American History in a Global Age*, ed. Thomas Bender (Berkeley: University of California Press, 2002), 168–91; Charles R. Hale, "Neoliberal Multiculturalism: The Remaking

of Cultural Rights and Racial Dominance in Central America," *PoLAR: Political and Legal Anthropology Review* 28, no. 1 (May 2005): 10–28; Marilyn Lake and Henry Reynolds, *Drawing the Global Colour Line: White Men's Countries and the International Challenge of Racial Equality* (New York: Cambridge University Press, 2008).

32 Jack O'Dell, "Foundations of Racism in American Life," in *Climbin' Jacob's Ladder: The Black Freedom Movement Writings of Jack O'Dell*, ed. Nikhil Pal Singh (Berkeley: University of California Press, 2010), 85–6; Aziz Rana, *The Two Faces of American Freedom* (Cambridge, MA: Harvard University Press, 2010); Corey Snelgrove, Rita Dhamoon, and Jeff Corntassel, "Unsettling Settler Colonialism: The Discourse and Politics of Settlers, and Solidarity with Indigenous Nations," *Decolonization: Indigeneity, Education & Society* 3, no. 2 (2014): 1–32; Lisa Lowe, *The Intimacies of Four Continents* (Durham: Duke University Press, 2015); Manu Karuka, *Empire's Tracks: Indigenous Nations, Chinese Workers, and the Transcontinental Railroad* (Oakland: University of California Press, 2019); Tiya Miles, "Uncle Tom Was an Indian: Tracing the Red in Black Slavery," in *Relational Formations of Race: Theory, Method, and Practice*, ed. Natalia Molina, Daniel Martinez Hosang, and Ramón A. Gutiérrez (Oakland: University of California Press, 2019), 121–44; Robert Nichols, *Theft Is Property! Dispossession and Critical Theory* (Durham: Duke University Press, 2020).

33 Paige Raibmon, "The Practice of Everyday Colonialism: Indigenous Women at Work in the Hop Fields and Tourist Industry of Puget Sound," *Labor* 3, no. 3 (Fall 2006): 23–56; Cindy Holmes, Sarah Hunt, and Amy Piedalue, "Violence, Colonialism, and Space: Towards a Decolonizing Dialogue," *ACME: An International E-Journal for Critical Geographies* 14, no. 2 (2015): 539–70; Adele Perry, *Colonial Relations: The Douglas-Connolly Family and the Nineteenth-Century Imperial World* (Cambridge: Cambridge University Press, 2015); Joanne Barker, ed., *Critically Sovereign: Indigenous Gender, Sexuality, and Feminist Studies* (Durham: Duke University Press, 2017).

34 Mahmood Mamdani, "Beyond Settler and Native as Political Identities: Overcoming the Political Legacy of Colonialism," *Comparative Studies in Society and History* 43, no. 4 (October 2001): 651–64; Mark Rifkin, "Settler States of Feeling: National Belonging and the Erasure of Native American Presence," in *A Companion to American Literary Studies*, ed. Caroline F. Levander and Robert S. Levine (Malden, MA: Blackwell, 2011), 342–55; Renée Hulan, "*Lieux d'oubli*: The Forgotten North of Canadian Literature," in *Canadian Literature and Cultural Memory*, ed. Cynthia Sugars and Eleanor Ty (New York: Oxford University Press, 2014), 54–67.

35 Audra Simpson, *Mohawk Interruptus: Political Life across the Borders of Settler States* (Durham: Duke University Press, 2014), 7.

36 Alexandra Harmon, Colleen O'Neill, and Paul Rosier, "Interwoven Economic Histories: American Indians in a Capitalist America," *Journal of American History* 98, no. 3 (December 2011): 698–722; John Munro, "Interwoven Colonial Histories: Indigenous Agency and Academic Historiography in North America," *Canadian Review of American Studies* 44, no. 1 (Fall 2014): 402–25.

37 David Rossiter and Patricia K. Wood, "Fantastic Topographies: Neo-Liberal Responses to Aboriginal Land Claims in British Columbia," *Canadian Geographer* 49, no. 4 (Winter 2005): 352–66; Aloysha Goldstein, "Where the Nation Takes Place: Proprietary Regimes, Antistatism, and US Settler Colonialism," *South Atlantic Quarterly* 107, no. 4 (Fall 2008): 833–61; Cliff Atleo, Jr., "From Indigenous Nationhood to Neoliberal Aboriginal Economic Development: Charting the Evolution of Indigenous-Settler Relations in Canada," *Canadian Social Economy Hub* (October 2008) http://socialeconomyhub.ca/sites/socialeconomyhub.ca/files/CAtleoCSEHubPaperoctober09.pdf (accessed May 10, 2022); Martha Stiegman and Sherry Pictou, "Recognition by Assimilation: Mi'kmaq Treaty Rights, Fisheries Privatization, and Community Resistance in Nova Scotia," in *Aboriginal History: A Reader*, ed. Kristin Burnett and Geoff Read (New York: Oxford University Press, 2012), 403–13; Isabel Altamirano-Jiménez, *Indigenous Encounters with Neoliberalism: Place, Women, and the Environment in Canada and Mexico* (Vancouver: University of British Columbia Press, 2013); David Lloyd and Patrick Wolfe, "Settler Colonial Logics and the Neoliberal Regime," *Settler Colonial Studies* 5, no. 2 (May 2015): 109–18.

38 Arthur M. Schlesinger, "The City in American History," *Mississippi Valley Historical Review* 27, no. 1 (June 1940): 50. Also see Andrew Heath, "Hidden Metaphors of Empire," *Neoamericanist* 5, no. 1 (Winter 2010): 8–12.

39 William Cronon, *Nature's Metropolis: Chicago and the Great West* (New York: W. W. Norton, 1991); Eugene P. Moehring, *Urbanism and Empire in the Far West, 1840–1890* (Reno: University of Nevada Press, 2004).

40 James Belich, *Replenishing the Earth: The Settler Revolution and the Rise of the Anglo-World, 1783–1939* (New York: Oxford University Press, 2009).

41 Tom Wilkinson, "The Writing on the Wall: The Language of Buildings," *Architectural Review* (January 23, 2019). Available online: https://www.architectural-review.com/essays/the-writing-on-the-wall-the-language-of-buildings (accessed October 21, 2021).

42 William Deverell, *Whitewashed Adobe: The Rise of Los Angeles and the Remaking of Its Mexican Past* (Berkeley: University of California Press, 2004), 133.

43 "Application No. 257: Application for Permit," July 25, 1911, St. Alice Hotel Clippings File, North Vancouver Museum and Archives.

44 Gesa Mackenthun, *Metaphors of Dispossession: American Beginnings and the Translation of Empire, 1492–1637* (Norman: University of Oklahoma Press, 1997), 11.

45 "Opening of the St. Alice Hotel," *Express* [North Vancouver], March 19, 1912, 8.
46 Molly W. Berger, "The American Hotel," *Journal of Decorative and Propaganda Arts* 25 (2005): 6.
47 Adele Perry, *On the Edge of Empire: Gender, Race, and the Making of British Columbia, 1849–1871* (Toronto: University of Toronto Press, 2001); John Sutton Lutz, *Makúk: A New History of Aboriginal-White Relations* (Vancouver: University of British Columbia Press, 2008); Renisa Mawani, *Colonial Proximities: Crossracial Encounters and Juridical Truths in British Columbia, 1871–1921* (Seattle: University of Washington Press, 2009).
48 Tina Loo, "Dan Cranmer's Potlatch: Law as Coercion, Symbol, and Rhetoric in British Columbia, 1884–1951," *Canadian Historical Review* 73, no. 2 (1992): 125–65; Cole Harris, "How Did Colonialism Dispossess? Comments from an Edge of Empire," *Annals of the Association of American Geographers* 91, no. 1 (March 2004): 165–82.
49 Nicholas Blomley, *Unsettling the City: Urban Land and the Politics of Property* (London: Routledge, 2004), 128–9.
50 Quoted in Jordan Stanger-Ross, "Municipal Colonialism in Vancouver: City Planning and the Conflict over Indian Reserves, 1928–1950s," *Canadian Historical Review* 89, no. 4 (December 2008): 542.
51 One of those dockworkers was Dan George who, long before his performance as Old Lodge Skins in *Little Big Man* (1970) earned him an Academy Award nomination, worked for years as a longshoreman on Burrard Inlet's docks. Members of the Squamish Nation formed the core of Local 526 of the Industrial Workers of the World. See Rolf Knight, *Indians at Work: An Informal history of Native Labour in British Columbia, 1858–1930* (1978; Vancouver: New Star Books, 1996), 247–9.
52 "Pub Law Trap, Say Indians," *Vancouver Province*, December 13, 1951, 17; "Magistrate's Stand On Indians Scored," *Vancouver Province*, May 14, 1954, 2; "You Can Buy Indian Friend a Beer, but Not at Home," *Vancouver Sun*, October 14, 1959, 21; Mawani, *Colonial Proximities*, 122–61.
53 Robert Campbell, *Sit Down and Drink Your Beer: Regulating Vancouver's Beer Parlours, 1925–1954* (Toronto: University of Toronto Press, 2001).
54 The St. Alice acquired a permission to operate a beer parlor in 1949. Minutes of the Statutory Meeting of the Council held in the Council Chamber, City Hall, January 3, 1949, 4, City of North Vancouver Council Minutes Archive. Available online: https://www.cnv.org/your-government/council-meetings/council-minutes-archive
55 Glen Sean Coulthard, *Red Skin, White Masks: Rejecting the Colonial Politics of Recognition* (Minneapolis: University of Minnesota Press, 2014), 116.

56 Hackworth, *Neoliberal City*; Katherine Mitchell, *Crossing the Neoliberal Line: Pacific Rim Migration and the Metropolis* (Philadelphia: Temple University Press, 2004).

57 "Sleepless Nights," *North Shore News*, November 22, 1981, A3; "From Shabbiness to Showpiece," *North Shore News*, January 31, 1982, A1; "A Night on the Streets," *North Shore News*, October 31, 1984, A1, A14–15; "Lonsdale Revitalized Just in Time for Expo," *North Shore News*, November 8, 1985, 3; "Development Needed," *North Shore News*, January 3, 1988, 6.

58 "Indians Claim Entire N. Shore," *North Shore News*, December 2, 1981, A1, A4; "North Van City Wants to Settle Indian Issues," *North Shore News*, January 16, 1983, A5; Jack Davis, "Native Citizens Being Degraded," *North Shore News*, February 13, 1983, A7; "Concern Over NV Indians," *North Shore News*, July 13, 1984, A3; Jack Davis, "Native Rights and Wrongs," *North Shore News*, April 17, 1985, 7; "Taxpayer Doesn't Owe a Thin Dime to the Indians," *North Shore News*, December 6, 1985, 6; "Squamish Band Demands Land," *North Shore News*, March 2, 1986, 2.

59 Doug Collins, "Where Do the Land Claim Payouts End?" *North Shore News*, April 18, 1984, A 8; Collins, "Colonel Collins' Last Stand," *North Shore News*, July 29, 1984, A8; Collins, "Give Indians Independence," *North Shore News*, August 28, 1985, 8; Collins, "Get This Straight," *North Shore News*, July 5, 1987, 9. For Collins on the Holocaust, see, for example, Collins, "How Big *Was* the 'Holocaust,'" *North Shore News*, August 29, 1984, A8; Collins, "Worm Working in Doug's Apple," *North Shore News*, May 19, 1985, 8.

60 Interviews conducted by the author and by Blackfoot geographer Michael Fabris with former patrons of the St. Alice.

61 "Victory for Rufus Park," *North Shore News*, October 7, 1981, A1, A10; "Battle of the Century Continues," *North Shore News*, April 28, 1985, 1; Meeting Minutes, North Vancouver City Council, October 3, 1988, City of North Vancouver Council Minutes Archive.

62 "North Vancouver Landmark to Face the Wrecker's Ball," *North Shore News*, December 14, 1988, 3; Meeting Minutes, North Vancouver City Council, September 11, 1989, City of North Vancouver Council Minutes Archive.

63 Cressey Development Corporation, "Heritage Potential of the St. Alice Hotel," October 13, 1988, Mayor Loucks' Correspondence (1988), Subseries II, North Vancouver Museum and Archives.

64 Hadani Ditmars, "A Multi-Billion Dollar Real Estate Project Is Rising on Native Reserve Land in Vancouver," *Architectural Digest* (September 29, 2021). Available online: https://www.architecturaldigest.com/story/vancouver-real-estate-native-reserve-land

65 "Senákw Vision," senakw.com/vision (accessed October 18, 2021).

11

Germany, the Environment, and the End of Communism: A Conversation

Julia Ault and Thomas Fleischman

In early December 2021, Julia Ault and Thomas Fleischman met over Zoom to discuss their recent books, East Germany, the environment, and 1989's legacy. Ault's *Saving Nature under Socialism: Transnational Environmentalism in East Germany, 1968–1990* was published by Cambridge University Press in 2021. Fleischman's *Communist Pigs: An Animal History of East Germany's Rise and Fall*, with the University of Washington Press, was released in 2020. We asked Ault and Fleischman to reflect on 1989's significance in East German and environmental history, the year's status as a moment of transformation, and the relationships between race, space, time, nature, and capital since 1989. While certain texts, such as Günter Schabowski's press conference of November 9, 1989, have had outsized (and unintended) consequences, Ault and Fleischman suggest other texts—Helmut Kohl's *Blühende Landschaften* (Blossoming or Thriving Landscapes) campaign slogan, the political platforms of various citizens' movements, and the posters and placards that sprang up in the streets—which illustrate the more complex and multivalent meanings of 1989 in the two Germanies.

> Julia Ault (JA): Would you want to start by saying a little bit about *Communist Pigs*, and why you wrote the book?
>
> Thomas Fleischman (TF): Sure. When I was beginning to look for potential dissertation topics, I was reading a lot about the environmental history of the GDR, and the collapse of the country in '89 looms very large in that historiography. I kept coming across explanations for that collapse that tended to fall into a Cold Warrior discourse that never sat right with me because it was bound up in a sort of Western triumphalism: that East Germany's environmental crimes were a result of socialist

megalomania, that the planned economies of state socialism were inherently backwards and irrational and could not help but pollute and destroy the environment, and so on. Being unsatisfied with that explanation, I wanted to figure out what really happened. What were the East Germans trying to build in their country, and why did environmental pollution problems occur in the ways that they did? These questions led me to look at agriculture—in particular, industrial agriculture. As I went digging for answers, most of what I could find about the topic was focused on collectivization drives and, specifically, their political consequences: the use and abuse of state power to force people to give up property. But there was very little about how farming actually worked. And so, by starting with the basics—asking "what did East Germans grow? How did they grow it? Where did they grow it? What did agriculture look like in 1949 versus 1970 versus 1985?"—I began to map a story of industrial development that increasingly appeared an awful lot like the industrialization of agriculture in Western Europe, but especially in the United States.

Communist Pigs is a history of industrial agriculture in East Germany, but from the perspective of animals, specifically three pigs, which I call the industrial pig, the garden pig, and the wild boar. These archetypes provide an alternative lens on to the development of East German agriculture because pigs are extraordinarily malleable in their physical form, in their behavior, and in their diet. I began to realize that reading what pigs look like, reading about where they live, what they eat, and how they live with other pigs is actually a useful way of understanding how people live with the environment, with agriculture, and with animals.

JA: I came to *Saving Nature under Socialism* from the perspective of environmental movements. I'd studied abroad as an undergraduate in Freiburg, which is known as the eco-capital of Germany, and then after college, I taught English in the former East Germany in a town called Jena. I wondered, "Why is no one talking about the environment here? What's going on? Why is there such a difference between these two places?" And so, I really focused my book on the evolution of environmental politics and protests in East Germany. I start in 1968, which is when the East German constitution included the right and responsibility to a clean environment, and carry the story through German unification in 1990. But I really didn't want to see East Germany in isolation. To me looking at transnational connections—whether it was physical pollution that crosses borders, or people, or ideas, policies, diplomacy—I really wanted to create a more regional context. I looked at West Germany—obviously German-German connections were important—but then I also wanted to look at how environmentalism developed in communism. For that aspect of the book, I looked east to Poland, which shared East Germany's second longest border, to see commonalities across Soviet Bloc countries. Basically, I aimed to decenter two notions: first that people only care about the environment in liberal democracies, and second, that people only care about it in a nation-state or national context. I examined at how physical environments, pollution, social movements, economic policies, and diplomatic considerations all transcended East Germany's highly militarized borders to create a regional and transnational understanding of environmentalism across and behind the Iron Curtain in Cold War Europe.

TF: Through a focus on a variety of texts, this volume—*Reading the New Global Order*—takes up global 1989 as a year of transformation but also one of continuity. More than three decades on, how do you think this change-versus-continuity question looks, when thinking about 1989 from the vantage point of German studies?

JA: Within German Studies, it depends a little bit on who you're looking at. In some ways, 1989 was not very important if you were living in Cologne or Munich [major cities in West Germany]. Your day-to-day life didn't change a whole lot, especially for white European Germans. For East Germans, a lot changed: employment opportunities and status, consumption, ability to travel. East Germans were initially excited about many of these opportunities, but they quickly developed new anxieties about job and social security as well as learning new political and economic systems. And then for the environment, the federal German government threw a lot of money at cleaning up environmental pollution in East Germany. But it came at the expense of economic downturns: a lot of factories were deemed not economically viable and were closed. But other industries did continue. For example, open pit coal mining of lignite—a low grade coal—continues to this day. They improved the desulfurization processes and implemented West German standards but mining still very much continues and is a significant reason why Germany has not further reduced its carbon emissions.

TF: I think that's a really excellent point. After 1989, East Germany basically ceased to exist within a year. And within four years, through economic reforms and privatization, all its major institutions and entities were wrapped up, and then that was that. But I think, as you point out with the lignite case, there were a lot of deep structures created by the Cold War, particularly when it came to the energy and security regimes that defined the borders of east and west that laid the groundwork for the economic development of those countries. Those things have not gone away. So, lignite is a perfect example as that cheap source of coal has become, ironically, more important now than it was in 1990, largely because of *die Energiewende*.[1] With the shuttering of nuclear energy, Germans had to find a reliable domestic source of energy, fossil fuels, and in this case, all they have in Germany, East or West, is lignite. That's a problem they're still dealing with, and that's not just an East/West thing. But then we also know, for example, that radioactive cesium, the nuclear fallout from Chernobyl, still persists in the environment of Central and Western Europe. Reactor Number Four, near Pripyat, is still burning; it's just covered in a giant sarcophagus. That crisis is ongoing. And then there's the footprint of the Iron Curtain, most recently discussed in Astrid Eckert's book *West Germany and the Iron Curtain*.[2] This famous, or infamous, militarized border has, in the post-socialist years, become one of the world's largest experiments in modern conservation through the creation of the so-called Green Belt. The idea that environmentalists can create a vast corridor of migration for wildlife, connecting the Baltic to the Black Sea and Mediterranean, is spectacular, but as Astrid shows, this particular configuration of nature was a product of Cold War security regimes. The East Germans thinned the forests on their side and prevented any kind of development, while in the West, economic neglect left the other side sparsely populated as well, as nobody wanted to invest money in building a factory right next to this border. In this way, the Iron Curtain created this particular environment, which is now, ironically, under threat of disappearing without the security regimes that maintained it in the first place.

JA: Just out of curiosity, agriculture after 1989–90 was obviously all privatized, but doesn't Mecklenburg still have some of the largest farms in Germany because they just sold off larger plots of collectivized land?

TF: Yes, I think one of the ironies is that industrialization hasn't stopped. It didn't stop in 1989 and, in many ways, because the former East no longer had to produce everything for one country to consume—you know, all the types of food that would need to be grown and eaten by East Germans within East Germany—now they've given over even more arable land to the cultivation and production of commodity crops that can be sold around the world. So a lot more of that land is now given over to rapeseed and wheat and corn production that was formerly reserved for potatoes and sugar beet and all these other crops that needed to be grown in East Germany. Without that restriction monocultures have expanded. Property holding—the number of people who own property in the East—has gone down. And most ironic of all, the scourge of livestock pollution has gotten worse since 1990. Livestock holdings have just continued to be consolidated so that there are fewer firms managing larger and larger stocks of animals.

German farmers can ameliorate or hide some of the worst pollution problems through capital and technology. But that hasn't stopped the pollution crisis at all. Look at a satellite image of the Baltic Sea and you can actually see the eutrophic dead zone spreading from one shore to another. Industrial agriculture still threatens the ecology of that body of water. The Baltic is probably worse off today than it was in 1990.

JA: Another aspect of continuity versus change around 1989 is specifically about environmental activists who were vocal and active in protests in the 1980s. Very few of them became prominent politicians or took up a public role in the 1990s. So many of them were involved in the citizens' movements in 1989, but because East Germany was incorporated into a West German (Federal Republic) dominated system, they had to learn to navigate new dynamics when they were more familiar with protesting a dictatorship. That context left fewer opportunities for participation in established West German political practices and networks. Matthias Platzek in Brandenburg became well known, and Carlo Jordan floated around Berlin politics for a while, but many of them really don't become prominent on a federal level. That's another human legacy with an environmental impact: people from the east were not commenting on and setting policy about what happened to their own landscapes, because so much of this was done from the top down and from the outside.

TF: I think that's a really important observation. It speaks to the ways in which another layer is added to the erasure of East Germany in the wake of 1989. Not only was its economy, its political institutions, its culture rolled up, but its people were also sidelined, and not just the regime itself but experts, people who knew about East Germany's environmental problems, who knew them better than anyone in the West ever could. And yet these people weren't being consulted to formulate environmental policy.

JA: Yes, people working in various East German institutes and in the environmental ministry in East Germany, most of them (other than at the top levels) were more or less ignored. But let's turn to another question: what does the German 1989 look like if we put race front and center? Thinking, for example, here of Tiffany Florvil's *Mobilizing Black Germany*, an important study that features a periodization which crosses 1989 without focusing much on the fall of the wall story that looms so large in many other accounts.[3]

You know, one thing that's indirectly related—maybe not quite the direction this question was going—is that, in West Germany, the Green Party was the only major political party to oppose unification. It was actually very vocal in its opposition to German unification because it was concerned that a unified Germany would return to its racist, fascist past. Instead, the Greens suggested that West Germany could help to support a reformed East Germany in different forums but wanted to avoid unifying Germany and creating a potential return to this more racist past. And there were then, as we know, racist incidents—neo-Nazis in the former East Germany in the 1990s setting refugee homes on fire—that then led to a narrative that East Germany had not confronted its past the way West Germany had. Today, with the rise of the AFD, we might ask if either side learned. This question of having alleviated, or addressed and put to bed, the Nazi past, or a racist past, is very much still present. It was there then, and I think it was overlooked or whitewashed in the 1990s, but now we're looking back and realizing that this was always present on both sides of the Iron Curtain. We need to think about race and racism in 1989/90 more critically.

TF: One of the strange things about the history of the Greens and environmentalism in the twentieth century is that it made a lot of strange bedfellows out of the left and the right. The ascendancy of environmentalism to the top of reunified Germany's agenda in the 1990s allowed people who disagreed on fundamental political positions to actually talk to each other.

This opening created opportunity for progress on the environment but also significant dangers, especially in the ways that environmentalism was treated as an apolitical project. In this case, I'm thinking about Rudolf Bahro—the East German dissident and writer who later espoused ecofascist ideas, even calling for a "Green Adolf" in Germany to deal with environmental problems.[4] There is a way in which environmentalism can in fact cover up deep seated and fundamentally racist ideas.

JA: Yes, we absolutely tend to think of it as a left-leaning, progressive set of policies today. But there were environmental preservationist ideas at the heart of Nazi ideology, the blood-and-soil type rhetoric. Environmentalism is not inherently inclusive, or progressive, but can in certain contexts be very racist.

TF: If we were to read Günter Schabowski's press conference of November 9 as a text of 1989, how would we interpret it?[5] Is it too much of a stretch to connect the idea of immediacy, or immediate effect, with a sense of cultural or technological acceleration that seems to have pervaded much of the human experience since the end of the Cold War? Has 1989, or perhaps the fully global ascendancy of capitalist time it represents, had an impact on the idea of time itself?

JA: I've got two thoughts on this. I'll start by very specifically talking about Schabowski's press conference and then move out from there.

The opening of the Berlin Wall with Schabowski's misstep—saying "this is effective immediately"—I don't think that was really his intention. I think the East German leadership was still stumbling at this point. Erich Honecker had disappeared from the public eye about a month before, and there was a lot of internal turnover. It's seen as this big watershed moment, especially in the West because the Berlin Wall and Germany's borders were so iconic in Cold War mentalities and worldview. In a lot of ways, though, this narrative ignores the fact that there were actually much larger shifts going on in other parts of Eastern Europe, well before November 9, 1989. Poland had already had semi-free elections nearly half a year earlier, Hungary had opened its border to Austria, to Western Europe, over the summer. I think, if anything, Schabowski's press conference shows how behind East Germany was in terms of acknowledging the inevitable collapse of the SED's rule at that moment. In that moment, though, there was still great debate about what the future without SED-rule would look like. I'd insert a little contingency there.

But stepping back and thinking about immediacy and sense of time, the growing digital divide between East Germany and other parts of the world contributed greatly to its collapse, both directly and indirectly through the economic disparity it represented. We look too closely at the differences between communist and capitalist states in the Cold War, because it lends itself to a triumphalist narrative of capitalism that does two things: (1) it ignores connections during the Cold War and (2) it ignores the legacies of communism that continue to this day in many parts of the world. Cold War borders were far more porous than we tend to think. There are also those continuing legacies of communism around the world today. A friend and colleague Andrew Kloiber is writing a book about coffee culture in East Germany and its connections to the Global South. He demonstrates very clearly that East German investment in Vietnam and Laos, for example, turned them into the well-known coffee producers they are today.[6] We tend to ignore that the connections within or between Communist and non-aligned countries were important. This sense of timeline was erased in the 1990s and early 2000s because capitalism won. Now, scholars like Kloiber are shedding new light on those relationships.

TF: In retrospect I think the Schabowski press conference came to be seen as the moment that the dissolution of the GDR began to accelerate dramatically. It was this watershed moment that opened the door to the West, or more specifically to "Europe" for Eastern Europe. After November 9, the countries of the eastern bloc seemed to exist in a new timeline altogether, moving in their development toward their former foils in the West. It was at the Maastricht Treaty signing that the EU got together and laid out the new rules that would define both what "Europe" was as an economic and political space for its current members, and how new members, specifically the countries of Eastern Europe, could become part of "Europe." Suddenly a new time horizon presented itself to the countries of Eastern Europe. In order to work toward "Europe," to be included in the Europe of the EU, they all had to follow a certain set of economic and political reforms that were, in many ways, quite devastating for the countries of the former East. This so-called Washington Consensus demanded that new member nations had to reduce social welfare spending, balance their budgets, divest themselves of publicly owned industries, and keep inflation low. Not only did these reforms introduce austerity to the East, but also deindustrialization. And while these reforms were being undertaken, leaders in the East kept justifying these measures to their citizens by saying, "We're doing this for Europe, so that we can join Europe." In the meantime, the EU was constantly rewriting the rules and prerequisites for membership so that timeline was pushed further and further away.

Now, most of those countries joined the European Union by 2004. But at what cost? I think many people have come to understand that living in the Time of Europe, or the EU for Eastern Europe, has not been a time of increased prosperity that was pledged to them, but rather a time of painful economic and social upheaval, of wrenching transformation that I think has played a direct role in the rightwing backlash to "Europe" that's unfolding right now.

JA: I totally agree. With Germany being so central in European, and specifically EU, politics, there is a mentality about Eastern Europe—"Oh we did it right. But now you're trying to join and we're holding you to different standards." It held these countries to contemporary standards, rather than those of the 1950s and 1960s when Western European integration began.

TF: Are there any texts of the German 1989 that seem significant to you in retrospect?

JA: Yes, a couple of sets of texts stand out to me about 1989. One is that, in the fall of 1989, starting in September, there were citizens' movements that all come together, the most famous of them was probably the New Forum. The citizens' movements were trying to push back against the SED to create accountability. The citizens' movements came up with comprehensive platforms with various planks. They were complex. A lot of them did not emphasize or even mention unification. They did not advocate to become a Western-style capitalist democracy. Rather they wanted a "third way," something that was different from single-party dictatorship in East Germany but also different from the more capitalist West German model. They critiqued both communism and capitalism, and in a lot of ways they presented, or hoped for, an improved form of socialism. Within that context, one commonality that struck me as I read the platforms for my book was that virtually all of them highlighted the desire for a more ecologically just form of governance. Thirty-odd years later, that is something that resonates especially with a lot of younger people in Germany today. Many East German activists didn't really get the whole-scale environmental transformation that they wanted.

The other set of texts that I think are really interesting and don't get enough attention are the posters and placards that people carried in the demonstrations in Leipzig, Berlin, and other cities. They covered a whole range of issues. We tend to think about placards that demanded unification, "We are the Volk" that sort of rhetoric. But in reality, they talked about everything from human rights to travel restrictions to environmental problems to asking for aid from the Soviet Union ("Gorbi come help us"—a reference to Gorbachev's reforms). Some of them were really funny and witty. Some of them were direct and cutting. Some were just a plea for change. The common narrative of successful unification (that does need to be challenged in a lot of ways) overlooks the variety, and sometimes inconsistency, of what people had on their minds in that moment.

TF: I think that's exactly right. And it reminds me of another text. The year 1989 is a conjuncture of all these different events and forces, creating for a short time a wide range of exciting possibilities. And what was so shocking about what followed is how rapidly that window closed. For me, the text that really represents the foreclosure of radical, alternative futures was German Chancellor Helmut Kohl's infamous campaign slogan in 1990—*Blühende Landschaften*. This is the idea that, under the CDU (the Christian Democratic Union), a set of economic and political reforms would unfold in the east that would create "blooming landscapes" of economic progress and growth. This slogan marked the ascendancy of environmental discourse to the top of German politics. This seemed promising, especially in the wake of 1989 when radical environmental critiques of the GDR as well as West German capitalism were everywhere. But in the hands of Kohl, this language was cynically co-opted to promote a supposedly "apolitical" program of highly disruptive, neoliberal reforms in the former East. Kohl's "blooming landscapes" signaled the coming marginalization of a radical environmental program in a reunified Germany, encapsulating the ways in which most East Germans, and their expertise, would be completely ignored and sidelined throughout reunification.

But let me pose a different question: How important do you think 1989 is to global environmental history, in terms of the actual climate, and in terms of ideas about it?

JA: Something I should have mentioned before, and it came to me as you were talking, is how 1989–90 is often depicted as this moment of eye-opening awareness on the part of Western Europeans and people in the United States, or outside of the Communist bloc, about the horrors of communism and how polluted it was. In *Der Spiegel*—which is essentially the German version of *Time* magazine—every other issue was an exposé about how horrible the pollution in East Germany was. On one level, 1989 was important for clean-up, because there was a new sense of awareness. Germans in East and West already knew the devastation was real. They just didn't necessarily have the facts and figures at hand. In that respect, it was a moment of transformation. For example, all East Germany's nuclear power plants closed very quickly in 1990. Also, the federal government invested heavily in industrial cleanup projects. It was really important. On another level, though, Germans (East or West, in this case) could not or did not seize unification as an opportunity to re-envision what environmentalism could look like in the former communist bloc. It just reinforced capitalist modes of environmentalism and environmental protection, often depending on capitalist polluters to regulate themselves. So again, this West German or Western European triumphalism meant that East German or communist practices were not critically considered. There was nothing to be saved or learned from the other system. The 1990s represented this moment in which capitalism, in its victory in the Cold War, portrayed itself as both wealthier and cleaner. There was nothing to be learned from communism, and a decided lack of introspection.

In terms of global environmental discourse, 1989 is almost a blip between the Brundtland report that comes out in 1986 and the Rio conference in 1992. It's often overlooked in that international conversation about other environmental questions, which we should question and challenge.

TF: Yes, 1990 is certainly the moment where we move away from sulfur dioxide being the major pollutant that people are concerned with, to carbon dioxide at Rio, and greenhouse gases in general. That is when that pivot happens. But I think you're also right to point out the real tragedy of this—and this is something that's so great about your book—you're reminding your readers that there is a long and very real tradition of environmental thought in the East that seriously engaged with the problems of industrial development, that had real ideas about the underlying problems of industrial communism and industrial capitalism, and also their legacies. The nature parks that exist in Eastern Germany were created in 1990 by the SED regime, as one of the last acts before the country was completely dissolved. All of this is just to say that environmental thought, as you point out, was a real thing in Eastern Europe that was worth engaging with, and it's been completely overlooked, passed over, discounted. In many ways, the tragedy of 1989 is that there was this moment of tremendous possibility for change, and it was just steamrolled by Western triumphalism, and the institutions of the West run by capitalists.

JA: That's totally right. They're being run by capitalists, and they're being run by a particular type of capitalist, a neoliberal conservatism that gains dominance in the United States and Western Europe in the 1980s with Reagan and Thatcher, and with Kohl in Germany. It's not even the Cold War consensus, the sort of center-right of the 1960s and 1970s, it's a new form of anti-union, anti-environment, pro-economic, pro-privatization, that is a different brand.

TF: It's interesting because there seemed to be a real lack of alternative political projects by 1990—Gorbachev's reform communism was a failure and enthusiasm for the robust welfare states and industrial economies of the Miracle Years had waned since the multiple economic crises of the 1970s. By 1989, the only ideology that seems to have any viability was neoliberalism, despite the fact that the outcomes of Thatcherism in England were mixed at best. The collapse of communism gave it new life.

JA: Yes, neoliberal capitalism was definitely validated and got a new life in a way it might not have had without this crisis of communism coming to a head between 1989 and 1991, culminating with the collapse of the Soviet Union.

TF: Last question: the GDR was a relatively short-lived country and yet has much to tell us about the history of the twentieth century, as well as our own times, as evidenced by the fact that the field of GDR history is thriving, and rightly followed by scholars in other areas. Why do you think this is?

JA: Starting with the longer history, East Germany is fascinating. It captures a lot of people's imaginations. Thanks to Cold War media, films, books about spies, the Stasi, the iconic nature of the Berlin Wall. That's probably why there is continuing public interest. East Germany was also important as a successor state to Nazi Germany, moving from one dictatorship to another, from a fascist to a communist one. This continuity has had incredible staying power in people's memory and in their vision of what Germany is and where it's been in the twentieth century. Intellectually, a divided state has offered a sort of laboratory to examine two Germanies, a democratic and capitalist one versus a communist dictatorship with a planned economy. We only have so many cases of divided states in the world: Korea, Vietnam, (also China/Taiwan as Song-Chuan Chen examines) but really, it's one of very few cases where you can look so closely at it. And then, on a very practical and perhaps cynical level, I think accessibility to German archives has played an important role in the continued prevalence of East Germany. It's relatively easy to obtain grants to conduct research in Germany; archives are open and accessible to scholars in a way that's not necessarily the case in other parts of Eastern Europe.

TF: We also have to remember that because East Germany doesn't exist anymore, nobody is jealously guarding its secrets. Nobody cares about East Germany in that way or is worried about what might be found in archives, as opposed to the other successor states in Eastern Europe.

JA: That's sort of the blessing and the curse of East Germany, having been rolled into West Germany. The East German leadership was entirely gone, and a whole transition of new people came in. This was not the case in other places. The old elites didn't disappear in Poland, the Czech Republic, Slovakia, Hungary, etc. I think these are some of the practical reasons why East Germany has such prominence in the scholarship.

My last point is that East Germany, for its own sake, has been studied a lot, and I think very, very thoroughly and very well. What we need to do is expand our horizons to think about how East Germany fits thematically and geographically into larger contexts. I think that's where the scholarship should go and is going now.

TF: Yes, I would agree. On the one hand, it is unusual to study a country that didn't exist for very long and doesn't exist at all anymore. That can seem very provincial or even parochial. On the other hand, the forces that shaped larger events of the Cold War period everywhere were also present in East Germany, and in studying them in the GDR, we can challenge or upend a lot of the assumptions embedded in those grand narratives.

JA: Agreed. East Germans were great at creating records. There are lots and lots of records: information about what East Germans thought and did, about daily life, and about different aspects of the party and the state were doing. It's oddly self-reflective in a certain way—totally oblivious in others—but there are many records to work and engage with.

Notes

1. The *Energiewende* is Germany's ongoing transition to affordable, renewable sources of energy.
2. Astrid Eckert, *West Germany and the Iron Curtain: Environment, Economy, and Culture in the Borderlands* (London: Oxford University Press, 2019).
3. Tiffany Florvil, *Mobilizing Black Germany: Afro-German Women and the Making of a Transnational Movement* (Champaign, IL: University of Illinois Press, 2020).
4. Eli Rubin, "The Greens, the Left, and the GDR: A Critical Reassessment," in *Ecologies of Socialism: Germany, Nature, and the Left in History, Politics, and Culture*, ed. Eli Rubin, Sabine Mödersheim and Scott Moranda (Bern: Peter Lang, 2019), 183.
5. Günter Schabowski, Press conference, November 9, 1989. Available online: https://digitalarchive.wilsoncenter.org/document/113049 (accessed December 4, 2021).
6. Andrew Kloiber, *Brewing Socialism: Coffee, East Germans, and Twentieth Century Globalization* (New York: Berghahn Books, 2022).

Conclusion

Ned Richardson-Little

1989: World-Historical Fracture and a Return to More of the Same[1]

As early as 1990, the year 1989 had already become shorthand for several enduring grand historical concepts: the Return to Europe, the End of the Illusion, the End of History.[2] More than a year, 1989 was a "world-historical event, in the Hegelian sense," in the words of Vladimir Tismăneanu.[3] In the decades since, histories of 1989 have not only proliferated, but taken a turn to the global, illuminated the "long 1989" and, by the thirtieth anniversary, deconstructed, demythologized and, in some cases, dethroned 1989 as the great caesura in modern history.[4] But can the year 1989 itself be excavated from the meta-discourse surrounding such attempts to ascribe it a singular meaning within larger grand historical narratives?

As the chapters in this book reveal, 1989 sits uncomfortably as the totemic end of the Cold War, ushering in a world-defining end of history, but also as signaling and confirming long-term trends now made triumphant by the exhaustion of their competitors. Looking back on the volume to which this book is a sequel, 1989 takes on a very different character than 1944, which, as Kirrily Freeman wrote, "was—globally—a moment of comparative openness, of radical potential in which futures were glimpsed, imagined and even programmatically laid out in ways that were fundamental and far-reaching."[5] When examined through the lens of the many texts in this volume, the great caesura is visible, but so are the intersecting continuities that reach into the present. As a world-historical moment, 1989 is remarkably free of utopias, beyond the very limited visions inherent to liberal democracy and national self-determination. Here, we see an optimism for the realization of democracy and freedom in broad strokes from many corners of the globe, but so little that is programmatic or comprehensive as a project for global change. The question of what comes after the bipolarity of the Cold War order is laden with anxieties and fears for a world riven by ethnic conflict and devoid of higher purpose.

In terms of the lofty ambitions of freedom, texts from this year so often frame the situation as Jürgen Habermas did in 1990, as "catching up revolutions" merely fulfilling the demands of modernization by realizing parliamentary forms of liberal democracy.[6] Rather than a radical openness to the future, there is a sense across many of the book's chapters of narrowed possibilities: imaginaries closed to the new and retreating to the old—or at least to the well used. While 1944 marked the ascendancy of new lefts and visions of the public and collective good across a range of fields, those who pursued such goals in 1989 were a small and quickly marginalized minority. Instead, the idealistic notions of 1989 took the form of both a relinquishment of power by those institutions that could pursue such collective visions and a devolution of power, ostensibly, to the masses via democratic voting and consumption. What would come next was not to be decided by intellectuals and leaders, but by individuals expressing their desires through parliaments and markets. Yet, behind this optimism lurked the steady advance of neoliberalism and the long-term force of colonialism still in effect on the ground. There is a sense of emancipation from certain heavy burdens of collectivism, but little order to what would come from this newfound freedom, to fill the void.

Democracy and the Freedom for More of the Same

The year 1989 is awash in soaring rhetoric from political leaders touting the triumph of democracy across the world. At the start of the year, before the dramatic events that would unfold in Eastern Europe and China, US President Ronald Reagan spoke in his farewell address of a sea change in world affairs, naturally emanating from his administration's efforts in the United States: "Countries across the globe are turning to free markets and free speech and turning away from the ideologies of the past. For them, the great rediscovery of the 1980s has been that, lo and behold, the moral way of government is the practical way of government."[7] Similarly, Pakistani Prime Minister Benazir Bhutto spoke optimistically about the new era of peaceful transition to democracy, as had occurred in her country the year before, where the population demonstrated that "democracy is the greatest revenge."[8] In South Africa, the Apartheid regime became more vulnerable to the forces of democracy, as the Harare Declaration of the Commonwealth nations took a harder line against racism and embraced interference in the internal affairs of states violating basic human rights. As one anti-Apartheid publication put it, "the forces of the new South Africa—the South Africa of democracy, equality and peace—are once again on the march."[9]

In Eastern and Western Europe, the past became an anchor point for the tumultuous present. In France, Jean-Paul Goude staged a "revolutionary opera" as part of official celebrations of the bicentennial of the French Revolution. Reproducing many of the racial and orientalist tropes of the event itself, UCLA Professor Robert Maniquis described it as "a happy mixture of humanity. There were French schoolchildren, Scots bagpipers, bare-breasted Ethiopian women, Russians dressed in Constructivist costume, an American marching band, Chinese acrobats, ritual dancers from Singapore, and much much more."[10] In Goude's choreography, the Revolution was simultaneously a pivotal movement of French national history, a symbol of international friendship, and a universal event. In Hungary, at the ceremonial reburial of Imre Nagy (the prime minister who led the reformist movement crushed by the Soviets in 1956) on June 16, 1989, a young liberal named Viktor Orbán declared: "Today, 33 years after the Hungarian revolution and 31 years after the execution of the last responsible Hungarian leader, we have a chance to achieve in a peaceful way all that was [once] obtained through bloody fighting for the nation."[11] The moment promised a chance to realize the strivings toward freedom of 1956, but also the Hungarian nationalist revolution of 1848 against the Austrian Habsburgs.

Already in 1989, the possibilities for that freedom were largely set toward the path of liberal democratic market capitalism. In a still divided Germany after the infamous press conference—discussed by Julia Ault and Thomas Fleischman—that led to the fall of the Berlin Wall, a group of dissidents and intellectuals put out a plea to resist the "selling off of our material and moral values" that had already begun. Against the siren song of German reunification, they called for the realization of a new socialist alternative to West Germany that could reflect the "anti-fascist and humanist ideals with which we began."[12] Yet this call was overtaken by a competing ten-point plan for rapid reunification offered by West German Chancellor Helmut Kohl, which instead envisioned a fundamental transformation of East Germany toward a vision of continuity with existing institutions in the West and ongoing processes of Europeanization.[13] Kohl's was not a blueprint for a visionary new future, but the promise of an end to new experiments and a turn toward dependable forms of democracy and prosperity that already existed in finished form or had an established path forward. Similarly, Soviet leader Mikhail Gorbachev's vision of a "Common European Home"—in which he imagined the integration of the USSR into a new kind of pan-European political arrangement—was similarly doomed to failure. In contrast to Kohl's plan for the expansion of European structures eastwards, Gorbachev aimed at erasing the East-West divide and, in turn, diminishing the transatlantic influence of the United States via NATO, which would now be obsolete.[14] Here too, the institutions built up in the West during the Cold War held fast against this vision of radical change: NATO expansion was propelled forward without participation by the Soviets and, later, the Russians.

Beijing and Berlin in 1989 have been elevated as iconic representations of the two paths available in that fateful year. While the fall of the Wall ushered in democratic transition, tanks crushed such ambitions and maintained authoritarian rule in the People's Republic of China. Yet there were many other roads taken between these two poles: in other parts of the communist world, the transition to democracy was far less dramatic—and far less democratic. In contrast to the mass mobilizations in East Germany, Poland, and Czechoslovakia, the transition to democracy in Hungary came about through elite negotiations. In Romania, Nicolae Ceaușescu resisted change to the point of ordering mass violence, which only resulted in his own execution. In Bulgaria and Mongolia, parliamentary elections in 1989 and a new rhetoric of democratization removed the upper echelons of the nomenklatura, but also allowed for the legitimization of a younger generation of that same—ostensibly ousted—power structure. Further afield, the democratic transition in Latin America was also rockier than the rosy imagery of a seamlessly unfolding wave of freedom suggested. Although Brazil held its first democratic elections for president since 1964 in 1989, the victorious Fernando Collor would not see through his term, resigning in an attempt to avoid impeachment for corruption. Lebanon's long civil war concluded with the country occupied by Syrian and Israeli forces and with a peace agreement that promised only a "return to political normalcy."[15]

Histories of the collapse of state socialism in 1989 often gloss over the complications of justice and democratization outside of the socialist world. In particular, the focus on the People's Republic of China in that year obscures the interconnections of this history with Taiwan's trajectory. If 1989 marked the beginning of the reunification of the two Germanies, it led to the divergence of the two Chinas, as Taiwan set out on a course of democratization and continued independence from the People's Republic. As Song-Chuan Chen's chapter shows, this path was as complex and multifaceted as the histories of democratization in Eastern Europe. Here too, self-immolation as a form of protest played a crucial symbolic role, as it had in Czechoslovakia with Jan Palach's protest against the crushing of the Prague Spring in 1968 and Oskar Brüsewitz's demonstration against the suppression of religion in East Germany in 1976, among numerous examples.[16] Unlike the Berlin-Beijing narratives that fit neatly within a Cold War framework, the history of Taiwan's democratization brings up the difficult question of why—as a member of the "free world"—it needed democratization at all. On a smaller scale, the idea of freedom and liberation within the democratic West itself is key to the chapter by Frances Pheasant-Kelly on the documentary *First Tuesday: Free to Speak*. In this case, the 1989 liberation of the Guildford Four highlighted unjust imprisonment and the perversion of the rule of law in the name of a liberal security state.

Eurocentrism, Multiculturalism, and Identities

One counterpoint to the optimism of 1989 as a marker of freedom has long been the fear of revived nationalism and ensuing ethnic conflicts in the wake of the Cold War. To some extent, these fears were realized with the collapse of Yugoslavia and the bloody conflict and genocide that followed. Only a few weeks after Tiananmen, Serbian President Slobodan Milošević gave his infamous Gazimestan speech at a celebration of the 600th anniversary of the Battle of Kosovo. There, he positioned Serbia at the forefront of a civilizational struggle to defend Europe, to which Serbia had always belonged and, therefore, did not need to be returned.[17] Already in 1989, the opening notes of the coming Yugoslavian Civil War could be heard.

The growing Islamophobia that was essential to the Serbian national project at that time was not unique to the Balkans. As Rita Chin demonstrates in her chapter, British liberals also began to imagine Muslims as a civilizational threat. The moment in which liberal democracy had ostensibly triumphed globally was also a moment of crisis within the West as communism ceased to function as a viable outside threat. Ayatollah Khomeini's fatwa against author Salman Rushdie generated familiar fears, but expressed within the framework of a new kind of global conflict, providing a precursor to Samuel Huntington's larger concept of a "Clash of Civilizations."[18] In Western Europe, this islamophobia pointed to the fragility of the new liberal order, which both aimed to provide a social space for pluralistic difference and seemed to require an enemy "other" for ideological cohesion.

As multiculturalism as a social concept was being attacked as untenable through the Rushdie affair, the concept of intersectionality was coined by

Kimberlé Crenshaw—as discussed by Phanuel Antwi and Amira Ismail—and Stuart Hall began to question the deeper meaning of identity and culture, as Michell Chresfield's chapter demonstrates. Diagnosing a shift from "a struggle over the relations of representation to a politics of representation itself," Hall saw the increasing importance of multiple forms of identity but also, as Chresfield shows, the increasing commodification of identity, which she links to the rise of personal DNA testing. This interconnection of new identities, multiculturalism, and their simultaneous marketization could also be seen in the art world: *Magiciens de la Terre* (Magicians of the Earth), a contemporary art exhibit at the Centre Georges Pompidou in Paris in August 1989, was billed as the "first truly international exhibition, bringing together artists from all over the world."[19] This new engagement with contemporary art produced by artists outside the North American and European bubble represented a cultural shift, as "world art" normally displayed in ethnographic museums was now exhibited in a major center, on par with Western examples. But it was also an element in the rise of the truly globalized neoliberal art market that sought new product from all corners of the world. Artistic visions of the periphery were suddenly welcomed into the center via the mechanism of a booming global art market.

In the arts in 1989 more widely, questions of race and sexuality exhibited a split character, with the mainstream absorbing certain elements of the various social movements demanding justice and equality and the growing reactionary forces seeking to suppress them. Oscar winners of the year included a range of Hollywood films dedicated to examining racial discrimination at a safe distance through the filter of the past: *Driving Miss Daisy* featured an African American chauffeur's relationship with his wealthy Jewish employer in Georgia from 1950s to the 1970s.[20] *A Dry White Season* looked at police violence and the brutality of Apartheid, but was set in 1976, providing the necessary distance from a present understood to be improving, if only incrementally. The film's ban in South Africa was overturned by September 1989.[21] The historical epic *Glory* focused on the exploits of the first African American regiment of the Union Army in the Civil War—but from the perspective of its white commanding officer.[22] By contrast, Spike Lee's incendiary *Do the Right Thing*—with its examination of contemporary racism and police brutality, and its concluding riot in pre-gentrification Brooklyn—was met with critical acclaim, but also sparked panic from newspaper columnists that it would drive Black audiences to imitate its on-screen violence, and was subsequently shunned from major film industry awards.[23]

The year did, however, mark new milestones in the gay liberation movement and in depictions of homosexuality. In East Germany, where homosexuality had been decriminalized in 1968 but remained taboo, the first gay-themed feature film was released in theaters on the day the Berlin Wall was opened. One of the last films produced by DEFA, the East German state film agency, *Coming Out* reflected the shifting norms of the socially conservative country through the story of a male teacher publicly announcing, and eventually being accepted for, his homosexuality.[24] In the German Democratic Republic, the relative absence of the AIDS epidemic perhaps accounted for the film's focus on the professional acceptance of homosexuals in the workplace as its central issue. By contrast, the disease was an important theme in protest art in the capitalist West. In the United States, where there were an estimated 100,000 cases of HIV in 1989, Keith Haring produced his now iconic canvas *Silence = Death* which appeared months before his own death of AIDS complications early the next year.[25]

Although freedom of speech was ostensibly on the upswing with the collapse of official censorship in the Eastern Bloc, the religious right was also beginning to claim greater power to shape the art scene. In the United States, Robert Mapplethorpe—a photographer whose work on erotic and BDSM themes elicited controversy throughout his career—died from AIDS complications in March 1989, shortly before his retrospective show, "The Perfect Moment," was cancelled by the Corcoran Gallery of Art in Washington DC, leading to a national debate about the boundaries of obscenity, public arts funding, and censorship.[26] The efforts to censor artistic work on the grounds of obscenity followed earlier incidents in the preceding years involving art accused of blasphemy, including Andres Serrano's photograph *Piss Christ* (1987) in Australia, and the Martin Scorsese film *The Last Temptation of Christ* (1988)—based on the novel of the same name by Greek writer Nikos Kazantzakis, which was banned in more than a dozen countries.[27] In 1989, Madonna's *Like a Prayer* Pepsi commercial was personally condemned by Pope John Paul II; that the "Cola Wars" between Coke and Pepsi that Billy Joel sang about in *We Didn't Start the Fire* somehow managed to take on a religious bent in a year primarily remembered for the triumph of secular movements for freedom and democracy remains an enduring irony.[28]

Beyond the Cold War

While the year 1989 will forever be indelibly connected to the Cold War, several chapters also demonstrate the emerging twenty-first-century frameworks that were already coming into focus in that year, as well as those that are often overlooked due to the high drama in Berlin, Moscow, and Beijing. The divisions between East and West as defined by the Cold War may have been unravelling throughout much of the decade, but 1989 marked the final disintegration of the Soviets as the main existential enemy in the United States, even before the collapse of the USSR two years later.

In popular music, Paul McCartney released a Russian-language version of the 1968 Beatles hit "Back in the USSR" exclusively in the USSR (making it a treasured bootleg single in the West), and the Moscow Music Peace Festival—ostensibly to rally against drug and alcohol abuse—featured Mötley Crüe, Ozzy Osborne, and the Scorpions, whose song "Wind of Change" (1990) would become the unofficial anthem of the democratic transition in Eastern Europe. Although 1989 saw the arrival of the soon-to-be era-defining grunge band Nirvana, with their first album *Bleach*, album sales were also dominated by the comeback albums of several 1960s icons: Bob Dylan's *Oh Mercy*, the Rolling Stones' *Steel Wheels*, and Neil Young's *Freedom*.[29] Ironically, it was a cancelled tour of the Soviet Union that inspired Young's single "Rockin' in the Free World" on that album.[30] Roxanne Panchasi's chapter on the Greenpeace album *Breakthrough* shows the hopes of environmentalists that they could "build a global community and work towards a future transcendent of political and ideological division." In this way, the abandonment of nuclear armed preparedness and the ecological dream of living in harmony with nature had already eclipsed socialism as the late-twentieth-century universalist and transnational utopian movement.

Yet for others, the decline of the Cold War prompted the search for a new version of the same, albeit with much lower stakes. The turn to the drug war as a successor to the militarized conflict between East and West also appeared in popular culture before emerging as a site of foreign intervention by the United States. Instead of a volcano-laired supervillain bent on world domination, the 1989 version of James Bond, the fictional superspy, faced down a murderous Latin American drug lord in *Licence to Kill*.[31] Although his massively popular techno-thrillers had until then focused on Cold War submarines and spies, Tom Clancy shifted gears to a plot in the novel *Clear and Present Danger* centered on the complicity of American officials in the cocaine trade in Colombia.[32] Only a few months later, as Wassim Daghrir explores in his chapter, the United States launched an invasion of Panama—under the name *Operation Just Cause*—to arrest President Manuel Noriega for his involvement in international drug trafficking. This military action was rationalized by President George H. W. Bush in moral terms as both the most recent phase of the War on Drugs and a means of spreading peace and freedom. In contrast to Ronald Reagan's rhetoric of democracy spreading on its own, force was justified in this case as part of the realization of a natural state of freedom that was good for Panamanians but also good for Americans. The legitimization of the invasion of Panama was not a marker of a new kind of American foreign policy, but one pieced together with the spare parts already lying around. With the Evil Empire in Eastern Europe facing terminal decline, cocaine barons to the south would have to suffice as an existential threat in the Western imagination until Iraqi President Saddam Hussein invaded Kuwait in 1990. In geographic terms, as the space of conflict in central Europe receded, concentration shifted briefly to Latin America as an extension of 1980s Cold War conflicts in the region, before moving to the Middle East which would form the focal point for fears and fantasies that would only intensify after 9/11 a decade later.

Although Francis Fukuyama warned of the "End of History" with the ascendance of liberal democracy, as Molly Geidel explores in her chapter, David Harvey focused on the rise of the postmodern. In what had once been the heartlands of the industrial workers' movement in the West, widespread deindustrialization and demoralization had taken over. The dying automotive city of Flint, Michigan, became symbolic of this collapse in Michael Moore's 1989 debut documentary *Roger and Me* on the filmmaker's quest to interview the CEO of General Motors about the shuttered manufacturing plants of Moore's hometown.[33] Similarly, Don Mitchell's chapter notes the efforts of the city of Johnstown, Pennsylvania, to reinvent itself after the steel industry's departure, through shopping malls and heritage tourism that shifted the city from industrial modernism to consumerist postmodernism. It was this transition—not the fall of the Berlin Wall or the rolling tanks in Beijing—that David Harvey sought to elucidate and used to ascribe to 1989 its position as a pivotal year.

To pull the lens back even further, there is also the question of whether to focus on the end of the Cold War and the ideological struggle between capitalism and communism as the defining structural conflict of the era, or to look at the long durée of imperialism and settler colonialism. John Munro's chapter asks us to situate 1989 and the triumph of neoliberalism outside of a chronology stretching back to 1979, 1945, or 1917, and to place it instead in the context of centuries of European and capitalist expansion. In the case of the destruction of the St. Alice hotel in North Vancouver, Canada, this was a story that began in 1792 with the colonization of the region.

In the end, 1989 was a watershed political event that augured a new era of democracy but was also the advent of a neoliberal depoliticization of politics, an important moment for the realization of a new post-Cold War world with few grand visions and even fewer successes. It represented the triumph of the West, but also—as several chapters in this book demonstrate—the fragility of the new liberal order. Ultimately, 1989 represented the return of the old in new forms, a world on the cusp of something different, but one that for many felt like more of the same.

Notes

1. Many thanks to John Raimo, David Spreen, Gregory Bouchard, Lauren Stokes, and Carolyn Taratko for their helpful suggestions on the text.
2. Timothy Garton Ash, *We the People: The Revolution of '89 Witnessed in Warsaw, Budapest, Berlin & Prague* (London: Granta Books, 1990), 154; François Furet, "From 1789 to 1917 and 1989," *Encounter* (1990), 5; Francis Fukuyama, "The End of History?," *The National Interest*, no. 16 (1989): 3–18.
3. Vladimir Tismăneanu, "The Revolutions of 1989: Causes, Meanings, Consequences," *Contemporary European History* 18, no. 3 (2009): 271.
4. On the global turn, see George Lawson, Chris Armbruster, and Michael Cox, eds., *The Global 1989: Continuity and Change in World Politics* (Cambridge: Cambridge University Press, 2010). On the long 1989, Piotr H. Kosicki and Kyrill Kunakhovich, *The Long 1989: Decades of Global Revolution* (Budapest: Central European University Press, 2019). On re-evaluations from 2019, see Jennifer L. Allen, "Against the 1989–1990 Ending Myth," *Central European History* 52 (2019): 125–47; Paul Betts, "1989 at Thirty: A Recast Legacy," *Past & Present* 244, no. 1 (2019): 271–305; James Mark et al., *1989: A Global History of Eastern Europe* (Cambridge: Cambridge University Press, 2019).
5. Kirrily Freeman and John Munro, eds., *Reading the Postwar Future: Textual Turning Points from 1944* (London: Bloomsbury Publishing, 2019), 4.
6. Jürgen Habermas, "What Does Socialism Mean Today? The Rectifying Revolution and the Need for New Thinking on the Left," *New Left Review* 183 (1990): 5.
7. Ronald Reagan, *Farewell Address to the Nation*, January 11, 1989. Available online: https://www.reaganlibrary.gov/archives/speech/farewell-address-nation
8. Benazir Bhutto, *Address to a Joint Meeting of the US Congress*, June 7, 1989. Available online: https://www.americanrhetoric.com/speeches/benazirbhuttoUScongress.htm

9   "Seize the Moment," *New Era* 4, no. 2 (August 1989), cited in https://www.sahistory.org.za/archive/celebrating-and-commemorating-twenty-years-harare-declaration-kgolane-alfred-rudolph-phala
10 Robert M. Maniquis, "Parades, Parodies, and Paradigms: The Bicentennial of the French Revolution," *Environment and Planning D: Society and Space* 7, no. 4 (1989): 363–5.
11 Cited in Ignác Romsics, *From Dictatorship to Democracy: The Birth of the Third Hungarian Republic, 1988–2001* (Boulder, CO: Social Science Monographs, 2007), 396.
12 "Für unser Land," November 26, 1989. English translation by Max Hertzberg available online: http://www.coldwarcultures.group.shef.ac.uk/for-our-country/
13 Helmut Kohl, "Ten-Point Plan for German Unity," November 28, 1989. Available online: https://ghdi.ghi-dc.org/sub_document.cfm?document_id=223
14 Mikhail Gorbachev, "Europe as a Common Home," Address to the Council of Europe, Strasbourg, July 6, 1989. Available online: https://chnm.gmu.edu/1989/archive/files/gorbachev-speech-7-6-89_e3ccb87237.pdf; Marie-Pierre Rey, "'Europe Is Our Common Home': A Study of Gorbachev's Diplomatic Concept," *Cold War History* 4, no. 2 (January 2004): 33–65.
15 The Taif Agreement, approved by the Lebanese parliament on November 4, 1989. Available online: https://www.un.int/lebanon/sites/www.un.int/files/Lebanon/the_taif_agreement_english_version_.pdf
16 Sabine Stach, *Vermächtnispolitik: Jan Palach und Oskar Brüsewitz als politische Märtyrer* (Göttingen: Wallstein Verlag, 2016).
17 See Mark et al., *1989: A Global History of Eastern Europe*, 203.
18 Samuel P. Huntington, "The Clash of Civilizations?" *Foreign Affairs* 72, no. 3 (1993): 22–49.
19 Maureen Murphy, "From *Magiciens de La Terre* to the Globalization of the Art World: Going Back to a Historic Exhibition," trans. Simon Pleasance, *Critique d'art. Actualité Internationale de La Littérature Critique Sur l'art Contemporain*, no. 41 (2013): 1.
20 Bruce Beresford et al., *Driving Miss Daisy* (Majestic Films International, 1989).
21 Euzhan Palcy et al., *A Dry White Season* (Sundance Productions, 1989).
22 Edward Zwick et al., *Glory* (TriStar Pictures, 1989).
23 Spike Lee et al., *Do the Right Thing* (40 Acres & A Mule, 1989).
24 Heiner Carow et al., *Coming Out* (DEFA, 1989).
25 Keith Haring, *Silence=Death* (1989), Painting, Acrylic on Canvas, 40 × 40 inches, 101.6 × 101.6 cm.
26 Ingrid Sischy, "White and Black: Robert Mapplethorpe's 'Perfect Moment,'" *The New Yorker*, November 6, 1989.

27 Naomi Cumming, "Playing with Transgressive Light: Serrano's 'Piss Christ,'" *Literature and Aesthetics* 8 (1998), 45–59.
28 Billy Joel, "We Didn't Start the Fire," *Storm Front* (Columbia, 1989).
29 Nirvana, *Bleach* (Sub Pop, 1989); Bob Dylan, *Oh Mercy* (Columbia Records, 1989); The Rolling Stones, *Steel Wheels* (Columbia Records, 1989).
30 Neil Young, *Freedom* (Reprise, 1989).
31 John Glen et al., *Licence to Kill* (United Artists, 1989).
32 Tom Clancy, *Clear and Present Danger* (New York: Collins, 1989).
33 Michael Moore et al., *Roger & Me* (Dog Eat Dog Films, 1989).

Contributors

Phanuel Antwi is Assistant Professor in the Department of English Language and Literatures at the University of British Columbia. He writes, researches, and teaches critical race, gender, and sexuality studies, and material cultures. He has published in *Interventions, Small Axe, Journal of West Indian Literature, Cultural Dynamics,* and *Studies in Canadian Literature*. He is completing a book-length project titled *Currencies of Blackness: Faithfulness, Cheerfulness and Politeness in Settler Writing* and has forthcoming *On Cuddling: Loved to Death in the Racial Embrace* (2023).

Julia Ault is Assistant Professor of History at the University of Utah. Her research interests include environmentalism, the Cold War, and socialism in modern Europe. She has published on environmental policy and protest in East and West Germany as well as Poland. Her most recent book is *Saving Nature under Socialism: Transnational Environmentalism in East Germany, 1968–1990* (2021).

Song-Chuan Chen is Associate Professor in Modern Chinese History at Warwick University. His research interest lies in the field of historical and contemporary interactions between China and the West. His recent publications include "The Power of Ancestors: Tombs and Death Practices in Late Qing China's Foreign Relations, 1845–1914" (*Past & Present*, 2018) and *Merchants of War and Peace: British Knowledge of China in the Making of the Opium War* (2017).

Rita Chin is Professor of History at the University of Michigan, Ann Arbor. Her research interests include immigration, race, and cultural diversity in post-1945 Europe. She is the author of *The Crisis of Multiculturalism in Europe: A History* (2017), *The Guest Worker Question in Postwar Germany* (2007), and co-author of *After the Nazi Racial State: Difference and Democracy in Germany and Beyond* (2009). Her research has been supported by the SSRC, Woodrow Wilson International Center for Scholars, ACLS, the Institute for Advanced Study, and the Guggenheim Foundation.

Michell Chresfield is an Assistant Professor of Africana Studies at Cornell University. Her research interests include the history of science and the history of racial formation and identity-making in twentieth-century America. Her current research examines how Americans of mixed Black, white, and indigenous ancestry used social science, medicine, and the law to negotiate multiracial identities during the Jim Crow era and the rise of multiculturalism. She is currently working on a book based on this research, titled *What Lies Between: Social Science, Medicine, and the Making of America's Triracial Isolates*.

Wassim Daghrir is Associate Professor and PhD Director in the College of Arts and Humanities at the University of Sousse, Tunisia. He holds a PhD in American History, Politics, and Cultural Studies from the University of Paris, and a post-doctorate degree in American Civilization from New York University. He is the author of six books and several articles on US foreign policy, democracy, media, and popular culture.

Thomas Fleischman is Assistant Professor of History at the University of Rochester. He researches and writes about modern Europe, Germany, environmental history, and animals. His publications include *Communist Pigs: An Animal History of East Germany's Rise and Fall* (2020).

Kirrily Freeman is Professor of History at Saint Mary's University in Halifax, Canada. Her publications include *Bronzes to Bullets: Vichy and the Destruction of French Public Statuary, 1940–1944* (2009) and *Reading the Postwar Future: Textual Turning Points from 1944* (2020) with John Munro.

Molly Geidel is Senior Lecturer in twentieth-century US Cultural History at the University of Manchester. She is the author of *Peace Corps Fantasies: How Development Shaped the Global Sixties* (2015). She is currently working on two books, one on documentary film and development in the Americas, and the other on the counterinsurgent girl.

Amira Ismail holds a BA in History and an MA in International Relations from the University of Birmingham. Her interests lie in platforming the stories and agency of young people in policy areas that impact them through her work with Chatham House and the Esmée Fairbairn Foundation. She is currently working in the third sector to create equitable access to education for young people growing up in disadvantaged environments.

Don Mitchell is Professor of Human Geography at Uppsala University, Sweden and Distinguished Professor of Geography Emeritus at Syracuse University, USA. His research focuses on capitalist transformations of urban public space and agribusiness landscapes, homelessness, and shifting labor regimes. His most recent book is *Mean Streets: Homelessness, Public Space, and the Limits to Capital* (2020).

John Munro is Lecturer in US and International History at the University of Birmingham. He is the author of *The Anticolonial Front: The African American Freedom Struggle and Global Decolonization* (2017) and, with Kirrily Freeman, editor of *Reading the Postwar Future: Textual Turning Points from 1944* (2020).

Roxanne Panchasi is Associate Professor of History at Simon Fraser University. She is the author of *Future Tense: The Culture of Anticipation in France Between the Wars* (2009) and the founding host of New Books in French Studies, a podcast channel on the New Books Network. Her current research is focused on the culture and politics of nuclear weapons and testing in France and its empire after 1945.

Frances Pheasant-Kelly is a Reader in Film and Screen at Wolverhampton University, UK. Her research interests center on abject spaces, fantasy, and the medical humanities. Her publications include two monographs, *Abject Spaces in American Cinema* (2013) and *Fantasy Film Post 9/11* (2013), and she is the co-editor of *Spaces of the Cinematic Home: Behind the Screen Door* (2015) and *Tim Burton's Bodies* (2021).

Ned Richardson-Little is a junior project leader at the University of Erfurt. His research interests include the history of socialism, international law and international crime in modern Germany, and the democratic transition in Eastern Europe. His publications include *The Human Rights Dictatorship: Socialism, Global Solidarity and Revolution in East Germany* (2020).

Select Bibliography

Altamirano-Jiménez, Isabel (2013), *Indigenous Encounters with Neoliberalism: Place, Women, and the Environment in Canada and Mexico*, Vancouver: University of British Columbia Press.
Ash, Timothy Garton (1990), *We the People: The Revolution of '89 Witnessed in Warsaw, Budapest, Berlin, and Prague*, London: Granta Books.
Ault, Julia E. (2021), *Saving Nature under Socialism: Transnational Environmentalism in East Germany, 1968–1990*, Cambridge: Cambridge University Press.
Blomley, Nicholas (2004), *Unsettling the City: Urban Land and the Politics of Property*, London: Routledge.
Brown, Jeremy (2021), *June Fourth, the Tiananmen Protests and Beijing Massacre of 1989*, Cambridge: Cambridge University Press.
Brown, Kate (2019), *Manual for Survival: A Chernobyl Guide to the Future*, New York: W. W. Norton & Co.
Campbell, Robert (2001), *Sit Down and Drink Your Beer: Regulating Vancouver's Beer Parlours, 1925–1954*, Toronto: University of Toronto Press.
Chang, Hao (1992), *Chinese Intellectuals in Crisis: Search for Order and Meaning, 1890–1911*, Berkeley: University of California Press.
Chin, Rita (2017), *The Crisis of Multiculturalism in Europe: A History*, Princeton: Princeton University Press.
Ciccariello-Maher, George (2013), *We Created Chávez: A People's History of the Venezuelan Revolution*, Durham: Duke University Press.
Clover, Joshua (2009), *1989: Bob Dylan Didn't Have This to Sing About*, Berkeley: University of California Press.
Conlon, Gerry (1990), *Proved Innocent: The Story of Gerry Conlon of the Guildford Four*, London: Penguin.
Coulthard, Glen Sean (2014), *Red Skin, White Masks: Rejecting the Colonial Politics of Recognition*, Minneapolis: University of Minnesota Press.
Crenshaw, Kimberlé (1989), "Demarginalizing the Intersection of Race and Sex: A Black Feminist Critique of Antidiscrimination Doctrine, Feminist Theory and Antiracist Politics," *University of Chicago Legal Forum* 1 (8): 139–67.
Dean, Robert D. (2003), *Imperial Brotherhood: Gender and the Making of Cold War Foreign Policy*, Amherst: University of Massachusetts Press.
Derrida, Jacques (1994), *Specters of Marx: The State of the Debt, the Work of Mourning, and the New International*, New York: Routledge.
Duster, Troy (2003), *Backdoor to Eugenics*, New York: Routledge.

Eckert, Astrid (2019), *West Germany and the Iron Curtain: Environment, Economy, and Culture in the Borderlands*, London: Oxford University Press.

Fairclough, Norman (2003), *Analysing Discourse: Textual Analysis for Social Research*, New York: Routledge.

Fanon, Frantz (1967), *Black Skin, White Masks*, New York: Grove Press.

Fleischman, Thomas (2020), *Communist Pigs: An Animal History of East Germany's Rise and Fall*, Seattle: University of Washington Press.

Florvil, Tiffany (2020), *Mobilizing Black Germany: Afro-German Women and the Making of a Transnational Movement*, Champaign, IL: University of Illinois Press, 2020.

Forrester, Katrina (2019), *In the Shadow of Justice: Postwar Liberalism and the Remaking of Political Philosophy*, Princeton: Princeton University Press.

Fukuyama, Francis (1989), "The End of History?" *The National Interest* 16: 3–18.

Gilman, Nils (2007), *Mandarins of the Future: Modernization Theory in Cold War America*, Baltimore: Johns Hopkins University Press.

Goldstein, Alyosha (2008), "Where the Nation Takes Place: Proprietary Regimes, Antistatism, and U.S. Settler Colonialism," *South Atlantic Quarterly* 107 (4): 833–61.

Grandin, Greg (2006), *Empire's Workshop: Latin America, the United States, and the Making of an Imperial Republic*, New York: Macmillan.

Hackworth, Jason (2007), *The Neoliberal City: Governance, Ideology, and Development in American Urbanism*, Ithaca: Cornell University Press.

Hall, Stuart (1996), "New Ethnicities," in David Morley and Chen Kuan-Hsing (eds.), *Critical Ideologies in Cultural Studies*, New York: Routledge, 441–9.

Hall, Stuart (2000), "Conclusion: The Multicultural Question," in Barnor Hesse (ed.) *Un/settled Multiculturalisms: Diasporas, Entanglements, Transruptions*, London: Zed Books, 209–11.

Harris, Cole (2004), "How Did Colonialism Dispossess? Comments from an Edge of Empire," *Annals of the Association of American Geographers* 91 (1): 165–82.

Hartman, Andrew (2015), *A War for the Soul of America: A History of the Culture Wars*, Chicago: University of Chicago Press.

Harvey, David (1989), *The Condition of Postmodernity*, Oxford: Blackwell.

Harvey, David (1989), "From Managerialism to Entrepreneurialism: The Transformation of Urban Governance in Late Capitalism," *Geografiska Annaler* 71 (B): 3–17.

Hoganson, Kirstin L. (2000), *Fighting for American Manhood: How Gender Politics Provoked the Spanish-American and Philippine-American Wars*, New Haven: Yale University Press.

Holsey, Bayo (2004), "Transatlantic Dreaming: Slavery, Tourism, and Diasporic Encounters," in Fran Markowitz and Anders H. Stefanson (eds.), *Routes of Remembrance: Refashioning the Atlantic Slave Trade in Ghana*, Chicago: Chicago University Press, 144–60.

Jowett, Gareth S. and Victoria O'Donnell (2006), *Propaganda & Persuasion*, Los Angeles: Sage.

Karl, Rebecca (2002), *Staging the World: Chinese Nationalism at the Turn of the Twentieth Century*, Durham, NC: Duke University Press.

Kauanui, Kēhaulani (2016) "A Structure, Not an Event: Settler Colonialism and Enduring Indigeneity," *Lateral* 5 (1): https://csalateral.org/issue/5-1/forum-alt-humanities-settler-colonialism-enduring-indigeneity-kauanui/

Kendall, Mikki (2021), *Hood Feminism: Notes from the Women That a Movement Forgot*, New York: Penguin.

King, Michael (1986), *Death of the Rainbow Warrior*, New York: Penguin Books.

Knight, Rolf (1978), *Indians at Work: An Informal History of Native Labour in British Columbia, 1858–1930*, Vancouver: New Star Books.

Kosicki, Piotr H. and Kyrill Kunakhovich (2019), *The Long 1989: Decades of Global Revolution*, Budapest: Central European University Press.

Lawson, Chris Armbruster and Michael Cox (eds.) (2012), *The Global 1989: Continuity and Change in World Politics*, Cambridge: Cambridge University Press.

Leeuwen, Theo van (2008), *Discourse and Practice: New Tools for Critical Analysis*, New York: Oxford University Press.

Lipsitz, George (2011), *How Racism Takes Place*, Philadelphia: Temple University Press.

Lousley, Cheryl (2014), "'With Love from Band Aid': Sentimental Exchange, Affective Economies, and Popular Globalism," *Emotion Space and Society* 10 (1): 7–17.

Mackenthun, Gesa (1997), *Metaphors of Dispossession: American Beginnings and the Translation of Empire, 1492–1637*, Norman: University of Oklahoma Press.

Maniquis, Robert M. (1989), "Parades, Parodies, and Paradigms: The Bicentennial of the French Revolution," *Environment and Planning D: Society and Space* 7 (4): 363–5.

Mark, James, Bogdan C. Iacob, Tobias Rupprecht and Ljubica Spaskovska (2019), *1989: A Global History of Eastern Europe*, Cambridge: Cambridge University Press.

Martin, Ben L. (1991), "From Negro to Black to African American: The Power of Names and Naming," *Political Science Quarterly* 106 (1): 83–5.

Massey, Doreen (1991), "Flexible Sexism," *Environment and Planning D* 9 (1): 55–6.

May, John (1994), *Final Report of the Inquiry into the Convictions Arising from the Bomb Attacks in Guildford and Woolwich in 1974*, London: HMSO.

May, John and Michael Howard Brown (1989), *The Greenpeace Story*, Toronto: Prentice-Hall.

Maya, Margarita López (2003), "The Venezuelan 'Caracazo' of 1989: Popular Protest and Institutional Weakness," *Journal of Latin American Studies* 35 (1): 117–37.

McKee, Grant and Ros Franey (1988), *Time Bomb: Irish Bombers, English Justice and the Guildford Four*, London: Bloomsbury.

Mitchell, Don (1992), "Heritage, Landscape, and the Production of Community: Consensus History and Its Alternatives in Johnstown, Pennsylvania," *Pennsylvania History* 59: 198–226.

Mitchell, Don (2003), *The Right to the City: Social Justice and the Fight for Public Space*, New York: Guilford Press.
Mitchell, Don (2018), "Revolution and the Critique of Human Geography: Prospects for the Right to the City after 50 Years," *Geografiska Annaler* 100 (B): 2–11.
Mitchell, Katherine (2004), *Crossing the Neoliberal Line: Pacific Rim Migration and the Metropolis*, Philadelphia: Temple University Press.
Mitter, Rana (2004), *A Bitter Revolution: China's Struggle with the Modern World*, Oxford: Oxford University Press.
Pei, Minxin (2006), *China's Trapped Transition: The Limits of Developmental Autocracy*, Cambridge: Harvard University Press.
Naughton, Michael (2007), *Rethinking Miscarriages of Justice: Beyond the Tip of the Iceberg*, London and New York: Palgrave.
Nelson, Alondra (2016), *The Social Life of DNA: Race, Reparations, and Reconciliation after the Genome*, Boston: Beacon Press.
Ngai, Sianne (2020), *Theory of the Gimmick: Aesthetic Judgment and Capitalist Form*, Cambridge: Harvard University Press.
Nichols, Bill (1991), *Representing Reality*, Bloomington: Indiana University Press.
Olufemi, Lola (2020), *Feminism Interrupted: Disrupting Power*, London: Pluto Press.
Perry, Adele (2001), *On the Edge of Empire: Gender, Race, and the Making of British Columbia, 1849–1871*, Toronto: University of Toronto Press.
Poyser, Sam, Angus Nurse and Rebecca Milne (2018), *Miscarriages of Justice: Causes, Consequences and Remedies*, Bristol: Polity Press.
Prashad, Vijay (2012), *The Poorer Nations: A Possible History of the Global South*, New York: Verso.
Ramet, Sabrina Petra, Sergei Zamascikov, and Robert Bird (1994), "The Soviet Rock Scene," in Sabrina Ramet (ed.) *Rocking the State: Rock Music and Politics in Eastern Music and Russia*, Boulder, CO: Westview Press, 179–216.
Rauth, Robert (1982), "Back in the USSR: Rock and Roll in the Soviet Union," *Popular Music and Society* 8 (3–4): 3–12.
Reardon, Jenny, and Kim Tallbear (2010), "'Your DNA Is Our History': Genomics, Anthropology, and the Construction of Whiteness as Property," *Current Anthropology* 53 (5): 233–45.
Richardson-Little, Ned (2020), *The Human Rights Dictatorship: Socialism, Global Solidarity, and Revolution in East Germany*, Cambridge: Cambridge University Press.
Rodgers, Daniel T. (2011), *Age of Fracture*, Cambridge, MA: Harvard University Press.
Rushdie, Salman (1988), *The Satanic Verses*, New York: Vintage.
Rutland, Ted (2010), "The Financialization of Urban Redevelopment," *Geography Compass* 4 (8): 1167–78.
Said, Edward (1994), *Representations of the Intellectual*, London: Vintage.
Scott, Joan (2007), *The Politics of the Veil*, Princeton: Princeton University Press.
Simpson, Audra (2014), *Mohawk Interruptus: Political Life across the Borders of Settler States*, Durham: Duke University Press.

Sivanandan, Ambalavaner (1989), "New Circuits of Imperialism," *Race & Class* 30 (3): 1–19.

Slobodian, Quinn (2018), *Globalists: The End of Empire and the Birth of Neoliberalism*, Cambridge: Harvard University Press.

Stanger-Ross, Jordan (2008), "Municipal Colonialism in Vancouver: City Planning and the Conflict over Indian Reserves, 1928–1950s," *Canadian Historical Review* 89 (4): 541–80.

Stiegman, Martha and Sherry Pictou (2012), "Recognition by Assimilation: Mi'kmaq Treaty Rights, Fisheries Privatization, and Community Resistance in Nova Scotia," in Kristin Burnett and Geoff Read (eds.), *Aboriginal History: A Reader*, New York: Oxford University Press, 403–13.

Strauss, Julia (2019), *State Formation in China and Taiwan: Bureaucracy, Campaign, and Performance*, Cambridge: Cambridge University Press.

Wasserstrom, Jeffrey N. (1991), *Student Protest in Twentieth-Century China*, Palo Alto: Stanford University Press.

Weldon, Fay (1989), *Sacred Cows: A Portrait of Britain, Post-Rushdie, Pre-Utopia*, London: Chatto & Windus.

Wilkinson, Tom (2019), "The Writing on the Wall: The Language of Buildings," *Architectural Review*: https://www.architectural-review.com/essays/the-writing-on-the-wall-the-language-of-buildings

Wolfe, Patrick (2008), "Structure and Event: Settler Colonialism, Time, and the Question of Genocide," in Dirk Moses (ed.) *Empire, Colony, Genocide: Conquest, Occupation, and Subaltern Resistance in World History*, New York: Berghahn Books, 102–32.

Index

AIDS 59, 184, 247
Albania 25, 26, 35, 36
American Descendants of Slavery (ADOS) 92–4, 99, 100
Apartheid 185, 187, 242, 243, 246
Armstrong, Paddy 144, 150, 151, 153–6
Austria 39, 195, 233, 243
Ayatollah Khomeini 5, 9, 39, 42, 44, 50, 195, 245

Baltimore 62, 63, 64, 209
Beijing 7, 62, 119, 136, 214, 244, 245, 247, 249
Berlin 2, 12, 73, 75, 203, 231, 235, 244, 245, 247, 249
    1989 anniversary celebrations 6
    West Berlin 176
Berlin Conference 67
Berlin Wall 1, 72, 76, 102, 176, 177, 205, 233, 238
    fall of 1, 2, 8, 18, 39, 72, 163, 183, 204, 217, 233, 243, 247, 249
    footprint 7
Birmingham Six 145, 152, 155–8
Black Lives Matter movement 11, 32
Breakthrough 3, 11, 183–97, 198, 202, 248
Bush, George H. W. 5, 248
    1989 anniversary celebrations 7
    administration 18, 25, 33
    inaugural address (1989) 4
    Operation Just Cause speech 3, 10, 161–79
    "wimp factor" 8, 10

Canada 3, 108, 205, 214, 249
    cities in 208
    Greenpeace 198
    NAFTA 208
    settler colonialism in 5, 11, 212
Canadian Pacific Railway 212, 218

capitalism 2, 4, 9, 11, 31, 32, 36, 76, 185, 192, 233, 235–7, 243, 249
    disaster capitalism 218
    in Fukuyama 20, 29
    in Harvey 65–7, 72–3
    in Marx 62
    and neoliberalism 30, 204
    racial 10, 11
    and settler colonialism 209–10, 212
Chan I-hua 131
Cheng Nan-jung 121, 128, 129–35
Chernobyl 188, 189, 199, 230, 256
Chiang Ching-kuo (Chiang junior) 121, 126–9, 137
Chiang Kai-shek 119, 125, 126, 129, 137
China, People's Republic of 3, 25, 64, 76, 120, 128, 129, 131, 138, 197, 238
    authoritarian 137, 244
    Communist revolution in 68
    Imperial era 123–4
    intellectual activism in 121–6
    pro-democracy protests 6, 8, 10, 119, 136, 162, 242
    Republic of China on Taiwan 125–6, 130
    state capitalism in 62, 215
Clover, Joshua 31, 32, 185
Cold War 4, 5, 18, 24, 25, 39, 76, 121, 124, 126, 135, 144, 165, 192, 204, 247
    end of 27, 39, 102, 187, 204, 233, 241, 248, 249
    footprint of 1
    and modernization 9, 19, 20
    periodization 205, 218
    policy 22, 68, 188
    post-Cold War era 161–2, 164–5, 171–2, 177–8, 250
    status quo 11, 143, 185, 227, 236–8, 242
    structures 229, 230, 244–5

colonialism 4, 5, 205, 207–9, 242
  settler colonialism 209, 211, 212, 217, 218, 249
Communism 2, 4, 73, 124, 176, 178, 204, 220, 235, 236, 249
  collapse of 1, 4, 11, 39, 192, 237
  containment of 126, 161, 245
  environmentalism under 229
Condition of Postmodernity, The (Harvey) 3, 8, 9, 59, 65, 66, 70, 72
Confucianism 121
Conlon, Gerry 144–50, 152–7
Conlon, Guiseppe 147, 148, 149, 155
consumption 63, 67–9, 92, 134, 185, 208, 229, 242
Contras 24, 164
Crenshaw, Kimberlé 3, 8, 10, 101–2, 103–15, 203, 246
Crown America 59–64, 71

deindustrialization 59, 60, 62, 234, 249
"Demarginalizing the Intersection of Race and Sex" (Crenshaw) 3, 10, 101, 102, 108
Derrida, Jacques 9, 18, 19, 28, 67
DNA 5, 81
  testing 8, 10, 79, 80, 81, 82, 84, 86–93, 95, 246
drugs 150, 151, 177
  trafficking 163–6, 170, 171, 248
  war on 171, 178, 248

East Germany, *see* German Democratic Republic (GDR)
École Polytechnique massacre 108, 115, 203
End of History and the Last Man, The (Fukuyama) 18, 28
"End of History, The" (Fukuyama) 3, 4, 8, 9, 17–25, 27–9, 31, 197, 241, 249
Europe 39, 53, 70, 229, 234, 245–6, 249
  Eastern Europe 1, 3, 5, 192, 233–4, 242–4, 248–9
    collapse of communism in 39
    deindustrialization in 73
    environmental concerns in 230, 236–8
    idea of 234
    immigration from 60
    return to 241
    Taiwanese radicals in 125
    US strategy in 177
  Western Europe 39, 230, 233, 237, 243, 245
    agriculture in 228
    immigration to 9, 40, 43, 51–53
European 11, 40, 80, 89, 244
  capitalism 212, 249
  colonial powers 67
  languages 122
Europeanization 7, 243

Fanon, Frantz 112–13
fatwa 5, 8, 9, 39–40, 42–6, 48, 50, 52, 245
First Tuesday 3, 8, 10, 143–7, 152, 155, 157, 245
  "Auntie Annie's Bomb Factory" 147
  "The Guildford Time Bomb" 149
  "A Case That Won't go Away" 152
  "Free to Speak" 153
Ford, Henry 68
Fordism 68–72, 75–6
Foucault, Michel 67, 73, 207
French Revolution 6, 183, 243
Fukuyama, Francis 3, 5, 8, 9, 17–33, 36, 73, 197, 204, 249

General Motors 101, 108, 249
gentrification 5, 7, 207–8, 215, 217, 246
Germany 1, 3–6, 11, 186, 195–6, 201, 227–39, 243
  Federal Republic of 229–32, 235–6, 238, 243
  German Democratic Republic (GDR) 6, 143, 227–39, 243–245, 246
Ghana 6, 90–2, 105
  Year of Return 6, 91
glasnost 102, 188
globalization 32, 76, 204
Gorbachev, Mikhail 7, 8, 20, 63, 188, 189, 235, 237, 244
Greenpeace 3, 5, 11, 183–91, 193–7, 248
Guildford Four 1, 3, 5, 8, 10, 143–57, 245

Habermas, Jürgen 242
Hall, Stuart 3, 10, 12, 80, 83, 103, 203, 246
Harvey, David 3, 8, 9, 30, 62–76, 203, 249
Hill, Paul 144, 147, 150, 152, 154

Honecker, Erich 233
Human Rights 127, 134, 204, 235, 243
   Human Rights Day 6, 127, 130, 134
   Human Rights Now! 187
Hungary 39, 233, 238, 243, 244
Huntington, Samuel P. 20, 120, 245

immigration 9, 28, 29, 47, 48
   anti-immigration 9
Imperialism 12, 25, 67, 162, 249
   aggression 4, 5, 178, 212
   and capitalism 67
   and Cold War 2, 205, 185
   nuclear 187
   "urban imperialisms" (Schlesinger) 209
India 39–41, 144
Indian Act 212
Indigenous people 3, 88, 129, 193, 216, 218
   communities 88, 212, 215, 219
   culture 32, 211
   dispossession 7, 212
   evictions of 11
   movements 32, 113, 205, 213–14
   oppression of 5, 209
Indigeneity 205, 208, 209, 212, 214, 219
International Monetary Fund (IMF) 25, 27
intersectionality 5, 8, 10, 101–15, 245
Iran 3, 39, 42–4, 50, 51, 54
Iran-Contra 164
Irish Republican Army (IRA) 144, 145, 147, 149, 150, 151, 159
Islam 9, 26, 39–43, 45, 51, 52, 53
   fundamentalism 7
Islamophobia 46, 245

Japan 124, 125, 128
   Japanese-Americans 26
   invasion and occupation of Taiwan 128, 129
   Japanese language 17
Johnson, Lyndon 22, 35
Johnstown (Pennsylvania) 6, 59–65, 67, 69, 71, 73, 75, 249
   flood 6, 59, 60
   Flood Museum 61, 75

Kanesatake resistance 108, 214
Kennedy, John F. 22, 163
Kohl, Helmut 7, 227, 235, 243

liberalism 17, 20, 24, 40, 51, 53, 73, 204

Maguire Seven 145–9, 152, 154–5, 157
Marx, Karl 20, 24, 36, 62, 64, 66–8, 70, 195
Marxism 9, 28, 63, 65, 73, 74, 75, 80
May Fourth movement 6, 127, 131, 136
Melodiya Records 184, 189, 191, 192, 196, 200, 201
modernism 66, 67, 68, 70, 74, 249
modernization 19, 27, 36, 122, 242
   modernization theory 9, 19, 20, 22–7, 29, 204
Montreal massacre, *see* École Polytechnique massacre
Moscow 189, 190–2, 197, 199, 201, 204, 247–8
multiculturalism 9, 40, 46–53, 55, 81, 83, 245–6
music 11, 31, 183–7, 189–92, 196–7, 204
   and modernity (Harvey) 66
   pop 5, 11, 248
   rock (Fukuyama) 17, 31

neoliberalism 29–35, 70, 207–9, 218–20, 242, 249
   and decolonization 29
   gentrification 7
   transition to 27, 76, 204–5, 237
"New Ethnicities" (Hall) 3, 5, 10, 80–4, 94
Noriega, Manuel 10, 162–7, 169, 171–4, 248
Nylon Cheng Liberty Foundation 132, 133

Oka crisis, *see* Kanesatake resistance
Operation Just Cause 3, 10, 161, 163, 165, 171, 248

Panama 2, 3, 5, 10, 12, 161–7, 170–8
perestroika 63, 102, 188
Poland 8, 229, 233, 238, 244
postcoloniality 27, 209
postmodernism 65–7, 72–4, 76, 249
postmodernity 6, 70, 72

racism 7, 93, 215, 232
   Apartheid 243, 246
   intersectionality 101
   and modernization 22, 23, 24, 26, 207

Rainbow Warrior (vessel) 187, 193
Rainbow Warrior II (vessel) 187, 193, 194
Rainbow Warriors (record) 3, 11, 184–7, 192–7, 198
RAND corporation 17, 18, 20, 23
Reagan, Ronald 63, 176, 237, 242, 249
    administration 18, 20, 25, 162, 164, 165
    election campaign 61
    policies 28, 144, 163
    war on drugs 171
reparations 25, 85, 92, 93
reunification 7, 11, 236, 243, 244
    diasporic 91
Richardson, Carole 144, 150–6
Rushdie, Salman 3, 5, 8, 9, 39–43, 45–53, 54, 245

Sacred Cows (Weldon) 9, 40, 50, 52, 53
Satanic Verses, The (Rushdie) 8, 9, 39–43, 45, 46, 48, 50, 51, 52
Schabowski, Günter 6, 227, 232–4
slavery 79–80, 82–3, 86, 111
    legacy of 24, 89, 92
    reparations for 25, 80, 85, 92–4
Slobodian, Quinn 29, 30, 207, 220
Soja, Edward 73–4
Solidarity 8, 39
Sovietology 20, 35
Soviet Union (USSR) 3, 39, 175, 235, 237, 248
    Breakthrough 183–4, 188–92, 197–8
    "clients" (Fukuyama) 23–4
    collapse of 35, 177
    withdrawal from Afghanistan 7
Spivak, Gayatri Chakravorty 84
Squamish Nation 11, 211, 212, 213, 215, 218, 225
St. Alice Hotel 3, 8, 11, 203, 205–19, 249

Taiwan 6, 7, 10, 119–21, 124–38, 238, 244–5
    pro-democracy movements in 3, 5, 6, 8
Thatcher, Margaret 8, 9, 18, 28, 41, 49, 63, 195, 237
Tiananmen Square 8, 75, 245
    legacy 1, 6

    massacre 10, 73, 120, 136, 183, 214
    protest 59, 61–2, 65, 119–20, 138, 203
Title VII 101, 108, 109, 113

United Kingdom (UK) 3, 120
    Greenpeace 186, 191, 193, 198
    immigration to 9, 39–42, 44, 47–8
    intersectionality 107
    policing in 10, 143, 145, 157
    race 83, 91
    release of *Satanic Verses* 40
    Third Way politics 36
United States (US)
    agriculture in 228
    Cold War aggression 18, 20, 22, 24
    Civil Rights 69, 108
    empire 2, 12
    fatwa in 43
    feminism in 144
    and Ghana 91
    HIV 247
    interventionism 174–8
    invasion of Panama 3, 5, 10, 161–72
    Iraq War 11
    and NATO 244
    and modernization 23, 31–2
    neoliberalism in 53, 208, 218, 237
    policing in 158
    policy 17, 28
    presidential rhetoric 4, 174–6
    relationship with Taiwan 125, 126
    racism in 7, 81–3, 85
    school system 26
    and the Soviet Union 39, 248

Vancouver 203–5, 210–18, 249
    Expo 86 208, 215
    gentrification of 3, 7
    Greenpeace 198
    Indigenous dispossession in 7
    Olympics 8
    transformation of 11
Venezuela 143

Weldon, Fay 8, 9, 40, 50–3, 56
West Germany *see* Federal Republic of Germany

Yugoslavia 144, 245

www.ingramcontent.com/pod-product-compliance
Lightning Source LLC
Chambersburg PA
CBHW062123300426
44115CB00012BA/1792